THE
COLOR
PYNK

THE WILLIAM & BETTYE NOWLIN SERIES
in Art, History, and Culture of the Western Hemisphere

THE
COLOR
PYNK

Black Femme Art for Survival

Omise'eke Natasha Tinsley

AFTERWORD BY Candice Lyons

University of Texas Press ⌄⌄ Austin

Requests for permission to reproduce material from this work should be sent to:
Permissions
University of Texas Press
P.O. Box 7819
Austin, TX 78713-7819
utpress.utexas.edu/rp-form

∞ The paper used in this book meets the minimum requirements of
ANSI/NISO Z39.48-1992 (R1997) (Permanence of Paper).

Library of Congress Cataloging-in-Publication Data
Names: Tinsley, Omise'eke Natasha, 1971– author.
Title: The color pynk : black femme art for survival / Omise'eke Natasha Tinsley.
Description: First edition. | Austin : University of Texas Press, 2022. |
Includes bibliographical references and index.
Identifiers: LCCN 2022002695
ISBN 978-1-4773-2115-7 (cloth)
ISBN 978-1-4773-2644-2 (paperback)
ISBN 978-1-4773-2563-6 (PDF)
ISBN 978-1-4773-2564-3 (ePub)
Subjects: LCSH: Lu, Kelsey. | Monáe, Janelle. | Huxtable, Juliana, 1987– | Mock, Janet,
1983– | Tourmaline. | Moore, Indya. | Feminist aesthetics. | Feminism and the arts. |
Womanism. | African American sexual minorities. | African American feminists.
Classification: LCC BH301.F46 T57 2022 | DDC 111/.85—dc23/eng/20220518
LC record available at https://lccn.loc.gov/2022002695

doi:10.7560/321157

FOR MY COUSIN

ANNA ELIZABETH STAPLER

APRIL 11, 1988—SEPTEMBER 13, 2021

IN LOVING MEMORY

CONTENTS

THE
COLOR
PYNK

PROLOGUE

For Alice Walker

Dear Ms. Alice Walker,

I wish I had known you in 1984. I wish my younger self, who was in junior high in Richmond, California, that year, had known you and your books were in my reach. That year, I read George Orwell's *1984* for extra credit and found parallels in the Ronald Reagan–engineered world around me; I found many, many more in the Trumpocracy's "alternative facts" a quarter-century later. That year, for reasons that now seem equal parts outlandish and (on good self-compassion days) touching, I volunteered for the Democratic Party and campaigned door to door for Walter Mondale and Geraldine Ferraro. On November 7, the day after Reagan landslid Mondale, I went to school dressed in head-to-toe black, complete with my Catholic mother's black lace mantilla draped over my hair. I wish I had known you, because then I would have known so many other ways to use Blackness and Sunday clothes as protest. While Reagan waged war on Black mothers, unions, and queers, you, Ms. Walker, responded with peaceful protest published between two covers. *The Color Purple* (1982), *You Can't Keep a Good Woman Down: Stories* (1982), *In Search of Our Mothers' Gardens: Womanist Prose* (1983), *Horses Make a Landscape Look More Beautiful* (1985), *To Hell with Dying* (1988), *Living by the Word* (1988): all broke ground like revolutionary petunias during Reagan's toxic Teflon presidency. In years to come, I read them. They weren't Orwellian. They were round, full, dirt rich, musical, moon drunk, womanish, Black, painful, sweet.

I am very, very grateful I knew you in 2016 and had known you (in the form of your writing) for several Black feminist decades. There are so many ways—and a clever title wasn't one of them!—your work made it possible for me to write this book, *The Color Pynk*; and so, to survive the Trump years by contemplating beauty. I know you have many, many things to do, many poems to write, and many speeches to give, so you will probably never read this. Still, I want to start this book by thanking you for just a few of the gifts you've left for me.

Thank you for "Everyday Use." If I'm trying to be fancy—and sometimes I do like to be fancy!—I'd say this book is about Black femmes' embodied protest in the Trump era. But if I'm keeping things simple, I could say it's about the clothes some Black femmes wore, the hairstyles other Black femmes wore, and the way still other Black femmes did their makeup while Donald Trump was in office. These things are all very, very transitory; are all Black femme ephemera, Black e-femme-era. The clothes went back into closets after photo shoots, braids were unbraided, makeup was taken off and lipsticks worn down to a nub; even Trump's presidency—thank goodness!—is gone with the wind. But your story "Everyday Use" taught me the beautiful things Black women make, and the beautiful things we drape ourselves in, aren't important because they last forever. In your story, Mama's college-educated daughter, Dee, comes back to visit her family on their farm and snatches up her grandmother's quilts so she can hang them on her walls as art. But Mama snatches the quilts back, telling Dee she's promised them to her youngest daughter, Maggie, as a wedding gift. "Maggie can't appreciate these quilts. She'd probably be backward enough to put them to everyday use," Dee huffs furiously. "Maggie would put them on the bed and in five years they'd be in rags. Less than that!" Mama replies simply, "She can always make some more. Maggie knows how to quilt."[1]

The art this book's Black femmes create isn't important because it's timeless, or transcendent, or however white people explain why Mona Lisa and her high-art cousins are in museums. It's important because it *teaches us how to quilt*. It teaches us how to take the scraps at hand and make them into something beautiful, something that keeps you warm and insulates you against forgetting. The particular pink pants or multicolored headscarf or president I describe might have disintegrated by the time you read this: maybe "in five years they'd be in rags. Less than that!" But so what? When we need to stitch something together that filters the colorlessness of the next Reagan, Bush, Clinton, or Trump, we'll know how. You taught me this: surviving through art is an everyday practice of "the well-turned phrase, the cute shape, the scalding humor that erupted like bubbles in lye."[2]

Thank you for the word womanist. While I was learning many, many old words in sixth grade, you invented a new one. The purple-filtered cover of your first collection of essays, *In Search of Our Mothers' Gardens*, opens to a four-part definition of *womanist*. Parts one through three talk about "a black feminist or feminist of color," "a woman who loves other women," and a Black woman who "loves herself. Regardless." But the final part made me think most: *Womanist is to feminist as purple is to lavender.*[3] David Bradley of the *New York Times Magazine*, who probably wasn't used to Black women inventing words, asked you to explain why you did. "I just like to have words that describe things correctly. Now to me, 'black feminist' does not do that," you told him. "I need a word that is organic, that really comes out of the culture, that really expresses the spirit that we see in black women. And it's just . . . womanish. You know, the posture with the hand on the hip, 'Honey, don't you get in my way.'" You went on teaching: "You see, one of the problems with white feminism is that it is not a tradition that teaches white women that they are capable. Whereas my tradition assumes I'm capable. I have a tradition of people not letting me get the skills, but I have cleared fields, I have lifted whatever, I have done it. It ain't not a tradition of wondering whether or not I could do it because I'm a woman."[4]

When that interview was published—also 1984—I needed someone to show me how Black women invent words when language gets too small for us. I went to Black schools in Richmond for K through twelve, but I wasn't assigned a novel by a Black woman until Zora Neale Hurston's *Their Eyes Were Watching God* lit up my freshman English syllabus at the University of California, Berkeley. By the time I discovered that Black women create our own words, I was *starving* for them. So this book collects, curates, coaxes, contemplates, caresses some words and phrases

Black femmes made up because we need them: *pynk, biologically female penis, Luthereal, fempower, interfertility industrial complex.* I'm following Black femmes who walk in your tradition, Ms. Walker, and it's never led me wrong.

Thank you for the Queen Honeybee, Shug Avery. The Color Purple is Celie's story, yes, but the character who looks "like the love thoughts of women," who arrives "like a bee to a blossom—a pear tree blossom in the spring"[5]—is Shug Avery, the jazz-singing, pleasure-cultivating, pink-loving Black femme to Celie's shy stud. "First time I got the full sight of Shug Avery long black body with it black plum nipples, look like her mouth, I thought I had turned into a man," Celie writes in her letter to God.[6] Real-life Black femmes melt for Shug too: see ourselves in her and love her fiercely. "She was the kind of woman I could see myself being," journalist Danielle Young writes in her open love letter to Shug, "free to come and go as she pleased, fearless enough to ask for and get what she wanted."[7] "I immediately took to Shug due to the description of her as a racy and wild woman in disposition, as well as her aesthetic, which was always flashy and bold," writes professor Kaila Adia Story, conjuring Shug and Audre Lorde's Afrekete as twin models for Black femme pleasure.[8] Atlanta-based performer Clover X declares her "femme role model is the sexy, sexual Shug Avery of Alice Walker's *The Color Purple* because 'she is everything a woman isn't supposed to be.'"[9] And self-described Black femme writer, sweetener, and creator Junauda Petrus embodies her love for Shug: "I have Celie and Shug tattooed on me because that was the first time I saw black queerness, black femme queerness, tenderly and sacredly—through Alice Walker's vision."[10]

Shug showed us Black femme love that was never passive, weak voiced, backgrounded, jealous, sometimes-y, self-abnegating, sour, thin; that was abundant, exploratory, songful, deep colored, unpredictable, independent, sweetening, womanish. "Because," as your friend and my teacher Barbara Christian wrote, "what we can even imagine, far less who we can reach, is constantly limited by societal structure," few of us had seen a Black femme character like Shug when you imagined her; and for those of us who knew our love could be all those things—but had no mirrors to reflect those possibilities—*The*

Color Purple offered "a way of knowing that I am not hallucinating, that whatever I feel/know is . . . an affirmation that sensuality is intelligence," as Barbara testifies.[11] Following in the footsteps Dr. Christian left for us, I wrote *The Color Pynk* with the intention of "learning from the language of creative writers, which is one of surprise, so that I might discover what language" we need to love ourselves hardest.[12]

Thank you for many, many other things too, Ms. Walker. For Zora Neale Hurston. For artists without art forms. For giving Grange Copeland three lives. For flowers. For talking to Black yoga teachers (I am one) about orchids. For CODEPINK. For loving your chickens and dogs. For taking care of truth. I hope you will accept this gratitude I'm offering, in the form of a little pynk book.

Black Femme-inist
(with apologies, love, and reverence to Alice Walker and
E. Patrick Johnson)

1. n.—A Black-identified member of the LGBTQIA+ community who embodies resistive femininity. Believes that the dismantling of misogynoir, femmephobia, and transmisogyny are necessary for Black freedom. Knows that Black freedom is necessary for the dismantling of misogynoir, femmephobia, and transmisogyny. Can be cis or trans, binary or nonbinary, AFAB (assigned female at birth) or AMAB (assigned male at birth). Is creative with race, gender, and sexuality, recognizing that creativity is not a luxury for those of us who are Black, queer, feminine, and never meant to thrive.

2. adj.—Loves other Black femmes, erotically and politically. Practices collaborative solidarity. Recognizes the reality of nonbinary vaginas and biologically femme penises. Knows love is a bustling highway and not a one-way street.

3. adj.—Unapologetically Black and beautiful. Enjoys roses while they're still here. Loves stars and STAR. Loves love. Loves themself. Regardless.

4. Femme-inist is to feminist as pynk is to pink.

Femme-inist Is to Feminist as Pynk Is to Pink

If it's not informed by radical black women I don't want to be part of it.

Elle Moxley, founder and executive director
of the Marsha P. Johnson Institute

write a new freedom song! one that honors the Black ancestors whose lives and choices honored your potential existence. write a song of freedom that makes you feel joyful when it comes through you, one you can march and dance to.

adrienne maree brown, writer, pleasure activist, and doula

nspired by radical Black femmes, *The Color Pynk* transcribes a futuristic, joy-tinted freedom song for the twenty-first century. Its premise is simple: this book is a loving, lingering note on Black femmes' poetics of survival in the Trump era and beyond. During the crisis in US feminism that followed Donald Trump's defeat of Hillary Clinton, Black femme intellectuals insisted with increasing urgency that the particularity of our racialized (Black), gendered (feminine), and sexual (queer) imaginations offers an important vantage point from which to challenge heteropatriarchy. *The Color Pynk* engages Black femme cultural production of 2017 to 2020 that colorfully, provocatively imagines freedom in the stark white face of its impossibility: the music of Janelle Monáe and Kelsey Lu, the fashion of Indya Moore and (F)empower, and the films and videos of

Tourmaline and Juliana Huxtable. While this book focuses on a specific slice of the twenty-first century, its inspiration (like its title) comes from the Reagan-era work of Alice Walker. In 1983, at the beginning of the long Reagan-Bush years, Walker collected nonfiction written between 1966 and 1982 in the volume *In Search of Our Mothers' Gardens: Womanist Prose*. The collection opens with her history-making definition of *womanist*, which starts, "A black feminist or feminist of color," and ends, "Womanist is to feminist as purple is to lavender."[1] Composing this definition in a time of "things hoped gone forever but now 'back with the wind' . . . the KKK, obscene national leadership,"[2] Walker met the return of the old with a new, elder-inspired model and name for Black women's solidarity and self-freeing. As *The Color Pynk* engages Black femme representations in music, film, television, social media, art, and fashion, it honors how and why femme-inist is to feminist as pynk is to pink: a way of knowing the world that disrupts conventional meanings of race, gender, and sexuality in the color-deepening, loving tradition of Black queers who, in Walker's words, are "turning madness into flowers."[3]

This book is designed as a triptych. Its first part, "Pussy Power and Nonbinary Vaginas," muses on singer Janelle Monáe's infamous "vagina pants," actor Indya Moore's self-described "nonbinary vagina dress," and Black femme body politics that embrace "promiscuous and polymorphic arrangements of femininity and feminine desire."[4] The second part, "Hymns for Crazy Black Femmes," thinks through Black femme disability politics in the work of musician Kelsey Lu and filmmaker Tourmaline, who conjure protective hairstyles and head wraps as metonyms for the lovingly handled twists and colors of neurodivergence. The book's final part, "Black Femme Environmentalism for the Futa," explores alternatives to white environmentalism in the bright-colored survival gear of artist collective (F)empower and the transspecies makeup of artist Juliana Huxtable. Each section considers how Black femme-inism visualizes radical alternatives to mainstream feminist political platforms. And each section looks at how Black femme artists use bodily adornment—clothing, hairstyles, makeup—as metaphors for the deeply colored, richly textured differences that Black femme perspectives make. This focus takes seriously that "femme *makes* esthetics political," as femme theorist Rhea Ashley

Hoskin notes, and that a "Black femme esthetic can push back against a white norm that has systematically excluded them, making the donning of feminine accoutrements an act of defiance."[5] *The Color Pynk* is about those overlooked, daily acts of Black femme defiance: about how, as Black femme writer Reneice Charles tells us, "crop tops and bodysuits with the word femme scrawled across them in neon pink" are a means to "defy the notion that my femininity is for or about anyone but me."[6]

You know what Charles means by "neon pink," but what color is *pynk*? Not a "real" color (is it?), pynk represents something very real to me: the nuances of Black femme thought. Janelle Monáe first seduced me with pynk's pleasure-soaked tones in her 2018 video "Pynk," whose description promises, "PYNK is a brash celebration of creation. self love. sexuality. and pussy power! PYNK is the color that unites us all, for pink is the color found in the deepest and darkest nooks and crannies of humans everywhere . . . PYNK is where the future is born."[7] Declaring the track among the best of 2018, *Pitchfork*'s Eve Barlow gushed, "Flirty and delicate, wishful and raw, 'PYNK' finds Monáe building a future worth believing in." Barlow rightly (if whitely) appreciated how "the song's genre-bending sonics and the video's femme-dominated utopia" create "a multisensory, radical journey into a new dimension of queer sexuality . . . using a color synonymous with girlishness to discuss the future of gender."[8] But Monáe's pynk *isn't* the girlish pink Barbie wears. To mix a new color, Monáe cuts pink's phallic *i* and replaces it with yonic *y*—playing with and against "clean white, liberal-feminist" 1970s spellings of *womyn* favored by trans-exclusionary lesbians.[9] Not *pink* as in slang for *vulva*, pynk doesn't "believe that all women need to possess a vagina to be a woman," Monáe tells *People*. "I wanted Pynk to be a celebration of women who are unique, distinct, different, may be different from one another but when they come together they create something magical and special."[10] The pynk-bathed femmes of Monáe's video are unique, distinct, different, yes, but share a highly melanated commonality: all are visibly African descended, since the artist "wanted to show *us*, in particular Black women, all celebrating each other."[11] Unlike the pink cheeks of peaches-and-cream, white-girl skin, pynk is the "darker shade'a Femme" that Bajan Canadian femme TJ Bryan searches for.[12] Not a physical tint you can differentiate from *pink* by its chroma or saturation, pynk is the color of the Black femme imagination: a metaphor for how Black femme-inism distinguishes itself from Black feminism by its queerness, and from white femme-inism by its Blackness.

An analogous color to Alice Walker's purple, pynk is a neutralizing shade for misogynoir. *Misogynoir*—a term coined by Moya Bailey, who glosses it as a "visual representation of anti-Black misogyny"—is its own color synthesis: "a portmanteau of 'misogyny,' the hatred of women, and 'noir,' the French word for 'black,' which also carries a specific meaning in film and other media."[13] In *Misogynoir Transformed: Black Women's Digital Resistance*, Bailey explores how Black folx counter misogynoir through *digital alchemy*, or "the ways that women of color, Black women, and Black nonbinary, agender, and gender-variant folks in particular transform everyday digital media into valuable social justice media that recode the failed scripts that negatively impact their lives."[14] But while alchemizing the dross of misogynoir into Black feminist vibranium is necessary to Black femme science, its magic is insufficient to create the color pynk. Misogynoir isn't a color that stigmatizes all Black femmes, Bailey makes clear: "Not all nonbinary Black femmes experience misogynoir because they are not read as Black women in public. For some femmes, homophobia and femmephobia might be the lens through which they become targets of violence. Black femmephobia is an important form of oppression to discuss, but it is not a synonym for misogynoir."[15] Like *Misogynoir Transformed*, this book meditates on how "those of us on the margins of Black womanhood"—femmes, enbies, demigirls, #GirlsLikeUs for whom "'woman' is not what we name ourselves"[16]—create videos, social media profiles, public performances, and digital archives to counter dominant visual culture that assaults us at the intersection of race and gender. But *The Color Pynk* focuses on the creativity of those of us who must recolor femmephobia—"the devaluation, fear and hatred of the feminine: of softness, nurturance, dependence, emotions, passivity, sensitivity, grace, innocence and the color pink"[17]—to create visions of ourselves that look like love. Creating these visions is an act of *pynking*: if *to pink* means "to perforate in an ornamental pattern," or "pierce, stab," *to pynk* is to weaponize Black femme ornament, aesthetics, and piercing insight to poke holes in a social fabric whose edges have always been too straight.[18]

These next pages offer a primer on how to tell *pynk* from *pink*: how to tease out Black femme-inism's gender-specific, race-specific, and desire-specific contributions to the ongoing project of *getting free*. I outline just a few of the many, many reasons why the vehicle *pynk* and its tenor *Black femme* represent a very smart, very Black, and very queer gender. In other words, why Black femme perspectives are important to dismantling white-supremacist heteropatriarchy; why pynk, like Black, is "where the future is born."

PYNK POETICS

Cotton candy, tutus, flavored lip gloss, Valentine's hearts, classic Bubblicious: a certain shade of pink is a very, very girly color. When my daughter Nia was two and toys, dresses, dance shoes, and potty seats were marketed to her only in that shade, she called it "pink light"—but mainstream feminists like Peggy Orenstein and Petula Dvorak imagine it as pink *lite*, "a tiny slice of the rainbow,"[19] lacking in substance and flavor, "cute and fun" but not suitable for "serious stuff."[20] Very girly pink was also the color I chose to wear to my PhD oral exams. Convinced I wasn't smart enough for this degree and my fakery would be exposed in five minutes, I dived into my high-femme, double-Pisces uncommon sense to assemble an outfit designed to make me feel most like myself and so (maybe?) most confident: a diaphanous pink dress with red roses and matching pastel cardigan, pink peep-toe heels, and a pink flower my girlfriend tucked behind my ear for luck. When I entered, one committee member laughed, "La vie en rose!"; when I surprised only myself by passing with flying colors, another remarked I'd done a great job except for my fashion sense. A pretty color, pink isn't supposed to be a smart one. My committee (which included not a single Pisces) supported me, believed in me, and wanted to deflect the misogynoir that would come straight for me if I went into academia not knowing what blush pink and high femme mean there. Kaila Adia Story, the Audre Lorde Chair in Race, Gender, and Sexuality at the University of Louisville, finds her hoop earrings, décolletage, and bold lipstick lead students to "challenge my knowledge, my credentials, my queerness, and

even my feminism, based upon my preferred aesthetic and gender performance. My false eyelashes, lipstick, perfume and, at times, racy form
of dress all signify to students, particularly my White and queer identified students, that I am there to entertain, party, and/or be their friend."[21]
Like pink, "femmes," Laini Madhubuti writes, are "supposed to be lite;
obsessed with clothes, hair, and makeup."[22]

But *pynk*—a color that visualizes Black femmes as smart because of,
not despite, our femme-ininity—doesn't come in lite. "The word *pynk* is
spelled with a *y* so it's something different; it's not what you think," Janelle
Monáe explains in a radio interview. "Pynk is the color of our *brains*."[23]
Black femmes wear our brains on our sleeve when we pynk up; walking
into rooms aggressively womanish, perversely pleasure tinted, or unapologetically crazy, we perform intelligence in a frequency that masculine-of-
center, straight, and neurotypical folk don't always see—because its shades
aren't what white ableist heteropatriarchy expects. These frequencies don't
denigrate *making sense of the world* through the neuroprismatic rather
than the normie, the creative rather than the literal, the sensuous rather
than the abstract, the floral dress rather than the power suit. Adapting
the words of my teacher Barbara Christian, I'd say femmes "of color have
always theorized—but in forms quite different from the Western form of
abstract logic. And I am inclined to say that our theorizing (and I intentionally use the verb rather than the noun) is often in narrative forms, in
the stories we create, in riddles and proverbs, in the play with language,
because dynamic rather than fixed ideas seem more to our liking."[24] Black
femme fluency, in figures "both sensual and abstract, both beautiful and
communicative," is a source of great pleasure for me, as someone who
loves figurative language—so much so, some exes complained my constant speaking in metaphor makes me hard to understand.[25] For them,
my accumulation of metaphors was as excessive as other markers of my
femmeness: my collection of statement earrings or platform shoes impractical for driving, for example. In fact, *figuration* means, in one definition,
representation in excess of literal meaning. Always representing in excess
of straight logic, femme gender expressions challenge folks to correct for
myopia that sees femininity as heterosexual availability. And the Black
femme, who, according to Kara Keeling, "defies the specular logic that

generally organizes 'lesbian,' as well as that which organizes 'black' and 'woman'"—who's smart enough to color outside commonsense visions of what queer *and* Black look like—models a bountiful array of possibilities for accumulating meaning beyond the normative.[26]

Let me cite just two modes of Black femme figuration I routinely see overlooked as serious intellectual practices. The first is the art of throwing shade, a genre Black femmes literally invented. In the second month of Trump's presidency (coincidence?), *Merriam-Webster's Dictionary* announced its addition of the phrase *throw shade* via a Tweet with a gif of ballroom legend Dorian Corey. The Tweet's screen grab from *Paris Is Burning* and its bright-yellow caption—Corey's famous line, "Shade is: I don't tell you you're ugly but I don't have to tell you because you know you're ugly"—acknowledge Black transfeminine folk as creators of a rhetorical trope that had thoroughly permeated mainstream social media and popular culture by the 2010s.[27] An art form of the insult, *shade* distinguishes itself from *reading* or *trash talk* by how it makes meaning in excess of the literal, mobilizing metaphor, metonymy, and what Zambian writer Namwali Serpell calls *melodramatic irony*.[28] "Shade is shot through with the idea of irony," Samuel Delany elaborates. "The aspect of those phrases and rhetorical figures which we are not sure how to respond to—where language opens up, through a moment's hesitation, into an explosion of potentialities, some appalling, some unimaginably wonderful, and all of which seize power for the speaker and, however momentarily, articulate wildly subversive possibilities."[29] But when mainstream press outlets like the *New York Times*, *Time*, or NPR report on shade in the *RuPaul's Drag Race* era, they approach it as a colorful pastime, at best—feminine bitchiness, at worst—rather than an art form that tilts and twists, recolors and refigures how words and wordlessness signify. Shade is "not a natural topic" for literary analysis, Serpell speculates, because "it is black and femme—a fiercely private code for survival, a badge of pride within certain cultural cliques."[30] But wouldn't it be more accurate to say anti-Blackness and femmephobia keep *shade* from serious consideration in most of the whitewashed, boys' club cultural cliques we call academia?

The second mode of too-often-dismissed Black femme figuration I'll evoke here—the one that centrally concerns me in *The Color Pynk*—is fashion metaphorics. Metaphors and shoes are two obsessions that, since grad school, have brightened my eyes and inspired me toward beauty. The former obsession earned me a PhD in comparative literature and tenured positions at three research institutions; the latter earned me unwanted attention from colleagues who stopped me with inane questions as I rushed to and from teaching, the library, or my office: *How do you walk in those? Aren't those hard to get around in?* One crucial element of shade is that it's at once verbal and nonverbal; the simile *her wig laid like Whitney Houston's third cousin* could be accompanied by the gesture of averting your eyes and stroking your own edges, say.[31] Well, Black femme metaphor is verbal and nonverbal too, elaborated in both how we adorn our words and how we adorn our bodies. Colleagues emboldened to ask about my gold stilettos or peacock-blue platforms simply expose their illiteracy in femme fashion metaphorics: they don't see I'm balancing on weapons made of precious metal, floating on the color of the ocean, refusing to walk on the same ground they do. Why do my books on metaphor look smart to them and my shoes look stupid? Why don't (usually poorly dressed) intellectuals appreciate Black and Latinx femmes' "creative labor in everyday performances of public body presentation[?]" queries performance scholar Jillian Hernandez: our "embodied performances and creative practices that . . . embrace ostentatious styling, hyperfemininities and hypermasculinities, raunch, grotesquerie, camp, voluptuousness, glitter, pink, and gold"?[32] As my brown femme mentor Kewal Hausmann says, "Straight logic makes no sense."

From sneakers to slips to nipple piercings to Fenty Beauty to sista locs, Black femmes curate shoes, clothes, jewelry, accessories, makeup, and hairstyles as metaphors for all kinds of things. If we're feeling extra *meta*, we may use them as metaphors for femmeness itself. In an interview for Laura Harris and Liz Crocker's 1997 anthology *Femme*, Barbara Cruikshank employs this metaphor to invite Joan Nestle to think through differences between woman and femme: "Let's think of becoming fem as a kind of garment. If you are making this transition from woman to fem, what do you first take off in order to put on your fem garb? What is it to take off being a woman?" "That is so smart," Nestle remarks on Cruikshank's line of inquiry, responding, "All the garments of public responsibility as symbolized by my work clothes. For the last thirty years, it has meant putting down my satchel with all my student papers, all the memos and requests of college teaching. It means divesting myself of pantyhose, slacks, pumps, bra. It means giving my body its own time when it is dressed only in garments of surrender."[33] For myself and other Black femmes engaged in this book—many of whom, like Story, know Black queer battle fatigue all too intimately—*surrender* isn't a dress we choose to put on. Instead, when we take off the straight, bougie, respectability-conscious constrictions of womanness, we imagine slipping into garments of *Black femme freedom*.

This last phrase is the alliterative, assonant expression of Black cisfemme historian Jessica Marie Johnson. Documenting how eighteenth-century Louisiana *femmes de couleur* manifested a more expansive idea of liberty than state-issued free papers could grant, Johnson evokes Black femme freedom as an imaginative "freedom rooted in their relationship to African descent, their sense of themselves as women, and their capacity to belong to themselves and each other . . . a promiscuous accounting of blackness as future possibility and femme as stealing a bit of sweetness for themselves."[34] To me, Kelsey Lu's braids look like freedom rooted in their relationship to African descent; Tourmaline's flower crowns look like femmes stealing a bit of sweetness for themselves. Elaborated under the long, orange shadow of Trump's presidency—when, as Saidiya Hartman writes of the Red Summer of 1919, "nothing appeared more improbable and untimely than colored girls, not yet broken by want and deprivation, dreaming of what might be possible"[35]—the fashion metaphorics of the artists in this book aren't "just" clothes, hair, and makeup (the trinity associated with femme liteness). They are, as Tourmaline imagines, *black femme freedom dreaming*. "When I refuse to make myself smaller to accommodate the demands for respectability put forward by mainstream institutions—when I wear sheer dresses and chokers to art openings and airports alike, when I don't tuck, when I am my fullest and freest self in the most public of places—I'm freedom dreaming," she writes. "I am expanding in the power of my unruliness and refusal to conform to violent and oppressive normativity."[36] Thottishly, unpassingly, translucently, savagely wearing the color pynk is "putting dreaming to the test of material practice," as Jill Casid offers; is "dreaming with the materials of the quotidian" as "a life plan."[37]

"NEGRESS" PYNK

Sugar Ray Robinson's flamingo-pink Cadillac, Cam'ron's Killa Pink mink coat, Lil' Kim's pastel-pink python boots, Kamala Harris's AKA-pink *Vogue* cover: a certain shade of pink is a very, very Black color. In 1936, Italian fashion designer Elsa Schiaparelli popularized an ultra-bright magenta later known as "shocking pink"—a color that, she recalls, came to her in a vision. "The colour flashed in front of my eyes. Bright, impossible, imprudent, becoming, life-giving, like all the light and the birds and the fish in the world put together . . . a shocking colour, pure and undiluted," she wrote in her autobiography. "It caused a mild panic amongst my friends and executives, who began to say that I was crazy and that nobody would want it because it was really nigger pink. What of it? Negroes are sometimes strikingly smart."[38] Schiaparelli's racist, backhanded compliment aside, the use of that racial epithet to describe "a dark hue of a particular color as in nigger brown, nigger grey or nigger pink" persisted late into the twentieth century, linguist Paulina Mormol finds[39]—even if calling a "deep, vivid pink . . . 'Nigger pink' would have been the vulgar version, used by children with neither background nor charity in their parents' hearts," Elinor Rufus Hughes opined in 1953.[40] Black folk themselves often embraced associations with vibrant pinks that color-shy white people avoided, testifies Guyanese writer Beryl Gilroy. "When I came to Britain I wore a plain pink dress with a large white bow and got stared at. People wore sensible colours—pink got dirty in the grime of the '50s," she remembers. "Everyone was wearing grey and black and we brought bright colours. We were used to wearing bright colours. We would walk along dressed to the nines and bouncing with confidence—people had never seen the likes of us."[41]

Pynk is an unapologetically femme and feminist shade of (what I'll call) negress pink. In white heteronormative common sense (the kind Kewal already told us *makes no sense*), Black femme-ininity is as nonsensical as pink in an English winter. Black people are assumed masculine—and queer AFAB people are assumed masculine—so to be Black *and* queer *and* feminine all at once would "explode common sense from the inside."[42] My husband, Matt Richardson, and our friend Marlon Bailey posit, "Misogyny and antiblackness coalesce into an endeavor that seeks to render black femininity into a pure absence. To identify as black and feminine equates to annihilation."[43] Seen through a whitewashing filter, Black queer femme-ininity disappears; but refocused through a pynkening filter, femme-ininity stands out as a very, very Black gender. Unlike woman, femme can be (but is not always) a nonbinary gender.[44] For artist and activist Joshua Allen, being a Black nonbinary femme means being "wholly uninterested in living my life in accordance with the social norms connected to the gender binary";[45] for sex educator Ericka Hart, it means refusing to "subscribe to any notion of man or woman" and creating a gender that's "something in between or something outside of or something around or under" those two poles.[46] And while the queerness of nonbinary femme experience creates new trajectories and pynker paths of *between and outside and around and under*, Blackness in the Americas has never fit into dominant "social norms connected to the gender binary."

Certainly, since the Baptist Church began promoting respectability politics in the early 1900s, Black folk have tried to condense our expansive genders in the hopes of mitigating anti-Blackness by acting like the ladies and gentlemen we could never be. But no matter how arduously African Americans twisted ourselves toward normativity, "it could not be denied that what it meant to be a man or a woman in the Negro world diverged wildly from what was to be expected in the world at large," Hartman ventriloquizes white judgment.[47] In working-class and rural families where women were breadwinners, play aunties and grandmothers raised children together, and matrimony was unnecessary to create families; "the gender non-conformity of the black community, its supple and extended modes of kinship, its queer domesticity, promiscuous sociality and loose intimacy, and its serial and fluid conjugal relations" meant whole communities moved *between or outside or around or under* prescribed man- and womanness.[48] Because of this, Hartman imagines that for Harlem Renaissance lesbian dancer Mabel Hampton, crossing from Black straight to

Black queer gender was as subtle a move as going from cherry blossom to shocking pink. "Did she have to be a woman? Did she have to be a man? Did she have to be anything at all, besides someone who loves women? What a woman could or should be was incredibly fraught, especially for a black woman. Even if she wore a dress or a skirt, she wasn't the same kind of woman as a white woman; and no matter how hard she worked or how many people she supported, she would never be considered the equal of a man," Hartman ponders from Hampton's point of view. "What was it that a colored woman was supposed to be? Whether they had bobbed hair or not, wore pants or dresses, had husbands or not, it didn't seem to matter; they all fell in between the categories or failed to conform to them."[49] In the introduction to their anthology *Brazen Femme*, Chloë Brushwood Rose and Anna Camilleri imagine, "Femme might be described [as] 'femininity gone wrong'—bitch, slut, nag, whore, cougar, dyke or brazen hussy."[50] If this is the case for Black femmes, it connects us to—rather than separates us from—Black cis and straight women, whose genders could just as accurately be described as "femininity with 'mistakes' . . . defiant in its 'failure' to occupy the intersecting norms of patriarchal femininity."[51]

The familial link between nonbinary and cisgender Black femininities takes center stage in Katori Hall's series *P-Valley* (2020–), where beard-sporting, wig- and lipstick-adorned Uncle Clifford (who uses she/her pronouns) holds together a hard-struggling cadre of dancers working at her strip club, the Pynk. Located in the fictional Mississippi town Chucalissa, the waterfront building that houses the Pynk is a precarious, debt-riddled family inheritance from Uncle Clifford's grandmother, Ernestine. Once a juke joint—a midcentury Dirty South space with ample room for "people who are complicated in their gender, queer characters, lesbians, gay men. . . . In them juke joints, they was doin' everything, and they didn't have the hang-ups that we have today," Sharon Bridgforth testifies[52]—the Pynk was originally a cotton mill owned by Ernestine's parents. "Of all things, Uncle Clifford chose to create a strip club. Why is it not a drag club or a restaurant?" Uncle Clifford's portrayer, Nico Annan, asks in an interview. "She is a dancer and her need for that unbridled freedom is why the women fly on the pole. In the world, day to day, we don't have the same level of freedom, so you wanna swing the pendulum to the total other side and live in such freedom and express that. That's what's going on in the club."[53] Annan, a gay man, vividly remembers reading the script for the first time. "It said something to the effect of, 'Uncle Clifford emerges from the shadows, eyelashes dancing like butterfly wings and nails like evil talons. She is equal in measure, masculine and feminine. Uncle Clifford.' And I was just like 'Wow,'" he recounts.[54] Annan actively mobilizes fashion metaphorics to highlight Uncle Clifford's choreography of Black femme freedom. "The imagery of the butterflies, the metamorphosis that lies within there, the strength of eagles. I thought about height, I thought about flight. So always even in some of my costumes and wardrobes, I worked very intricately with our designers. . . . I always wanted a little feather, a little sense of that flight."[55]

Birds of pynk feathers flock together. Uncle Clifford is an unapologetically fierce mother peacock to her often-struggling dancers, offering childcare for a newborn whose mother comes to work with a split lip, employing a Black lesbian couple and accommodating their pregnancy, offering to spend money she doesn't have to bail a dancer out of jail. "Femininity gone awry, gone to town, gone to the dogs": this is how Brushwood Rose and Camilleri describe *femme*, but it's also how Chucalissa's churchgoing folk view both Uncle Clifford (whom they address as "he/she" and "it") and the dancers at the Pynk.[56] "These girls, these girls. Ain't no orphanage for hos," Uncle Clifford explains her commitment to her employees.[57] Clear that she's not a woman like them but also that she's not unlike these women, Uncle Clifford creates a Black feminine, trans-inclusive, sex-work-positive flock at the Pynk. "There is an art to flocking: staying separate enough not to crowd each other, aligned enough to maintain a shared direction, and cohesive enough to always move towards each other," adrienne maree brown remarks of what humans can learn from birds.[58] The diversity of the Black femininity that flies through the Pynk is a source of pride for Uncle Clifford, who consoles aspiring rapper Lil Murda when he gets into a fight over a dancer: "The Pynk got everything. . . . We got white bitches, redbone bitches, high-yellow bitches, midnight-blue bitches, Molly, hot wings, Tums after the hot wings." "Seem like the Pynk got everything but the one thing I really need," Lil Murda replies slowly, running his eyes down Uncle Clifford in her red silk dragonfly-print jacket and reaching over her shoulder to slip his finger inside one of her curls. Yes, Lil Murda:

without Black femme-ininity, the color spectrum of Black femininity is incomplete. "This little nigga tryna make me blush," Uncle Clifford laughs nervously, adding her own color to the Pynk.[59] Overflowing with brown, red, yellow, and blue, the Pynk is a very, very Black space whose beauty is only complete when Uncle Clifford's colors can be seen in the flock.

Personally, I don't believe including all feminine people under the umbrella *femme* benefits those of us who hold this label as a shield to deflect trans- and queerphobia—and who need it to find one another. In one of *P-Valley*'s most visually stunning scenes, Uncle Clifford stands at the edge of a cotton field under her *own* umbrella—a red lace parasol whose fabulousness brings an oncoming tractor to a halt. But I also believe that denying the intimate connections between Black femme-ininity and Black cis and straight womanhood can do nothing but leave us all more vulnerable. "Our situation as Black people necessitates that we have solidarity around the fact of race," the Combahee River Collective wrote in their groundbreaking 1977 statement. "We reject the stance of Lesbian separatism because it is not a viable political analysis or strategy for us. It leaves out far too much and far too many people, particularly Black men, women, and children."[60] Femme theorists often point out how much cis and straight sisters can learn from us: "A femme perspective is not only vital, but also uniquely equipped to reconfigure and analyze dominant culture, while also challenging and exposing the deeply ingrained femmephobic meanings attached to femininity. Femme theory is thus a framework for dislodging these prescriptions of femininity; checking what assumptions might be held about femininity and feminine people," Hoskin suggests.[61] But Black femmes have so many lifesaving, binary-cracking, world-expanding gender lessons to learn from Black women too. "I'm a femme like my mother and my grandmother," performer Veronica Jenkins claims. "Hardworking handywomen who can repair a leaky faucet or change the spark plug in a car, who curse like sailors, who get dressed up for church, who can cook like gourmets when we need to and order pizza when we aren't . . . who like reading waaay too much to be attentive mothers to toddlers . . . who know how to cornrow and plait and make a scene when it's necessary—yeah, that's the kinda femme I am."[62] The very, very Black pynk kind, who knows how to make a wayward way out of no way.

STAR PYNK

Triangles, double moons, handkerchiefs, pansies, roses while we're still here: of course, of *course*, so many shades of pink sing queerness without saying a word. Writing this book, I spent uncounted hours gazing at very, very queer pink pantsuits, pink eye makeup, pink ribbons, pink altars, pink survival gear, even pink HuCows. But the sources of femme pinkness that drew me in deepest . . . that I returned to again and again like a river . . . were the gowns, flowers, and aura of Stonewall veteran, activist, artist, model, and performer Marsha P. Johnson. I fell into rose-colored time warps watching her on Tourmaline's Vimeo, Randolfe Wicker's YouTube, and Michael Kasino's love letter of a documentary, *Pay It No Mind*. On February 14, 2019, I brought art supplies to my Femme Theory class at Harvard so students could make valentines for Miss Marsha and leave them in public places. I entreated my amazing Harvard colleague Robert Reid-Pharr, who knew Marsha in the 1980s, to tell me stories. Gifted with a chance to moderate a conversation with CeCe McDonald and Elle Moxley in February 2021, I asked these brilliant women to talk about their love for the Queen Mother. Marsha P(ay It No Mind) Johnson *is* the color pynk to me—the femmebodiment of all its queer nuances, loving generosity, and improbable joys. One of Mother Marsha's most circulated images—the header on the Marsha P. Johnson Institute website and the model for murals in Dallas, Denver, Portland, and Jersey City—shows her smiling radiantly in an off-the-shoulder fuchsia taffeta dress, haloed by a crown of roses, carnations, daisies, peonies, and baby's breath. In one of my favorite images she poses at Gay Pride in a shimmering, rose-gold gown, crowned with a wide-open wreath of pink and red flowers and adorned with a lavender sash embossed STONEWALL. In these and other images that live on my screen, Miss Marsha is always fabulously, fantastically ornamented to the hilt in ways that *look like love*.

Let me be more specific, though: Mother Marsha is gorgeously ornamented in ways that look like *Black love*. Everyone knows Black people love shiny things, right? That "aesthetical Negroes [are] content to waste money on extravagance, ornament, and shine."[63] That "things that bling, shine, or shimmer, that emit light are especially privileged" in the "everyday aspirational practices of black urban communities, who make do and more with what they have, creating prestige through the resources at hand," as art historian Krista Thompson elucidates.[64] In his influential, unabashedly racist 1908 treatise "Ornament and Crime," Viennese architect Adolf Loos was indulgent of so-called Kaffirs' love of the ornamental since, unlike "modern man," they "have no other way of attaining the high points of their existence."[65] Twenty-first-century racists are less tolerant of African American accumulation of "bling, shine, and shimmer." Noting derision of Hurricane Katrina survivors' jewelry, Humvees, Louis Vuitton bags, and flat-screen TVs, Lisa Marie Cacho observes, "Poor African Americans are not only represented as unentitled to 'luxuries'; they are also denied the power to decide what constitutes a 'luxury' and the power to define what they need and what they can live without."[66] Not (only) luxuries, ornaments can be lifesaving shields more resistant than levees. "The ostentatious display of things might be interpreted as a protective means. We might understand the use of material goods and the production of blinding light as a shield or apotropaic, simultaneously reflecting and deflecting the deidealizing gaze on black subjects," Thompson offers.[67] "The beauty of black ordinary, the beauty that resides in and animates the determination to live free, the beauty that propels the experiments in living otherwise," Hartman states in no uncertain terms, "is not a luxury; rather it is a way of creating possibility in the space of enclosure, a radical art of subsistence, an embrace of our terribleness, a transfiguration of the given. It is a will to adorn, a proclivity for the baroque, and the love of too much."[68]

For Black trans women, transfeminist scholar Eve Lorane Brown describes, the *beauty of black ordinary*—the "extravagance, ornament, and shine" of hormone therapy, hair extensions, contouring kits, or other everyday accessories of black femme-ininity—saves lives in more immediate ways. White trans women forgo makeup, breasts, or shaved legs and walk through her majority-Black Oakland neighborhood unharassed, she notices, benefitting from residents' knowledge that interfering with *any* white person risks police intervention. The same isn't true for Black trans women. "No matter how unclockable" a trans femme of color might be, "no matter how well she could blend in, she still carried that seed of fear about being found out . . . fetishized, ridiculed, rejected, or attacked," Janet Mock writes. "We don't have to search for too long to watch footage of a girl being attacked on public transit or in the restroom, or read a story about the killing of yet another black or Latina woman."[69] Femme tech— manicures, wigs, foundation makeup, dresses, waist trainers, handbags, hormone therapies, plastic surgeries—are "'luxuries' [that] may be re- garded as meeting basic physiological and safety needs for African Amer- ican trans women," Brown concludes.[70] Diving into ornament as a daily practice of beauty and safety, Treva Ellison remarks, Black trans femmes engage "the sartorial, the expressive, and the performed" with a view to "reworking and repurposing the signs, symbols, and accoutrements of Western modernity" in ways that guard against "Black femme subjection, abuse, and premature death."[71]

But Marsha's pink, shiny, frilly, plastic, floral femme tech wasn't cu- rated to blend seamlessly with—well, *anything*. She stood out, always. Queen Mother wasn't shy to walk through town half en déshabillé: "She'd be coming up Christopher Street with the rolled-down stockings, fuzzy slippers, her wig in beer-can rollers: 'Hello, everybody! What a wo-o- onderful morning!'" Sasha McCaffrey laughs.[72] When fully dressed— gloriously "over the top with the jewelry, flowers in her hair, very creative looking, very commanding of attention," performer Ron Jones recalls[73]— Marsha embodied the Black aesthetic Hartman lyricizes as the "tendency to excess, the too much, the love of the baroque; the double descriptive: down-low, Negro-brown, more great and more better; the frenzy and passion; the shine and fabulousness of ghetto girls."[74] Like her spiritual daughter Tourmaline, Marsha dressed as her "fullest and freest self in the most public of places": "I remember seeing Marsha walk down the street in a miniskirt that she had made with nothing on underneath and it was clearly see-through. *Clearly!*" Rick Shupper emphasizes. "She wasn't the kind of queen you questioned her drag," Martin Boyce explains thought- fully. "Because she had very little. And, you know, she wasn't a well- dressed, coordinated kind of queen. She put on what was available and what, you know, fulfilled her idea of being a woman to some extent. It was a very, very natural look—and all her own."[75] A self-described STAR (Street Transvestite Action Revolutionary) who cofounded the nation's first house for trans youth, Marsha often had little besides her look to call "all her own." "Years ago I had to get some of my stuff out of the trash can and bring it home and wash it. I've never been an extravagant-type drag queen who can go out to a fancy store and buy expensive dresses," Marsha explained in 1992. Quick to show friends how to transform a discarded gown with "a cut here and scissors here and a razor blade here for the bottom, and . . . glitter," Marsha turned a trip "to a Salvation Army" store into "an art form because she knew for five dollars, maybe three dollars, you should be able to get an outfit," actor Agosto Machado recalls with reverence.[76]

"No people can live off of flowers, nor gain strength and robustness by devotion to beauty. No people can get their living and build themselves up by refined style and glittering fashion, or addiction to harmonies, colors and delights that please the senses," Hartman channels early-twentieth-century racial uplift messages.[77] But Marsha *got her life* exactly that way. Her loving friend and roommate Randy Wicker recalls, "Maybe she'd take her last ten dollars and go out the door and come back twenty minutes later with this big bouquet, ten dollars' worth of flowers. And I'd say, 'Marsha, what are you doing wasting your last ten dollars on flowers!?' And she'd go in my back room and be putting them in her hair and making this incredible arrangement: 'Oh don't worry, Mr. Wicker, these flowers gonna make me a lot of money!' And they would." Nearly all of *Pay It No Mind*'s interviewees remember Marsha's mystical connection to flowers with reverence. "I'd go to the flower district and they'd have these big tables where they sort lilies and things, and Marsha would be *sleeping* under them. I saw this more than once. And I would say to the guy there, 'Why is she here?' and the guy would just say: 'Oh, she's holy,'" Thomas Lanigan-Schmidt recounts, shaking his head in awe. "She would stay there and they'd give her, Marsha, the leftover flowers, tons and tons of flowers, daffodils."[78] Day-old roses, lilies, carnations, jasmine, and baby's breath interlaced with plastic flowers, tinsel, netting, faux fur, mirrors, sequins, and faux pearls in Marsha's hair, offering an exuberant, unapologetically over-the-top vision of Black femme-ininity that "disrespects notions of proper taste and decorum and celebrates the feminized and exaggerated."[79] Making art out of *literal* excess (flowers), Mother Marsha's overfull, fresh and artificial, riotously colored crowns are a study in why Hernandez claims "pink poses threats to the patriarchal aesthetic values of Euro-American culture."[80]

The ornaments of a very queer gender, Marsha's pynk flowers—pynk even when red, purple, or white—also symbolize a collection of very queer desires. "Flowers, of course, are the sex organs of plants," Naomi Wolf reminds readers in her unabashedly hetero- and ciscentric *Vagina: A New Biography*, opining that "lushly petalled, vulval flowers such as red roses . . . ordered thoughtfully in advance" naturally produce arousal in the (according to her) biologically distinct female brain.[81] But Marsha's lushly petalled, thoughtfully ordered flowers metaphorize a very different kind of desire. Her crowns visualize a headspace—a Black femme brain—that creates pleasure from cut flowers, yes, both those thrown away and those so precious you buy them with your last ten dollars; and also through plastic blossoms, electric lights, costume jewelry, holiday decorations. Marsha wears a Black trans aesthetics that, as L. H. Stallings writes, reorganizes the senses to "disturb forms, biological and otherwise," and "emancipates sexuality from nature and entrusts it to artifice, which opens up a world where the difference between the sexes, form, appearance, beauty, age and race" mean *differently*.[82] Marsha's crowns are undeniably erotic in Audre Lorde's sense of "creative energy empowered."[83] But (unlike Wolf's book, inspired by a change in her orgasms), Marsha's floral art was neither sexual nor sexually motivated. Over-the-top decoration wasn't the way to draw trade (clients or lovers), Marsha was clear: "The best way to do it was with your own natural hair . . . with just a little bit of makeup."[84] Not designed to enhance or represent her sex life, Marsha's ornaments multiplied because she enjoyed them in and for themselves. In *Sensual Excess: Queer Femininity and Brown Jouissance*, Amber Jamilla Musser intimates that *seeking pleasure in the ornamental* itself represents a queer desire: "After all, why separate orgasmic pleasure from pleasure in the decorative, and why give it priority?" she asks.[85] Perversely, self-pleasuringly ornamental, Queen Mother didn't wear flowers, pynk, or Black femme-ininity to attract any kind of lover or orgasm: she wore them as their own form of pleasure, expression, protest, and love. And that, children, is what makes the impractical pynk dreams of Black femmes so very, beautifully queer.

Like pink, pynk isn't a color that everyone favors—or even recognizes.
"Anyone studying pink today comes up against 'the color's inherent am-
bivalence,'" art historian Valerie Steele observes in the exhibition catalog
Pink: The History of a Punk, Pretty, Powerful Color. "Pink provokes ex-
ceptionally strong feelings of both 'attraction and repulsion' . . . and . . .
has been called 'the most divisive of colors.'" In fact, Steele notes, color
historians are divided about whether pink is anything more than a pale
shade of red: "Linguists say that pink is among the least common color
terms. A surprising number of books about color do not even mention
pink, and some people deny that pink is a 'real' color at all. It would probably be more accurate to say that pink is an anomalous color that often
seems unimportant."[86] People say the same things about Black femmes,
I know. Some deny cis femmes are "real" queers: I'm thinking of Black
studs at a house party who insisted femmes experience sexism while they
(studs) experience homophobia, or Black femmes at an Ivy League school
who declined to speak about queer gender since their femme presentations
(they said shamefacedly) made them "normative." Of course, people still
deny trans femmes are "real" women: when public figures like Chima-
manda Ngozi Adichie and J. K. Rowling negate trans-woman-ness, they
voice a transmisogyny that runs deep on both sides of the Atlantic. If you
don't believe in pynk—if you don't believe Black femmes are "real" queers,
women, or forces to be reckoned with—then please know, I haven't written
this book to convince you otherwise. When Janelle Monáe visited radio
host Jazzy McBee to discuss her album *Dirty Computer,* she owned, "With
this particular album I had to think about who I was okay with pissing off,
who I didn't really care about jumping ship or not supporting the message.
I had to think about that. And I had to think about who I wanted to celebrate."[87] When I decided to write *The Color Pynk*, I thought about those
same things.

I wrote this book to celebrate Elle Moxley, adrienne maree brown, Reneice Charles, TJ Bryan, Kaila Adia Story, Laini Madhubuti, Dorian Corey, Jessica Marie Johnson, Tourmaline, CeCe McDonald, Janet Mock, Eve
Lorane Brown, Amber Musser, Queen Mother Marsha P. Johnson: to celebrate all the Black femmes who have appeared in these opening pages, all
the Black femmes who will appear throughout the book, *all Black femmes*

everywhere. Black femmes who don't believe you're queer enough, I wrote this to celebrate you too. As Monáe says, "*This* is who needs the love. I'm going to write . . . to uplift *us*. Not try to be angry or please people, but really celebrate the people who need it."[88] I also wrote *The Color Pynk* for Black femmes' parents and godparents, siblings and sister-friends, cousins and play cousins, friends and lovers, spouses and exes, children and chirren: for everyone who believes that we are, as sister Black femme Pisces Isake Smith identifies herself, our "ancestors' wildest dreams."[89] Because I chose Black femmes to celebrate, I wrote in the language I use when we talk to each other. This may mean you come across a term or concept you don't know and I don't define because, as Monáe told McBee about pansexuality, "I think you should research it, Google it."[90] In other words, I'm asking readers who want to be in solidarity with Black femmes to do the work of becoming fluent in Black queer language and even, as my sibling spirit Jafari Allen suggests, of "becoming fluent in" our "(perhaps disparate or even contradictory) desires."[91]

Especially *this* desire. When *MadameNoire* asked Elle Moxley, "What is your biggest dream for Black women/Black femmes everywhere?" she replied gorgeously, "That we will love ourselves fully from our own eyes, and if we're lucky to love ourselves I hope we learn to love ourselves over and over again in new ways . . . and then just maybe we'll be able to apply that love to a Black woman before anybody else."[92] I wrote this book to be part of Ms. Elle's dreams; and I wrote this book in the hope you will want to be part of her dreams too. This is *la vie en pynk*.

PART ONE

Pussy Power and Nonbinary Vaginas

W e did it! We created a sea of pink!" pussyhat creators Krista Suh and Jayna Zweiman enthused in the afterglow of the 2017 Women's March. "Young and old, rich and poor. Educated and not, religious and secular. Straight and LGBTQ, every race and color. All wearing hand-made, knitted caps on a single day, awash in a sea of pink, arm-in-arm in solidarity for women's rights and in protest against the rhetoric used toward women and minorities in the previous year's state and federal elections."[1] Flush with craft-activist success, they reiterated their pleasure in the hat's name: "We love the clever wordplay of 'hat' and 'cat,' but yes, 'pussy' is also a derogatory term for female genitalia. We chose this loaded word for our project because we want to reclaim the term as a means of empowerment."[2] "The pink pussy hat is enticing and (almost) irresistible," Banu Gökarıksel and Sara Smith muse in their critique of the march. "Bright, clever, and beautiful—and yet."[3] And yet, not every feminist protesting Trump's inauguration felt empowered by the vision of solidarity knitted into the hats. South Asian feminist Amiya Nagpal cut to the quick: "The march conflated womanhood with having a vagina. The march conflated being a woman with having a pink vagina. . . . My vagina is not pink."[4] Transfeminist professor Cáel Keegan reminded, "Any time feminism starts centering people based on anatomy, that gets . . . dangerous for trans people."[5] The hat's creators well-meaningly justified, "We chose the color pink . . . because pink is associated with femininity. We did not choose the color pink as a representation of some people's anatomy. . . . It does not matter if you have a vulva or what color your vulva may be. If a participant wants to create a pussy hat that reflects the color of her vulva, we support her choice."[6]

But support for multicolored hats misses the stake of protests like Nagpal's and Keegan's, whose ultimate critique was not of the hat's pattern but of the model of solidarity it represents. These viewers saw in the Pussyhat Project a race-blind, ciscentric feminism "expanding" to include all races and genders in its folds without imagining what it would mean to meet Black and brown, trans and queer feminists on our own terms—terms that might unravel yarn-narrow foundations from which liberal feminism and hats were being spun. Black transfeminist Elle Moxley, director of the Marsha P. Johnson Institute and one of the hat's most blunt critics ("The hat won't prove anything," she says), usefully challenges models of solidarity that take a symbol of privileged femininity and ask marginalized feminists to identify with it.[7] "It is the responsibility of people who want to be in solidarity with Black women, and Black femmes to be self-reflective. . . . Solidarity is often dictated and controlled by people with power and privilege," she remarks.[8]

Even as some protesters espoused a one-knitting-pattern-fits-all feminism to usher in Trump-era resistance, other Women's March participants used their platforms to imagine Blacker, queerer shades of solidarity. Among the keynote speakers that day was singer Janelle Monáe, who addressed the crowd in a black sweatshirt that commanded protesters to "FEM THE FUTURE" as she chanted names of Black women who died in police custody. While black-clad, free-haired Monáe chose not to pink up as part of her protest that day, the next year she released a series of visual texts that envisioned unapologetic Blackness and unapologetic pinkness—that is, Black queer femme-ininity—in her own figurative landscapes. Monáe's video "Pynk" composed what Carmen Phillips calls "a black queer feminist love letter to springtime, being femme, [and] black and brown women's bodies" as her character forewent hats for internet-breaking (so-called) vagina pants.[9] Also speaking at the Washington Women's March was black-suited journalist Janet Mock, whose waterfall of brown curls needed no pussyhat as she called for all present to "break out of our comfort zones and be confrontational" on behalf of detained migrants, sex workers, and trans youth.[10] The following year, Mock worked closely with Indya Moore—a young nonbinary trans femme who had been a sex worker and was living in a group foster home during the march—on the history-making television series *Pose*. Mock became the first trans woman of color to write and direct a television episode, "Love Is the Message," which opened with Moore's character—ethereally beautiful transfemme Puerto Rican sex worker Angel—draped in multiple shades of pink as she explains to a white cis woman what it means to be a woman with a penis. On social media, Moore pushed Angel's conversation further: "Dear cis people, I hope you one day evolve beyond penises and vaginas," they pleaded shadily,[11] inserting "a radical point missing in mainstream" feminist campaigns like the pussyhat, where "trans women are often made to feel ashamed of their genitals if they don't have a vagina."[12]

In 2018, Monáe and Moore both darkened the pussyhat's millennial pink to new shades: Monáe dancing through videos in Black, femme-inist, pynk pussy pants, Moore hitting the red carpet in wild, decolonized, nonbinary, brown vagina dresses. Broadening mainstream feminism's color and gender palette, these artists challenge viewers to engage in the political work Moxley calls *collaborative solidarity*: organizing between Black cis- and transfeminists that stresses respect for differences as a means of establishing peer relationships. "Collaborative Solidarity goes beyond diversity and inclusion. It is about building community and camaraderie despite people's differing lived experiences and identity politics. It's about fostering clusters of connections."[13] I'm interested in Monáe's and Moore's pynk and decolonized brown figurations of the Black femme, then, *not* because they represent an identity subcategory largely invisible in popular culture. (They do.) I'm interested in how their literal and figurative color palettes visualize "clusters of connections"—between pink, pynk, and brown; vagina, pussy, and penis; feminine, femme, and nonbinary—that offer conceptual models for the kind of feminist solidarity we need now.[14] I engage the femme-inist figurations of Monáe and Moore not as models of *what* to think but of *how* to think across difference: with radical openness, playful world traveling, self-valued emotional labor, and commitment to ongoing transformation. As they model this political pliability, they fulfill the wishes of Black nonbinary femme writer Hunter Shackelford, whose favorite color is also pink: that femininity no longer be denied "queerness, nuance, gender deviance/complexity, sexual agency and visibility" and can "be seen as queer, as gender expansive, as powerful, as struggle, as magic, as conjuring, as complicated and as a spectrum."[15]

Janelle Monáe

Fem Futures, Pynk Pants, and Pussy Power

(For Omi Oshun's lessons in
Black joy, gold mirrors, and pynk for self-care)

t's hard to stop rebels who time travel.[1] Rebel with a cause in a chain-festooned motorcycle jacket and black double buns in place of a pussyhat, Janelle Monáe was invited to the 2017 Women's March on Washington to perform—but she did not come to play. "Hello, future," she greeted the crowd with gravitas. "I am so proud to stand here as a woman, an African American woman. My grandmother was a sharecropper—she picked cotton in Aberdeen, Mississippi; my mother was a janitor; and I am a descendant of them, and I am here in their honor to help us move forward and *fem the future*."[2] As the last phrase landed, she unzipped her motorcycle jacket to reveal her black sweatshirt with FEM THE FUTURE emblazoned in white caps. It was a phrase guaranteed to rivet my eyes to the sharp-tipped *F* and *M* pointing at Monáe's breasts. *Fem the future* as in *femme it up*, as in front-load our future with outrageous, hard-glinting, unapologetically queer femininity? As in, Janelle just said we need to wrest the future from the abuser of power in chief and will it to us nasty femmes who embrace woman- and girliness and queerness at the same time? "I want to say to the LGBTQ community, my fellow brothers and sisters . . ." Janelle continued.[3] By January 2017 we were years deep in rumors about Janelle's queerness and her video cameos, color-coordinated outfits, and girls' trips with beautiful Afro-Latinx actress Tessa Thompson (#Janessa!).

33

So was I crazy to think maybe, *maybe* Janelle might step onto the Women's March stage to hail queer femme folk and cast her lot with us?

A quick internet search traced Janelle's sweatshirt slogan to her fall 2016 #FemtheFuture brunch and clarified the hashtag *wasn't* a call to queers. "Fem the Future is a grassroots movement led by progressive millennials working together to advance the awareness, inclusion, and opportunities for women and those who identify as women through music, arts, mentorship, and education," Janelle explained to the press.[4] When I found out she was using the word *femme* in a way that hinted at queerness but stopped two letters short—stopped a "me" short—of embracing it, I was salty. Like everyone else, I'd watched Janelle dodge reporters' questions about gender and sexuality while sporting her signature tuxedos and androgynous black-and-white suits, always looking good enough to femme up for. Her tuxedos, she explained, stylized working-class (not stud) pride: "The tuxedo is a homage to my mother, who was a janitor, and my father, who drove trash trucks, and how they put on a uniform every day and turned nothing into something."[5] Her suits shouldn't be read as masculine because, she declared, "I don't believe in masculinity and femininity. I'd like to redefine how . . . women look."[6] And when asked about her love life she claimed only to date androids—apparently answering as Cindi Mayweather, the freedom-fighting ArchAndroid protagonist of her first albums. Now, my rational self appreciated the complexity and creativity of these answers, firm in my belief that Black queer folks should *never* have to lay bare our gender and sexuality for anyone to judge or fantasize about. But there was another part of me, a tender, fleshy part bruised by so many years without media images of Black femmes like me being loved by other Black women. And when Janelle demanded we #FemtheFuture but didn't declare her love for femmes, I despaired: if Janelle isn't publicly claiming someone as beautiful, talented, and accomplished as Tessa, what hope is there for the rest of us to be loved in ways all the world can see?

So at the end of Trump's first year in office, I was still secretly, completely unfairly salty with Janelle Monáe—even as I continued to shine love at Beyoncé and, for a fourth year in a row, taught a large lecture encouraging students to enter Black feminism through Beyoncé's music. On February 22, 2018, a student in that course, Gabrielle Sanchez, sent an email: "I just wanted to share Janelle Monáe's song that she released today because it is a true black feminist anthem, even using a phrase that's popped up in our class a few times: black girl magic. . . . It's called 'Django Jane' and the music video is amazing too." Can you believe I was trifling enough to file the video on my mental list of things to watch later? But April 10 I got an un-ignorable note from another student, Ana Mitchell. "I don't know if you've happened to see the video for Janelle Monáe's new song Pynk since it was released like three hours ago (lol) but it's cunnicentrism all over the place. Also, the Janelle/Tessa love is real." Cunnicentrism *and* real love for Tessa in the same video? Immediately I opened "Pynk" on my phone. And what can I say? Caroline Framke wasn't wrong when she rejoiced that "Pynk" takes the queer subtext of Monáe's earlier videos and "releases it into the desert for a joyous coming-out party."[7] Carmen Phillips was on point when she described the video as "a black queer feminist love letter to springtime, being femme, [and] black and brown women's bodies."[8] Two weeks later Janelle followed up with one of the most memorable coming-out statements I've ever read. *Rolling Stone*'s Brittany Spanos recorded, "'Being a queer black woman in America,' [Monáe] says, taking a breath as she comes out, 'someone who has been in relationships with both men and women—I consider myself to be a free-ass motherfucker.'"[9]

So yes, I'd been properly schooled in the art of watching this rebel who time travels, and the next day, when she released her emotion picture *Dirty Computer* free of charge, I streamed it on my (literally dirty) computer as soon as I dropped my daughter at school. "My name is Jane 57821. I am a dirty computer": Monáe delivers her first lines from a floating examination table in a facility called New Dawn, where "dirty computers"—outlaws like queers, punks, partiers, poly folk—are forcibly cleansed of their memories by the program Nevermind.[10] The guide assigned to her cleansing is her former lover Zen (Tessa Thompson), renamed Mary Apple 53, and as Nevermind operators scroll through Jane's memories (which cross the emotion picture as music videos) she desperately, lovingly tries to get Zen to remember their life together. Is near-future Jane still clothed in black and white? Sometimes, but in a white feathered dress topped with a black motorcycle jacket in "Crazy Classic Life" or a white crop top and black pants embroidered with red roses in "Make Me Feel." Does she wear suits? Yes, but in brilliant lavenders and pinks and reds and mosaic prints. "This project was about painting in different colours, not just black and white; going in and allowing myself to use all the shades of the crayon box," Janelle mused in an interview.[11] Black, white, and every shade of the crayon box, Jane femmes up Cindi's androgynous futuristic look: Jane femmes (up) the future. Now, I didn't and don't take this as Janelle's revelation of "real-life" femme identity. But I do take it as a visual declaration that imagining Black queer femininity, and loving Black femmes through perilous political times, is important to her political vision. In *Dirty Computer*, Janelle's choice to be seen as a girly-girl is less a gender expression than a political position. "I want it to be very clear that I'm an advocate for women," she explained to the *New York Times Magazine* about the album. "I'm a girl's girl, meaning I support women no matter what they choose to do."[12]

"A pretty young thang, she can wash my clothes / But I'll never ever let her wear my pants,"[13] Monáe satirizes toxic masculinity in *Dirty Computer*'s "Americans" (and echoes the Trump White House's infamous directive that female staff "dress like women").[14] But *Dirty Computer*'s femmes don't need permission to dress how they want and to wear their own pants, thank you very much. Clichés of dyke gender also imagine that since World War II made pants acceptable attire for women, butches never wear dresses and femmes (almost) never wear pants. In *Queer Style*, Adam Geczy and Vicki Karaminas declare, "The most publicly visible sign of lesbianism in the 1950s was the appearance of the butch or stud lesbian, with her stylized short hair, men's tailored suit or blue jeans. . . . Meanwhile, femmes appeared glamorous and wore make-up, tight dresses and skirts (rarely pants)."[15] But femmes' own memories tell more nuanced fashion histories. In their classic ethnography *Boots of Leather, Slippers of Gold: The History of a Lesbian Community*, Elizabeth Lapovsky Kennedy and Madeline Davis record stories of how in the mid-twentieth century, femmes *did* wear pants—just differently than studs. Joanna, remembering a time in the late forties when she and her slacks-clad butch were harassed on the street, explained, "I was wearing pants too but I had, like I had a blouse on. I had make-up on. So evidently we did look a hell of a lot [like a gay couple]."[16] It wasn't just her butch's gender that marked them as a

gay couple, she recognizes, but her femme-ininity—still visible in pants—
that queered them on the streets. Pearl recalled, "I would dress with high-
heeled shoes and skirt or a dress. That's the way I usually dressed. . . . Once
in a while I'd get real, I don't know if you'd call it brave or what, but I'd put
on. . . . I don't know if you remember when zoot suits were in style with the
long jackets and the chains and the pants that had real tight legs."[17] Real
brave, maybe, or real Black: since the zoot suit was popularized by African
American men, for a femme to wear one was to declare that neither pants
nor Blackness undercut her high-femme-ininity.

So femmes have *always* worn the pants, literally, and always have been
and always will be capable of wearing the pants, figuratively. In its dystopian near-future remix of our misogynoir present, *Dirty Computer* dig-
itizes *how to wear the pants like a Black femme*—not like a bro-dude or
a stud, understand, but like someone who at once plays with and weap-
onizes the femininity that was supposed to be her weakness. I'm going
to take these next pages to tell you what I've learned about Black femme
pants and Black femme power in the two Janelle Monáe videos my students rightly told me to study, "Django Jane" and "Pynk." Along the way,
I'll stop to pay homage to other Black femmes who wear pants in ways that
teach us all something about what it means to be Black, queer, a girl's girl,
and a free-ass motherfucker. And who, like time-traveling rebels Janelle
and Erykah Badu in "Q.U.E.E.N.," sing "Baby, we in tuxedo groove. . . .
Baby, here comes the freedom song."

SHUG'S PERFECT PAIR OF PANTS

A sea change comes for Alice Walker's protagonist Celie when she
leaves her abusive husband and moves to Memphis with her sugar,
lover Shug Avery. Because Shug is a singer and on the road for weeks
at a time, sometimes Celie finds herself rattling around Shug's big
pink house not knowing what to do with herself. Before Celie left her
husband, Shug advised her that "times like this, lulls, us ought to do
something different";[18] and she convinced Celie to make herself a pair

of pants, since "you don't have a dress do nothing for you. You not made like no dress pattern, neither."[19] While Shug is off singing for white folks to make money, then, that's what Celie does. "I sit in the dining room making pants after pants. I got pants now in every color and size under the sun. Since us started making pants down home, I ain't been able to stop."[20] Bolts of cloth and many patterns later, Celie has something special to present Shug: "Finally one day I made the perfect pair of pants. For my sugar, naturally."[21] When their friends and Shug's bandmates see those magically flattering pants they want their own pairs, of course, so soon Celie's sewn more pants than the dining room can hold. "One day when Shug come home, I say, You know, I love doing this, but I got to git out and make a living pretty soon. Look like this just holding me back. She laugh. Let's us put a few advertisements in the paper, she say. And let's us raise your prices a hefty notch. . . . You making your living, Celie, she say. Girl, you on your way."[22]

Miss Celie's perfect pants for Shug are a love offering from a butch to her femme, a soft, unwrinkling garment that makes Shug's life easier when she's on the road singing her independence; and that adoringly showcases her beauty in all its roundness, softness, and Blackness. "Once Shug put them on, she knock your eyes out," Celie admires. "She run round the house looking at herself in mirrors. No matter how she look, she look good."[23] It took a butch to design the perfect pair of pants, yes, but it took a pink-loving femme who looked reeeaaallll good in them to see their possibility and show the world their value. Shug encourages her lover to make pants as a symbol of emotional independence before she leaves her husband, then turns them into the means of her financial independence once she does. And her name is Celie's business address: "Folkspants, Unlimited. Sugar Avery Drive, Memphis, Tennessee."[24]

SEE JANE RULE

On January 30, 2018, Janelle Monáe "basically brought African royalty to Hollywood" when she arrived at the *Black Panther* premiere in a voluminous Christian Siriano skirt paired with a black crop top with royal blue and white puffed sleeves, topped by a beaded choker and gold-embroidered kufi.[25] Janelle had as many reasons as any Black woman to celebrate the release of a film about an African superhero, plus one: after the film's nationwide release, a trailer for *Dirty Computer* aired ahead of *Black Panther* in select, routinely sold-out theaters. The connection between the films—a live-action adaptation of a Marvel comic set in the fictional, never-colonized nation of Wakanda and a speculative fiction visual album in a dystopian, never-named colonial power—was more than coincidental. "Not a lot of people know this but *Black Panther* was filmed from Atlanta, so technically I'm from Wakanda! A lot of the cast are my friends and a lot of them came to Wondaland when I was making *Dirty Computer* and I gave them a preview of the album," Janelle explained, crediting the cast's enthusiastic response with giving her courage to release her new music. "I feel blessed really to be creating music and putting out an album during the same time as *Black Panther*. . . . *Black Panther* is through the lens of Afro-futurism. It's telling our stories in the future through our lens, and *Dirty Computer* is also telling our stories in the near-future through the lens of a black *woman*."[26]

Titular superhero King T'Challa on his throne, muscular and gleamingly black in his vibranium suit, a beam of light shining on his face: this image of strong African manhood, distributed worldwide on *Black Panther* posters, reminded us it was still possible to conjure a heroic Black future in the first year of Trump's reign. But what would it look like if the heroic Black future is femme? You see when you open "Django Jane," *Dirty Computer*'s first video release. Beginning in the dark, a tracking shot leads viewers to inlaid Moroccan doors that open as two Black women bodyguards allow entry to a room thick and soft with pillars, drapes, Persian rugs, and lush foliage. The lens stops in a medium shot of Monáe seated on a throne and dressed in a fitted pink pantsuit, surrounded by women in studded black leather jackets and pants; all wear the embroidered kufi

Monáe debuted at the *Black Panther* premiere. "The colorful tailored suiting and kufi-like accoutrements spoke to the sharp contemporary style of many metropolitans across the African continent," *Cultured* magazine's Darnell-Jamal Lisby muses, quoting Monáe: "When you see 'Django Jane,' the visual pulls from my ancestors, and there's me in the middle of so many Black women who have my back and whose back I have."[27] Monáe's ancestral vision projects into an Afrofuturistic feminist stronghold, where leather-suited women semicircle around Janelle like the Dora Milaje, Wakanda's all-female special forces, standing guard in T'Challa's throne room. The training and exploits of the Dora Milaje entered the Marvel Universe in Roxane Gay's series *Black Panther: World of Wakanda*, where protagonists Ayo and Aneka fall in love while fighting to protect Wakanda's royal family. "You did know this was a Marvel comic that centers two Black lesbians fighting for their beliefs and for a better way forward for Wakanda, didn't you?" speculative fiction blogger Sister from Another Planet joked after reading the comic. "Trust me, I'm as surprised as you are."[28]

While the *Black Panther* film sidestepped the comics' lesbian romance, the Dora Milaje of "Django Jane" lean into it. Quite literally, the Black women who "have [her] back" lean erotically toward their seated leader: one shot finds the eight leather warriors tilting their bodies to rest their heads on the enthroned, pink-suited Monáe, two heads resting in her lap, two on her shoulders, and four pressed to her face as she raps, "Running out of space on my damn bandwagon." If *Black Panther*'s directors had filmed T'Challa in a similar position with men warriors' heads cradled in his lap and caressing his face, of course—of course!—viewers would have immediately shouted its queerness. But a quick scroll through reviews assures me, almost no writer received Jane's relationship with her Dora Milaje the same way. Center screen on her throne, Jane's queerness remains shrouded in *femme invisibility*—which Sinclair Sexsmith glosses as "femmes not being recognized as queer because of their gender presentation."[29] Now, I could have gotten furious about how femme invisibility colors reviews that paint "Django Jane" as being about Blackness rather than queerness; after all, this misogynoir strain of femme invisibility is my own longtime nemesis. But instead, as I listened to Monáe rap, "Black girl magic, y'all can't stand it. . . . They been trying hard just to make us all vanish," I began to wonder: What if this song is a rallying call to all the magic Black femmes whose "dirty" queerness is constantly vanished from the eyes of our beholders? What if we view "Django Jane" as a vision of a future where femme invisibility becomes a superpower?

Yes, invisibility is a common fictional superpower for women in graphic novels: Invisible Woman, Matrix, Spectrum. And one of the Dora Mila-je's most powerful warriors wins her battles by staying strategically half seen: Nakia (played by Lupita Nyong'o), covert operations specialist and member of Wakanda's War Dogs, an elite espionage group where (according to Marvel Comics) "she excelled as a spy and spent more and more time away from her country as she delved deeper into missions that she believed helped not only Wakanda, but the greater cause of women, especially those being subjugated on the African continent."[30] The femme invisibility of "Django Jane" is this kind of Nakia-like superpower, a pynk cloak that enables wearers to work as secret agents on behalf of all queers. In "Can Femme Invisibility Be a Superpower?," Briana Shewan opens with a compelling picture: "It's the middle of the day. The air is crisp, the sun is shining and casting long shadows, the birds are chirping and there's the bustle of people moving about their routines. Femmes are in the mix, too, riding transit, working, attending school. Femmes, though, can't be seen. We navigate secretly, below the radar, making shit happen." Born out of femmephobia, femme invisibility becomes a weapon we wield to our advantage. "Sometimes it serves you to be invisible because it allows you to be selective about who you reveal yourself to. You can show yourself to those who can truly see you, love you, and support you," Shewan continues. "Taking your time while using your invisible superpower to determine if others share the vision of more expansive queer community helps keep you safe."[31] And wasn't that what Monáe was doing during those years of declaring she only dated androids while wearing black-and-white suits? "Jane Bond, never Jane Doe," she names herself for an überfamous secret agent in "Django Jane," then challenges, "Black and white, yeah that's always been my camo / It's lookin' like y'all gon' need some more ammo."

That camo became a cloak of invisibility that helped Monáe infiltrate a recording industry with little space for Black queer women artists in the 2000s. But it didn't keep *us*—Black femmes, even those who (like me) stayed salty—from seeing her. When Black Lives Matter cofounder and femme activist Patrisse Cullors joined Monáe for one of her Instagram Live Liberation + Elevation Talks, Cullors expressed appreciation for Monáe's earlier "camouflaged" music: "I've been following your work and your career for a while now and so much of your work, so much of your music, so many of the parts you've played have been such an inspiration to me and so many of us. There's a whole crew, community of mine that have played your music on repeat and [it] got us through *so many years of our lives*, coming out as young queer people." Even before this appreciation, Monáe and Cullors made clear that they *saw each other* as femme-presenting queers when they greeted each other with overlapping compliments: "You look *so pretty*! Look at you." "Thank you! Look at *you*, sis!"[32] *Look at you, I see you* in your cloak of femme invisibility: this is what the femmes in my life say to each other in lifesaving ways. I'm thinking of the brilliant femme friend who wears scarlet lipstick for early-morning Zoom because she knows I'll appreciate it. (I do, effusively.) Of the time I met Janet Mock and she complimented my shoes because she knew I picked them out just for her. Of all the sexy, silly, colorful Instagram posts tagged #Femme4Femme. Femmes seeing and loving ourselves in all our queer glory may be the apotheosis of our superpower. "What if as femmes we can see each other?" Shewan concludes. "What if we've confronted the villain in ourselves from years of roaming a patriarchal society and shed any internalized femme invisibility. What if to each other, we are glowing energy on the landscape. We send out beams of light that other femmes can see. For us, it's a radiant view."[33] When I go back to "Django Jane" now, I trace its coded trail of popular culture references and see beams of light pointing us to media exploring femme in/visibility as superpower.

First Monáe shouts out LGBT-inclusive Russian band Pussy Riot: "We gon' start a motherfuckin' pussy riot," she raps, glossing on *Genius* that "they're a protest punk band, and they've been deeply inspirational to me. They've been jailed because they are fighting for women's rights and the LGBTQI community."[34] Then she name-drops *Moonlight*, the 2016 Oscar-winning film where she made her acting debut: "We ain't hidden no more, moonlit nigga, lit nigga" plays with the title of the film about (semihidden) love between two Black boys, cowritten by Black femme-identified playwright Tarell Alvin McCraney. Next Monáe comes around to the television series *How to Get Away with Murder*—"I got away with murder, no scandal / Cue the violins and the violas"—and its lead actress, Viola Davis, whose power femme character Annalise surprised audiences in the second season when she revealed a woman lover. Not done yet, Monáe offers a gorgeous visual citation of *A Fantastic Woman*, the 2017 Oscar winner for Best Foreign Language Film and the first film with a trans lead to win an Academy Award. As she calls out "mansplaining," Jane peers between her naked legs to see her face reflected in a round mirror balanced on her crotch, replicating the position in which *A Fantastic Woman*'s transfemme protagonist Marina reflects her gender identity back to herself despite ciscentric attempts to erase her femininity.[35] Pussy Riot, Tarell, Annalise, Marina: Monáe sees the radiance of your beams of light and uses them to light Jane's way.

Unlike "Pynk," whose pastel, sparkling displays of femme-for-femme love are unmissably open and colorful, "Django Jane" makes viewers work for queer subtext. And why shouldn't we work, when Monáe herself has clearly worked hard to pen and spit fiercely clever, intertext-rich, wordplaying lyrics? The line-after-line, rapid-fire work of encoding and decoding queer references in "Django Jane" mirrors the ongoing, never-done work of coming out that femme invisibility entails. "Identities are stripped away every time I enter a new crowd and labels are placed on you before you can mention your name," Black femme Mariah Barber makes clear. "The closet also becomes a revolving door when you leave it in a skirt, lip and heel. You must constantly out yourself for your identity markers to be honored. . . . It can be exhausting, especially when there is a Q&A to follow. This manifests itself when people are bombarding you with questions, validating yourself constantly and having to correct other's preconceived notions."[36] Exhausting and enraging, too, to have to *over and over and over again* perform work I've never seen cis-het folk called to do. Moving through that anger and exhaustion and turning it into art is part of the Black femme superheroic work Monáe accomplishes in "Django Jane." "When I wrote songs like 'Django Jane,' it was important to get out my anger, to get out my frustration, to be deliberate about where I stood on certain issues," Monáe admits. "To make sure that women—black women in particular—knew that this is an album for us. This is for you. This is for me. It's about a journey through all these emotions," a journey she describes as "difficult" and "work in progress."[37]

To be a femme who wears the pants(uit) in "Django Jane" is to be a femme who works hard in every way: works on her craft, works through her feelings, works to see and be seen by other Black femmes. Jane's magenta suit is a work uniform too: a femme-fabulous version of the black-and-white suits Monáe sported in earlier albums to honor her working-class roots. "Momma was a G, she was cleanin' hotels / Poppa was a driver, I was workin' retail," Janelle raps her family work history as she and her Dora Milaje body roll dramatically, first to the right, then to the left. In her study of Monáe's gender-bending suits, Monica Miller reflects, "When we see her in the tuxedo, which is when we see her at all, we know that she is working. The uniform and its status as Monáe's only dress reminds her and us of both the quantity and quality of the work she's set herself to do: the tuxedo 'lets me know I still have work to do in our community,' work that she describes as inspirational and healing."[38] The pynking of Monáe's uniform in "Django Jane" visualizes that not only is it possible to be all femmed up and work: being a Black femme means you *have to work* with and against invisibility "in our community." Hard, creative, everyday work transforms Black women into superheroes, Monáe testifies of her mother: "My momma was a G. She was my superhero. She still is. She'd turn nothing into something every single day."[39] It transforms Black femmes into superheroes, too, as every day we turn *nothing* in our presentations that easily reads as queer into *something* we love and cultivate fiercely; every day, we challenge those around us to "reframe your vision and choose to see the concealed or what the gendered globe didn't teach," as Barber puts it.[40]

Being a superhero isn't, *can't* be a role anyone performs around the clock, though. When ceremony and battle are over, T'Challa takes off the Black Panther suit; and when Black femmes are tired of the weight of our invisibility cloaks, we retreat to "cultivate something no one else can see, visible only to" those we love, so that we can cultivate self-affirmation "that grounds us in everything we need to take on this world," Barber continues.[41] Superhero Django Jane may be the greatest of all time, but despite and because of that, she's only visible in "Dirty Computer" for a few short minutes. "If she the GOAT now, would anybody doubt it?" Jane repeats as the song closes and the camera retraces its steps, tracking away from Monáe and her court, retreating from the guards who shut the Moroccan doors behind them. Ending, for now, the moment these super-femmes let themselves be visible to the outside world.

PINK BRUJERÍA

Yes, they started as a skate crew, and no, they are not just here for fun and games. Brujas is a New York–based radical femme-of-color collective of skateboarders, artists, healers, and community organizers, who, in addition to hosting events such as queer "Anti-Prom" and "Fuck Summer Camp," launched their first streetwear collection, Brujas × 1971, in 2016. "We see 1971 as a combination of both the political DIY cultures that we were radicalized in in the Lower East Side, anarchist organizing where people sell T-shirts and throw parties to get their friends out of prison, and the really brash street and skate wear aesthetics that have been developing for ages," Brujas member Izzy Nastasia explained.[42] In addition to bike shorts, cheer skirts, and unisex draws, Brujas' current collection features bottoms simply called "soft skate pants" and touted as the "best skate pants ever made . . . feel like sweats look like work pants." The pants come in red to honor the group's radical politics, black to honor "the work of BLACK artists whose ancestors built the wealth that has been compounded and invested into many of the products flying around the Internet," and pink. "Pink is growing to be a tonal symbol of the new, gender-free punk-wave," the website explains the collective's predilection for this last color. "Pink actually provides gender neutrality within our space in the way of stark contrast to the otherwise normalized male dominance in parks. By re-appropriating a previous infantilizing market scheme into a politically radical, anti-capitalist context, we not only reclaim the right to skate in our rapidly gentrifying neighborhood, but also the power of softness."[43]

They also chose pink for the flyer announcing the launch of their special collection Each One Teach One, released in September 2017 during New York Fashion Week. The flyer was styled as a handwritten detention slip, issued to "Friends & Family" for "Defiance" and "Inappropriate/Abusive Language," and the box provided for "Administrator Comments" announced, "Celebrating the release of this collection during NYFW, BRUJAS presents a day of Teach-Ins on the Lower East Side, the birth place of our organization. The Teach-Ins will include workshops and lectures on topics from native New York plants movements to a writing workshop on 'Poems that Kill' to the history of Student Strikes with both educators and students sporting BRUJAS' Each One Teach One collection."[44] The collective's fashion-show-cum-teach-in publicized the radical potential of traditionally feminized reproductive labor, including caregiving and garment making, to remind us that femmes of color are not only powerful because we wear the pants: we're powerful because we made the damn pants before we put them on. Izzy calls out, "I think 'Brujas' as a brand and a crew is so significant: to name the group that and align yourself with heretics and other traditions that have been deemed deviant, and people whose reproductive labor is mined and extracted by capitalism."[45] In other words, *brujería* is as much a product of femme labor as it is a supernatural force.

PYNK LIKE PUSSY POWER

"Powerful with a little bit of tender," Monáe sings as she crawls through a line of Black women in leotards and brightly colored tights, pausing between a set of yellow-Lycra-ed limbs to press her cheek to and dance her fingers down one woman's thigh as she croons "tender." This is the video for "Make Me Feel," released on February 22 along with "Django Jane."

"A song of desire and freedom," the *Guardian*'s Rebecca Bengal called this first Monáe video to costar Tessa Thompson, noting that "gossip rags have wondered loudly whether" the video "could mean that Monáe and Thompson are dating, or that Monáe is 'finally' out of the closet."[46] On April 10, Monáe answered that wonder with the release of the overflowingly sapphic, unabashedly cunnicentric, pinker-than-a-pink-triangle visual for "Pynk." Queer Twitter responded with elation. "@JanelleMonáe and @TessaThompson_x just set me free in a way I never knew was possible. BLACK GIRLS LOVING ON EACH OTHER ALL 2018 #PYNK," Strong Black Lead testified.[47] "Congrats to Tessa Thompson and Janelle Monáe for eradicating heterosexuality," Danny Vegito joked.[48] And Dened Rey Moreno applauded the video's femmed future: "Y'all Janelle Monáe and Tessa Thompson are at it again blessing us queer girls and truly being the embodiment of #20GAYTEEN like what a time to be alive."[49]

"Paint the city pink, paint the city pink," Monáe foreshadowed in "Django Jane," and "Pynk" visualizes that pink metropolis as she "literally invent[s] a new color and share[s] it with us mere mortals."[50] The video opens with an extreme wide shot of a desert landscape filmed in infrared, hillsides and brush sloping inward in shades of rose and flamingo pink. The camera moves in tighter to a hovering pink Cadillac—a futuristic vision of Sugar Ray Robinson's famous fuchsia Caddy—carrying Jane, Zen, and two friends through the ever-pinker valley. They pull into the Pynk Rest-Inn, where signs promise "Last Chance: Food, Rooms" and "Grrls Eat Free and Never Leave"; where a Black woman wearing two shades of pink, a pink popsicle melting down her hands, snaps sugary fingers to draw in the travelers and usher in the song's rhythm. Instrumentation joins as the video cuts together shots of the travelers relaxing by an empty pool, drinking strawberry milkshakes and crossing fishnetted legs on its edge, and Jane posing in fluffy red and pink against the wind-rustled desert landscape. From her close-up the camera moves to a full shot of Jane in a line of seven women, five costumed in now-(in)famous billowing pink pants: pale-pink ruffles on outer thighs, darker-pink crepe on inner thighs that part in unison as dancers bend and straighten their knees to Monáe's first "Pynk . . ." These swelling pynk pants immediately broke the internet in a way the pink pantsuits of "Django Jane" never could. Resisting their coy branding as "vagina pants," Monáe explained, "Sometimes I think people interpret those as vagina pants, they call them vulva pants, they call them flowers, but it just represents some parts of some women. There are some women in the video that do not have on the pants, because I don't believe that all women need to possess a vagina to be a woman."[51]

Not vagina *anything*, the phrase "Pynk" attached to its pink, fluffy, wet, ruffled look is spelled out in bright lights at the Black women–only dance party later in the video. "Pussy Power," a pink neon sign proclaims as Jane spanks one of her dance partners and sings, "Boy it's cool if you got blue / We got the pynk." And as those of us who move in Black queer universes know, Black pussy power doesn't necessarily have anything to do with vaginas. Scholar Shoniqua Roach brilliantly sets out all the many things "pussy" means when Black queer folks speak that word: "Consider black queer rapper Fly Young Red's sonic invitation to 'throw that boy pussy', which explicitly aims to 'empower feminine men' and indexes the signifying power of 'pussy' to encompass black queer sex that does not necessarily involve female genitalia. We might also reflect on the ubiquity of the affirmation 'my pussy is fierce', as heard in queer and trans vogue and ballroom scenes. In this context, there is no necessary correlation between 'pussy,' anatomy, gender performance and sexual acts." Instead, Roach urges us to think of "black pussy . . . as a technology of black feminine survival": a mobilization of the erotic that enables a Black fem(me)-inine subject to "tap into modes of erotic agency otherwise denied to her" and "secure nominal black freedoms in the face of state-sanctioned infringements on black erotic life."[52]

Now, girls of color grow up in a world that tells us Black pussy is the opposite of a superpower—that deploying the erotic makes us vulnerable. And femmes' queerness doesn't inoculate us against this message. "The whole world told me that there is nothing more common and stupid than someone feminine of center with their legs open, wanting something more than a kick or a curse," Desi femme Leah Lakshmi Piepzna-Samarasinha reflects.[53] So early-career Monáe tried to perform pussy-free, strategizing a buttoned-up, unfleshy android persona to minimize her vulnerability as a Black woman in the exploitative music industry. "The persona, the androgynous outfits, the inflexible commitment to the storyline both on- and offstage, served in part as protective armor," she tells Brittany Spanos.[54] But as she created *Dirty Computer*, Monáe came to question whether this seemingly impenetrable persona always served her feminist politics. "There are people who have used my image to slut-shame other women: 'Janelle, we really appreciate that you don't show your body.' That's something I'm not cool with. . . . I have never covered up for respectability politics or to shame other women."[55] The virulently erotophobic, misogynoir rhetoric and policies of the Trump administration pushed her to move through her discomfort with vulnerability and develop a different "technology of black feminine survival." The Black pussy power celebration of *Dirty Computer*, she owns, is "a response to me feeling the sting of the threats being made to my rights as a woman, as a black woman, as a sexually liberated woman. . . . Black women and those who have been the 'other,' and the marginalised in society—that's who I wanted to support, and that was more important than my discomfort about speaking out."[56]

"Pynk" sounds different from Janelle's earlier songs, stretching into the breathy upper reaches of her vocal range as she sings over bubbling synths. The song credits nine writers, among them Monáe, featured artist Grimes, and Richard Supa and Steven Tyler of Aerosmith fame. The inclusion of these last two artists acknowledges Monáe's Black femme-inist reworking of the band's sexually suggestive 1997 hit "Pink," whose title and line structure "Pynk" plays with. But where Aerosmith's ode to genitalia reinforces the idea that "pink" is for men's pleasure ("Pink it was love at first sight. . . . Pink gets me high as a kite," Tyler sings),[57] Monáe changes the point of view on pink from straight white masculine to Black femme. "Pynk like the inside of your . . ." the song begins, skipping a wordless beat as the pink pants open. But as the verse continues, Monáe completes the line to reveal she's exploring Black femme-ininity not (just) as the inside of a body but as psychological interiority. "Pynk when you're blushing inside, maybe / Pynk is the truth you can't hide, maybe," Monáe sings, the last line delivered as Thompson's head emerges from between Monáe's pink-blossoming legs. These are the video's most intimate shots of Monáe and Thompson, the positions in which they're most vulnerable and interdependent: Monáe balances with legs spread and Thompson perches on all fours beneath her, each counting on the other's synchronous movements to keep from toppling over. And like many of the video's shots, the moment is campy, funny, and silly, with Thompson grinning broadly against the pink pants and batting her eyelashes before Monáe covers her face with her hand. In one outtake, Thompson falls over laughing in this position and Monáe ends up on top of her, hugging her and stroking her hair before she helps her up.

I want to spend a moment thinking about this erotic playfulness, which I see as both Monáe's expression of vulnerability and her imagination of Black femme freedom. Femme scholars like Ann Cvetkovich and Ulrika Dahl lay out the political importance of consciously inhabiting vulnerability, which, according to Dahl, "is predominantly understood as feminising and subsequently as negative, scary, shameful and, above all, something to be avoided and protected against." In the current political moment, she exerts, vulnerability stands to be productively rethought as a "daring openness" to be *pierced to the core* by difficult political and social issues, potentially opening space for new solidarities. But to be collaborative, vulnerability-based solidarities can't be race blind: the form of vulnerability that serves femmes "in the streets and in the sheets differs depending on racialisation, class position, age and body shape, not to mention location in the world and time of day."[58] Making ourselves vulnerable by publicly working through trauma, Amber Musser notes in her discussion of Black museumgoers subject to pitying white gazes at a Kara Walker exhibition, may be neither novel nor empowering for femmes of African descent. So what if, instead, we melt our pinkest feelings into a sweeter, gentler, more carefree Black girl color of vulnerability: playfulness?

"I think one thing that I love about Janelle that people might not always know about her because she is so, um, kind of poised and elegant is that she's so silly!" Thompson laughs in the mini documentary "A Revolution of Love." "She's like just a very silly human and has this real sort of childlike quality, and my work [with her] is the most exciting when I feel like it's just play."[59] *Just playing* from start to finish, "Pynk" imagines a literal and figurative rest stop where Black women perform neither remunerative nor reproductive labor. Black femmes work hard in "Django Jane," but in "Pynk" they play both hard and soft. "When you need a holiday, when you want to sip rosé /I just wanna paint your toes and in the morning kiss your nose," Monáe raps to Thompson in the song's extended version. No one at Pynk pays for lodging, no one fills the pool where the women lounge; all enjoy milkshakes, multiple costume changes, and dancing day and night. The cunnic images cut in are less sexy than silly: an oyster sprinkled with pink glitter, a donut with a finger poking through the middle, a fluffy cat, a juicy grapefruit. This playfulness turns the rest stop into a place where Black women connect: wearing different candy-colored outfits and fabulous hairstyles, the Pynk femmes are linked not by looking alike but by sharing how they cut up, relax, party, and enjoy. They femmebody the woman-loving attitude of playfulness María Lugones describes as "a particular metaphysical attitude that . . . involves openness to surprise, openness to being a fool, openness to self-construction or reconstruction and to construction or reconstruction of the 'worlds' we inhabit playfully."[60] Thompson echoes Lugones's theory of world traveling as she finishes musing on Monáe's silliness: "Inside of the space of make believe we have the ability in sort of an aspirational way to create the world that we live in. To create a world that is more joyful, that is more pleasantly challenging, that is more free. That's Janelle to me."[61]

The pleasant challenges of "Pynk" go deeper than the pants Thompson pokes her head through, we learn, when the dancers take the party to a room inside the rest stop. "Pynk like the skin that's under . . ." Jane sings as she rises dramatically from the pink-shag-covered bed, revealing what's under those pants: tighty whities with SEX CELLS in pink lettering at their center and copiously artificial pubic hair spilling from their sides. In her reading of Monáe's 2010 video "Cold War," which begins with a collar-bone-to-head shot of the artist removing her robe while the screen goes dark, Shana L. Redmond reminds us that Black women artists are at their most vulnerable when their clothes come off on camera.[62] And while the character Cindi manages her risk by never showing her unclothed body below the neck, Jane zooms in for a Black femme-inist pink shot that keeps playing with viewers on her own terms. As she continues to sing, the camera offers a medium close-up of another set of thighs in white briefs that declare, "GREAT COSMIC MOTHER," and zooms in to a third that challenge, "I GRAB BACK." This last phrase floated on signs at the Women's March, but the briefs in "Pynk" repurpose it with a spirit of literally cheeky play-fulness, linking it to a Black body rather than a disembodied sign; and with a visual reminder that Black pussy power isn't rooted in *whatever* may be inside "men's" briefs with feminist slogans, but in the practice of speaking back as a technology of Black femme-inine survival. And in case you missed her speaking truth to power the first time, Monáe repeats in "I Got the Juice," "If you try to grab my pussy cat, this pussy grab you back (hey)," then follows up with, "This pussy grab you back / Give you pussy cataracts."

Pastel, fluffy, neon, and playful as it may be at the Pynk rest stop, Black pussy power is *never* just feel-good sex positivity. It *always* has claws and can *always* grab back. "Black pussy power's ability to cultivate and sustain manifold forms of black survivorship," Roach makes clear, can mobilize femmes to "black feminist vengeance" as a form of erotic agency when it needs to.[63] The power of the erotic, Audre Lorde told us, is that "when we begin to live from within outward, in touch with the power of the erotic within ourselves, and allowing that power to inform and illuminate our actions upon the world around us," we become "less willing to accept powerlessness, or those other supplied states of being which are not native to [us]."[64] This is the spirit in which Amanda Duarte coined the slogan "This Pussy Grabs Back" during Trump's first presidential campaign. "To hear a presidential candidate bragging about sexually assaulting women, well, my pussy got really angry," she offers playfully and seriously. "She is tired of feeling violated and unsafe, and she isn't gonna take it lying down. I got this image in my mind of my pussy just snapping back at his disgusting tiny hand . . . and thought, let's rally the pussy troops."[65] The playfulness of "This Pussy Grabs Back," Duarte makes clear, isn't a distraction from feminist protest: it's a queer, off-center strategy of attack against heteropatriarchy's heavy-handedness. As Inger-Lise Kalviknes Bore, Anne Graefer, and Allaina Kilby note in their study of the slogan, creatively mobilizing "productive tensions between anger and joy" creates resilient feminist communities: "Energised by funny and biting political commentary, the key value of humorous images like the #WomensMarch posts is not their contribution to political debate and deliberative exchange of knowledge. Instead, it is the possibility that they can help sustain activists' energy by reminding them that they are part of wider communities of feminist feeling, and by helping them overcome despair through defiant, unruly laughter."[66]

Did you laugh when the camera zoomed in to Jane's SEX CELLS briefs and you saw a curly weave spilling out of her drawers, femmes? Did you giggle when Jane and Zen crawled to each other across a bridge of brief-clad, hip-circling femme asses? If so, then you stopped at the Pynk Rest-Inn to gather forces on your journey to Black femme freedom. After years of clarifying that the pynk pants are *not* vaginas, Monáe revealed in a 2020 interview what they *are*: "I wanted something that moved and represented a time portal . . . a cool-looking shape that blurred the lines, but also felt erotic."[67] Pynk pants, rest stops, and pussy power are doorways to another, erotic Black femme-inist way of being: one where, Kara Keeling lovingly writes, we glimpse the figure of the "Black femme . . . serving as a portal through which present (im)possibilities might appear."[68] "I wanna fall through the stars / Getting lost in the dark," Jane sings riding through the desert with her crew, looking up at the sky as if anything might be possible. Since the opening of the Pynk rest stop, many of us have checked in to enter that portal with Jane—to recharge by imagining a silly, frilly, fluffy, sweet, *different* future falling from the stars to reach us dirty computers. Black queer feminist writer, lawyer, social justice advocate, and yoga teacher Candace Bond-Theriault kept *Dirty Computer* on repeat during the June 2020 civil rights protests to "remind me that we must continue to cultivate resilience and celebrate our lives": "*Dirty Computer* is a Black queer feminist love note to Black, queer, and femme America that reminds us we can celebrate blackness and march in the street to support #BlackLivesMatter, while falling in love with ourselves and others at the same time that we fight against the patriarchy."[69] "Sunny, money, keep it funky / Touch your top and let it down," Jane sings as she bobs at the edge of the empty pool, scissors-kicking backward with her line of femmes to release into a playful, sisterly vulnerability and come back to declare, "Boy it's cool if you got blue / We got the pynk." Pynk, the color that unites us all; pynk, where the future is born.

ANYA NUTTZ, WET AND CREAMY

"I'm feeling a little cunt," Boston-based "gender fluid floozy" and drag performer Anya Nuttz captioned a picture of themself sitting on a snowy sidewalk, rocking a white bodysuit, thigh-high blue snakeskin boots, and a teal wig on March 9, 2019.[70] An assigned-female-at-birth queer performer who favors a short natural, backward baseball caps, and loose jeans offstage, Anya Nuttz came to drag not as the king people expected, but as a queen whose femmeness has nothing to do with vagina and everything to do with Black pussy power. "Gender is up here" (pointing to an image of a brain) "not down there" (pointing to a drawing of briefs), their November 2016 Facebook cover page declared, and their drag costumes femmebody this truth with a wicked sense of humor.[71] In a May 18, 2017, Instagram post they side-eye the camera in a black bodysuit whose crotch is spilling over with a cascade of tangled-at-the-top, braided-at-the-bottom pink hair tracks. Instead of tucking the tracks' glueable edges inside her bodysuit, she lets them flap out, putting their artifice on maximum display and captioning the shot, "Rapunzel, Rapunzel, let down your (pussy) hair."[72] At "Unleash the Peach: A Queer Variety Show and Dance Party," held in Cambridge on March 8, 2019, Anya creamed the stage to Rihanna's "Birthday Cake": they bounced up and down on a yellow cake with white frosting to the beat of Riri's cake-cake-cake-cake until their inner thighs and the stage were both slick with frosting. "Wet and creamy," they captioned the video on Instagram, and drag performer Natalia Heaux answered, "Moist and dreamy."[73] The femme pleasure Anya Nuttz lets us witness onstage isn't clitoral or vaginal, peach lovers, it's store bought and sugar-cream frosted.

"#Hyperqueen #hyperqueendrag," Anya tags their cake post, their raunchy-sweet humor illustrating Rachel Devitt's claim that a hyper (female-to-femme) queen "performs a heightened femininity . . . at once campy and earnest, parodist and ecdysiast," and that "parodying the gender they are assumed to have allows fem drag queens to critique the connection between biology or body and gender or performance."[74] Case in point: an April 2018 mirror selfie of Anya with Beyoncé-esque blond spiral curls sweeping their face, pink eyeshadow and lipstick setting off glitter-dusted cleavage lunging out of a peach robe, and unevenly aligned yellow letters superimposed to spell "they/he." "What's a they/he?" a comment from a fellow drag performer facetiously asks, rightly insinuating that questioning how gender is put together is exactly the hyperqueen point.

WAKANDA FOR LOVERS

Camp was the theme of the 2019 Met Gala, and to no one's surprise, Black queers slayed the event. Actor and screenwriter Lena Waithe walked the carpet in a double-breasted suit whose pinstripes were lyrics from Black queer club anthems and whose back carried a bold-stitched message: "BLACK DRAG QUEENS INVENTED CAMP."[75] Janet Mock worked a metallic gown festooned with Josephine Baker–esque silver feathers for her first-ever Met Gala appearance, telling *Elle*, "What I love so much about this particular theme is that my people created it. Everyone else is kind of coming here to put on a show, and I think that for a lot of queer and trans people, doing the most is just our everyday."[76] Not to be outdone, Janelle Monáe arrived in a Christian Siriano gown styled as an abstract face, one side black and white, with red lips at the knee, the other a pink skirt, with a beaded eye—that blinked!—covering her left breast. And she made her high camp literal by crowning herself with four precariously stacked top hats. "Known for her affinity for tuxes as much as her iconic vulva pants, Monáe often plays with gender through fashion, especially on stage or on the red carpet," *Bustle*'s Katie Dupere pointed out. "By mixing a femme gown with a masculine top hat (or four), Monáe pulled together the polar opposites of gendered fashion into one cohesive look. And the result is Camp AF."[77] Stitched into a single garment, Monáe's tuxedoed-worker side and pink-blossoming playful side carefully balance and complement each other, while her blinged-out boob winks dramatically, making sure we all know there's more to her queer gender than meets the eye.

Monáe didn't attend the event with Tessa Thompson, fueling ongoing dyke-drama speculation that Tessa had left Janelle for another actress. But Janelle sent gay Twitter into fireworks when she was seen at the party whispering and dancing very, *very* close to longtime friend and *Black Panther* star Lupita Nyong'o. Transfemme-inist writer Mari Brighe summed up the online mood when she tweeted, "I've never seen anything excite and unify queers quite like this news. I'm fairly sure that Janelle and Lupita are now the benevolent and eternal Queens of All Queers. I, for one, excitedly pledge my fealty."[78] As 2019's speculative Black queer supercouple, the queen of Wakanda loving America's dirtiest computer would spectacularly fem the future, and beautifully Blacken it too. Since she burst into the Hollywood spotlight with her 2014 Oscar win, Nyong'o has been an outspoken opponent of colorism and open about how it affected her self-image. "I hope that my presence on your screen and my face in magazines may lead you, young girls, on a beautiful journey," she wished at the 2014 Essence Women in Hollywood luncheon. "That you will feel the validation of your external beauty, but also get to the deeper business of being beautiful inside."[79] Much as I love #Janessa, part of what made the world look at the couple and see Thompson as femme to Monáe's butch, I fear—along with Monáe's suits—was Thompson's long, loose hair and lighter skin tone, which colorism has always correlated with fem(me)inine beauty (just as tall, *dark*, and handsome has been associated with masculinity). #Janita, though, with its images of Janelle adoring someone whose dark skin, short natural hair, and continental Africanness are part of the shimmer of her femme-ness: it's not the final frontier for Black femme freedom, maybe, but it's somewhere closer.

#BlackAndPynk forever.

Indya Moore

Nonbinary Wild Vagina Dresses and Biologically Femme Penises

(For Juana, in anticipation of more sexual futures,
lipstick-stained laughter, and brown femme joy)

"I met Indya Moore three years ago at a film screening, where, eyes brimming with tears, [they] told me [they] loved me," Janet Mock reverently profiled the actor and model for *Time*'s 2019 list of one hundred most influential people. "A year later, we came together again for *Pose*, a trailblazing series that changed the landscape of television and our lives. Writing [their] character Angel proved healing for me as a trans woman who had walked in those same platform shoes, longing for more than the crumbs society had thrown girls like us. . . . [They are] the living embodiment of our wildest dreams finally coming true."[1] When Moore arrived on the red carpet for the Time 100 gala, they looked like Black femmes' wildest dreams bloomed even more wildly. Moore stunned in a sheer Iris van Herpen mermaid dress, whose intricate pleats ruffled the skirt and sleeves opened like beige, brown, and copper seashells. Styled as a gilded, Haitian-Dominican-Nuyorican rebirth of Botticelli's *Birth of Venus* and rising cornrowed from their own shell, the artist shielded their crotch with a modesty panel but let the brown of their nipples set off the brown swirling at their hips. "And then, a nonbinary Wild Vagina bloomed," they captioned the first red carpet picture of themselves they posted on Instagram, then elaborated for the second, "Wild decolonized unlady unclassy 100% commando nonbinary Vagina for Time 100."[2] ("That's not your typical pink vagina dress," Danielli admired on *mitú*.)[3] Mirroring Mock's graciousness in recognizing Moore as the future, Moore dedicated their moment to Black and Latinx trans big sisters and elders. "Thank you @TIME. An unspeakable Honor. Thank you @lavernecox, @janetmock . . . Marsha P [Johnson] & Silvia Rivera for making this transsexually dreamy moment possible."[4]

In their work together in 2018 and 2019, Moore and Mock both honored and made Black trans history. Their series, FX's *Pose*, is a first-of-its-kind period drama revolving around Black and Latinx trans women and gay men in the 1980s New York house-ballroom scene. One article on the series explained ball culture for those unfamiliar: "Balls originated as safe gathering places in NYC for those primarily within the black and Latino communities who identified as LGBTQ. A talent competition of sorts, participants don elaborate, self-designed costumes and divide themselves into groups (or houses) to walk, dance, strut, vogue and pose their way down the runway for trophies."[5] Bringing this underground culture to the small screen, *Pose* featured scripted television's largest-ever trans cast and received American Film Institute, GLAAD Media, and Peabody Awards in its first season. "Nothing like this has ever happened in the history of American television where our demographic can see itself for six months straight as the lead characters on national television," ballroom legend and filmmaker Elegance Bratton appreciated.[6] Mock became the first trans woman of color credited with writing and directing a television episode when "Love Is the Message" aired July 8, 2018, inspiring Janelle Monáe to post, "I love you Janet. You are what we have been waiting for. Genius."[7] Mock's favorite character, Angel, became the breakout role for Bronx native Moore, who began modeling at fifteen while living in foster care and left their final group home months prior to their *Pose* audition. "Seeing so many trans women acting and performing was something that was major and amazing to me," Moore acknowledges. "Knowing that we have a trans writer also made me feel safe about the stories that I would portray. I didn't have to worry about recycling stigmatic ideas through the stories that I was telling, because there were people who shared the experiences that the stories were about writing them."[8]

When the pilot's first shot widened to Angel, reclining open-legged on a chaise lounge, wearing calf-high pink platform boots, tube socks, black fishnets, cutoff shorts, and a rainbow-striped sweater, I leaned in closer to the screen. Moore's feather-adorned, Afro-haloed, tender-hearted, love-seeking character became the highlight of every episode for me, and of course when I finally joined Instagram that summer (don't judge my lateness!) I followed them. I soon discovered what their other 238,000 followers already knew: Moore often posts multiple times a day and *never* posts anything but the realest content. Small talk and fluff are not for them, they explain to *Elle*: "When I'm around people having conversations about their day, I'm looking at them, like, 'What could they possibly be talking about? How are we not talking about deconstructing white supremacy right now? How are we not trying to save trans people?'"[9] So I joined their "legion of fans . . . thanking [Indya] for being forever a teacher, for doing the exhausting work of explaining [their] radical perspective" on gender, race, and sexuality, and I recognized their forever teaching by regularly presenting their posts as theory in my spring 2019 Femme Theory class at Harvard.[10] Then one April day I was walking down the Cambridge streets scrolling through Instagram and came across Indya in their nonbinary wild vagina dress and, *and*: remember Beyoncé's lyric, "Know where you was when that digital popped . . . stop the world, world stop— carry on!"[11] Like that, my Black femme world stopped for Moore's dress, then rebloomed, wi(l)der.

Earlier I compared Moore's emergence in their nonbinary vagina dress to the birth of Venus, a Roman syncretization of the Greek goddess Aphrodite. Deity of femininity, beauty, and eroticism, Aphrodite was not of woman born: she rose from foam (*aphros*) that floated upward when Kronos cut off his father Uranus's testicles and threw them into the sea.[12] Yes, this hyperfeminine goddess is the byproduct of supernatural testes. Similarly transforming commonsense understandings of reproductive bodies, Moore's levitation as a nonbinary vagina is what Treva Carrie Ellison calls "Black femme flight": "the re/appearances of queer femininity that disorganize and confound the categories we often use to make sense of the world."[13] Analyzing mid-twentieth-century media representations of Black gender-nonconforming folk, Ellison traces print culture's role in solidifying rather than simply reflecting "ideas, like the idea that Black womanhood is cohered through the presence of the vagina."[14] Almost three-quarters of a century later, Moore mobilizes the more widely accessible space of social media to participate in the form of Black femme flight that Ellison (citing adrienne maree brown) identifies as "flocking," which "creates the possibility for Black trans and queer aesthetics through collective practice."[15] Moore's skill in flightfully captioning photos of their Black body—the kind of "real life" images of breasts and crotch bulges that, many users imagine, should convey gender without explanation—decolonizes gender by showing that "Black penises and vaginas are simultaneously pendulous flesh, terrains of cultural maneuver, and imaginative surfaces for the desire of others," as Ellison writes.[16] And Black queers respond by recognizing Moore's simultaneous divinity and humanity and, by extension, our own. The first comment on Moore's Time 100 posts came from Janelle Monáe—"breathtaking"—followed by Laverne Cox's rave: "Stunning, just stunning. Work! Congratulations darling!" Actor Stephen Conrad Moore revered, "This dress is poetry . . . it's a song from a Black heavenly angel" (earning a pleased "Ugh" from Moore). Queer sex educator Erika Hart burst out, "Oh shit!!!!!!!!!!!!!! You better be a nonbinary vagina!!" and intersex activist Pidgeon Pagonis appreciated, "This is actually so effing important and miraculous and I'm overjoyed THANK YOU."[17]

Joining this Black excellent company flocking to Moore, I'm turning these next pages into a much longer response to Moore's brilliant social media theorizing than Instagram would ever allow. Remember when Moore explained to the whole internet what a biologically female penis is? If you don't, I'm going to tell you all about it. Do you have ideas about what a wild decolonized nonbinary vagina looks like? If you do, I'm going to invite you to compare them to what Moore's helped me imagine. As I follow Moore in their cultural maneuvers through the "imaginative surfaces" of Black penises and vaginas, like the actor themself, I stop to pay homage to their Black and Latinx trans elders' and older sisters' wisdom in talking about trans genitalia. In season 2 of the Netflix prison drama *Orange Is the New Black*, Laverne Cox's character, Sophia, is the only inmate with sufficient knowledge to educate others on the workings of a vagina because she "designed one herself."[18] While this line is played for laughs in the series, the flurry of thought raised when Moore designs a nonbinary vagina from haute couture suggests maybe we all should stop (world, stop!) and take it more seriously.

VENUS XTRAVAGANZA

"I don't think there was . . . an image that had more of an impact on me than seeing Venus Xtravaganza sitting on that pier smoking a cigarette," Janet Mock told *TV Guide* about the influence of Jennie Livingston's 1990 documentary, *Paris Is Burning*, on her screenwriting. "You can't write and make up characters like that. They're all so real about the little humble goals that they wanted and I think that is what the lasting impact of that film is."[19] A member of the House of Xtravaganza and "main daughter" of Mother Angie Xtravaganza in 1987 when Livingston shot *Paris Is Burning*, Venus—born in New Jersey in 1965 to a Puerto Rican and Italian family—moved to New York at fourteen to transition. There, she turned tricks and snatched trophies for the House of Xtravaganza as a famously beautiful femme realness queen. "Some of them say that we're sick or crazy, and some of them think that we're the most gorgeous special things on earth," Venus smiles to the filmmaker, dressed in a summery white top and pants while reclining on a girlish twin bed with a flowered spread. "I don't feel like there's anything mannish about me, except maybe what I might have between me down there"—she laughs—"which is my little personal thing. I guess that's why I want my sex change, to make myself complete."[20] Venus was found strangled in a hotel room on December 25, 1988, during filming, a tragedy prefigured by the haunting image of her smoking on the pier at sunset as she speaks with the audio of her voice muted. Deeply marked by Venus's story, Mock finds the documentary's treatment of her death hollow: "The most heartbreaking part of *Paris* is the death of Venus Xtravaganza. Her body is just disposed of, without talking about what happened to her. If Pose were to do a storyline like that, we would show the consequences, the mourning."[21] When *Pose* pursued such a story line in season 2, Mock ensured the focus of Candy Ferocity's death remained how "women in this community band together. From getting her body from the morgue, making sure she looks her best, making sure that they scrape up all their pennies to throw her a funeral, to reaching out to her parents who show up, to give everyone that great healing moment that we all wish that we had."[22]

But before writing an alternative version of Venus's death in season 2, Mock writes two alternative possibilities for Venus's continued life in season 1. In one, Venus gets the vagina she wanted. "The Fever," the show's fourth episode and the first where Mock is given an exclusive writing credit, introduces a character named Aphrodite Xtravaganza. Aphrodite floats into a ball soundtracked by Sheena Easton's "Sugar Walls," just returned "refreshed" from "Bangkok"—vaginoplasty—to win grand prize for Femme Queen Realness. "It's like I finally felt whole," she describes the surgery. "There's nothing compares . . . to when you look between your legs and see nothing there." Encouraging another character to pursue surgery, she asks, "How lucky are we? We create ourselves."[23] The importance of this rebirth of Venus was not lost on viewers familiar with *Paris Is Burning*. "I don't believe in an afterlife, but I would like to think Venus is with her mother, Angie, elated to see the character created in her likeness achieve all that eluded her in her too-brief life," Jeffry Iovannone imagines. "Thanks to Janet Mock, Venus Xtravaganza lives."[24] In Mock's second rewriting, Venus doesn't have surgery—but she finds a way to live rather than die through sex work. Also a young trans Puerto Rican street prostitute when we meet her in the first episode, Moore's character, Angel, transitions to safer, more affirming work in a peep show. "It's safe behind the glass. Money is good. And, I like being admired," she explains.[25] Like Mock's experience of stripping, when "dancing in the club gave me greater confidence in my body,"[26] Angel's choice of sex work to affirm her autonomous femme-ininity testifies to LaMonda Horton-Stallings's point that "what has been labeled as sex work can be as important an element of self-definition to various trans folk as surgery has been in certain narratives."[27]

In its first season, *Pose* had eight one-hour episodes to convey the complexity of trans women's relationship to their sexualized bodies—a complexity flattened into easy jokes or facile tragedies in most media. Of course, no show can represent more than a fraction of the ways trans women and trans femmes know, love, and care for their bodies in so short a time. By bringing five trans actors of color into starring roles on prime-time television, though, the show facilitated public platforms—interviews, awards show speeches, expanded social media followings—for more transfeminine folk to represent their own bodies in ways viewers, listeners, and followers could flock to. As I made myself into one of Indya Moore's students on Instagram, I followed Mock's invitation to reflect on how many possible rewritings there can be of the once-tragic story of the trans woman of color and "what I might have between me down there." There are so many stories, and, as Saidiya Hartman writes of Black women in another context, "in all of them she is called Venus."[28]

A FEMME PENIS

Radiant in bubblegum lipstick, salmon feather wrap, and ruffle-draped fuchsia dress contrasting the dark window behind her, Angel opens the history-making *Pose* episode "Love Is the Message" in something not unlike the "typical pink vagina dress" Danielli describes. At the end of the previous episode, Patty (Kate Mara), wife to Angel's lover, Stan—having discovered her husband's affair and the posh apartment he rents for Angel—slipped into a ball, introduced herself to her cowife, and asked to talk. "Love Is the Message" opens with the women filmed in silhouette through the smudged glass of a diner window, then cuts to the interior and Angel's point of view as she faces Patty. From point of view to setting, Mock frames this meeting with Angel in a position of power. Angel's power includes her confidence-imbued trans reveal to Patty, who takes her for a cis woman. Mock notes, "She says with such confidence and assuredness, 'No, honey. I'm a transsexual'—with no shame, with no guilt. She's like, 'No, this is who I am. Your husband came for me.'"²⁹ Still disbelieving, Patty protests, "You're a woman"—and Angel swiftly answers, "One hundred percent." When Patty demands Angel "prove it" by showing her "dick," Angel calmly rejoins, "I'm here to talk, but I got boundaries. I'm not bothered by any part of who I am, except that. Everything I can't have in this world is because of that *thing* down there. If you want to see who I am, that's the last place you should look."³⁰

Unlike their character Angel, Moore publicly maintains they *don't* identify as 100 percent woman—or 100 percent *any* gender. "I don't identify as a woman. I don't identify as a man," Moore explained in conversation with Ericka Hart at Essence Fest 2019. "I don't identify within the binaries of those things. My choice to identify as such, even though I typically express myself in feminine ways, is to constantly disrupt the notion of the gender construct."³¹ Also differently from their character, Moore ruffles conservative and trans-exclusionary feathers by professing not only that women can have penises, but that those penises are as *biologically female* as cis women's vaginas. "The biology of trans women may be different than that of a cis woman, but that doesn't make trans women less biological, less woman, or less biological women. Trans women aren't synthetic or parody women," they educated in a series of February 2019 tweets. "If a woman has a penis, her penis is a biologically female penis," they continued, explaining the last phrase for the confused: "A biologically female penis is a non artificial penis (eg: dildo, vibrator) that is part of a biological (human) woman's body."³² Ana Valens noted in the *Daily Dot* that "with Moore's viral tweets—[their] original Saturday post sparked over 4,000 retweets and 20,000 likes—[they are] forcing cisgender Twitter users to address their hidden biases against trans bodies."³³ Predictably, while many celebrated Moore's tweets, others lost their mind. A response video from "Fawning Girl" began by zooming out from a screenshot of Moore's tweet, then rapidly cutting together "scientific" anatomy diagrams overlaid with audio static as the host stammers, "Biology—how do you make—how—what—" before a computerized voice interrupts: "We're sorry, but . . . Fawning Girl has stopped running."

Undoubtedly, Calvin Klein's promotional team had read—and were hoping to capitalize on—the actor's viral tweets when they chose Moore as the face of the label's June 2019 Pride capsule line. Moore modeled for a series of photo and video underwear ads for the company that year, beginning with the "I Speak My Truth in #MyCalvins" campaign. The video spot for that campaign begins with the camera looking from above on Moore modeling white briefs and an unbuttoned white shirt on a balcony, then interweaves shots of them reclining on a blanket, rubbing thighs together as they gently cup their breasts, leaning playfully over the ledge, and dancing languidly as their voice-over plays: "I used to tell my friends, I'm ugly before 10 a.m. and I'd warn them to just not look at me. But not anymore. I won't wait to be free. I speak my truth in my Calvins."[34] From Victoria's Secret to Hugo Boss, mainstream "underwear is marketed in an incredibly gendered way, with branding that relies heavily on stereotypes and advertising imagery that is often alienating, or even triggering, for many people—particularly those who already grapple with being misgendered in their everyday lives," queer journalist Bailey Calfee remarks.[35] But Moore's ads for trendsetting underwear brand Calvin Klein refuse masculine/feminine, male/female binaries. They move through the video wearing "menswear" clothing staples—a white dress shirt (with buttons on the right side to indicate it's "for" men) and white trunks with "Calvin Klein" emblazoned across the waistband—but lean against the window with head tilted and right hip jutting out, striking a pose whose "recoiling of weight through the hips" Black queer dance scholar Tommy DeFrantz categorizes as "traditionally feminine."[36] And their unbuttoned shirt reveals round, braless breasts, while their legs open into a V that draws viewers' eyes to a soft bulge in their trunks. Moore speaks proudly of these ads that feature, according to journalist Jada Yuan, "a subtle crotch bulge to go along with [their] pert breasts"; Moore underscores, "I think that's so important!"[37]

Not allowing costuming, gesture, or "pendulous flesh" (to return to Ellison's term) to identify them as woman or man in this video, Moore finesses elements of voguing that—for those fluent in its Black queer movement vocabulary—choreograph them as *femme*. (Moore, like femme queen Venus, is a member of the legendary House of Xtravaganza.) Vogue femme, Christina Tente describes in her master's thesis on the dance form, is a "contemporary voguing style, characterised by hyperbolic femininity, soft moves, dramatic poses, and cunty energy. It emphasises feminine movements and it includes five elements: hands performance, catwalk, duckwalk, spins and dips, and floor performance."[38] Moore describes their own experience of vogue femme, more poetically, as "a language, a hobby, a job, a lifestyle, a culture, a sport, an art, a dance, a safe space, it is a beautiful-twirling-geometric intersection of Afro-American and Latin-American culture."[39] In their "I Speak My Truth in #MyCalvins" spot, Moore gives viewers hands performance while perched gracefully on the balcony's edge. The ball of their left foot balanced on the ledge, right leg extended to the floor, and thighs in an open V, their right hand holds the railing while the left circles on the soft, limp wrist characteristic of vogue femme. At this moment—also the beginning of the voice-over that "speaks truth"—Moore seems at once grounded and ready to fly, their crotch bulge, breasts, and ballroom hands gesturing toward femme flight. In the companion video "Convention Killer," Moore—now advertising a black lace bodysuit from Calvin's "womenswear" line—again gives us hands performance along with floor work, rolling and twisting with arched back and circling wrists as they dance in a mirrored glass cage.[40] A black shirt tied around their waist swings between their legs as they work vogue performance style "soft and cunt," which "consists of clean, soft, and smooth hand/arm movements in a fluid and flowing way."[41] Mobile hands, *not* pendulous flesh of any kind, are the body parts that tell stories of gender in vogue femme, Tente argues: "The hands mark every presence and activate all bodies, from the voguers to those who came to look or judge. . . . They frame the face, create boxes and flows of energy, they tut, twist and draw eights, they tell a story, point to certain parts of the body that need to be looked at and admired."[42]

For voguers and spectators alike, ballroom recognizes (at least) six genders. My friend and colleague Marlon Bailey lists them as follows:

1. Butch queens (gay men)
2. Femme queens (male to female transgender people at various stages of reassignment)
3. Butch queen up in drags (gay men that dress and perform as women)

4. Butches (female to male transgender people at various stages of reassignment)
5. Men (males born as male and that live as men but do not identify as gay)
6. Women (females born as female and live as female and are straight, lesbian, or queer)[43]

While Bailey uses the terms *female* and *male*, he clarifies that these terms signify differently in ballroom culture than in the straight world. "Community members view the category of sex as open and unfinished," he explains, and "hold the fundamental belief that sex categories are malleable and that the body can be altered through various means, such as reconstructive surgery, hormonal therapy, or padding."[44] Moore's styling and posing in the Calvin Klein videos use hands performance to point to ways Moore alters not only the body itself but their understanding of what their body *means*. In the "Convention Killer" spot, their hands deftly circle both their face and upper thighs as "parts of the body that need to be looked at and admired."[45] Their vogue femme hands point to their crotch in a way that, in the words of my brilliant Femme Theory student Elijah Ezeji-Okoye, "begs us to imagine a biologically femme, non-binary penis": that is, Moore's voguing femme choreography in their slightly bulging Calvins "allows us to include the biology of the penis in a more representative femme-ininity while resisting the gender binaries that are imposed upon us from birth."[46]

I love Ezeji-Okoye's idea that Moore dresses and dances a biologically femme penis, which aligns with Moore's self-identification as "nonbinary, femme," and decidedly *not* female. I also love that when I write something like this—*Moore gestures toward her biologically femme penis with soft and cunt hands*—I'm putting together words that make little sense in relation to each other in straight common sense but signify generously in Black queer world making. Like *Black pussy* in Shoniqua Roach's theorizing, *cunt* and *cunty* don't reference genitalia in ballroom. *Cunt* and *pussy* are "criteria for gender performance in ballroom culture, as opposed to insults or demeaning expletives hurled at women and femme queens," Bailey points out. (Comedian D. L. Hughley once called Moore a pussy for objecting to his homophobic jokes, to which they responded, "Pussy's are warm, have depth and are strong enough to take a beating. . . . Pussy is absolutely complimentary to who I am.")[47] Bailey notes, "When these terms are used, the speaker does not typically say 'you are a cunt.' Instead, the speaker says, 'give me pussy' or 'you look cunt,' meaning give me femininity in your performance and self-presentation."[48] In Bailey's examples, *cunt* functions as an adjective rather than a noun: and while concrete nouns suggest "permanency, stability, fixity," as Gloria Wekker writes of Dutch nouns describing sexuality, adjectives—whose semantic role is *change*, modification of a noun's meaning—are more supple, more suited to the malleable, unfinished understanding of sex and gender Bailey attributes to ballroom.[49] *Cunty* is a descriptor Moore themself uses, as in their tweet about Janet Mock's work on *Pose*: "Goddess @janetmock teleported from the universe of infinitely cunty magical stuff and crushed some sugar, some spice and everything transsexual & softly blew the contents with her hand using her holy afro futuristic breath unto the book of Pose. & then our cast was born."[50] Nobody's cookie-cutter, heteronormative femininity, the *infinite cuntiness* in Moore's fabulous description is a femme-ininity that multiplies gender possibilities like grains of sugar, births *something new* with hands and mouth instead of uterus, and creates beautiful Black femme futures that were never supposed to exist.

When Calvin Klein released the Pride line May 14, Moore, in paid partnership with the clothing brand, posted several underwear ads to Instagram without captions except promotional hashtags. But two days later Moore released other images from the shoot without Calvin Klein's sponsorship and with very pointed captions, including "Deconstructing white supremacy & colonial Heteronormative patriarchy & Gender violence In #MYCALVINS."[51] As important as Moore feels their femme penis Calvin Klein ads (as I call them) are, however, they also recognize limits to the decolonial work their mainstream modeling can effect. "There are ways that I can shift our social and political landscape through the stories I tell on screen and off," Moore reflects to *i-D*'s Jess Cole for the magazine's 2020 "Up + Rising" series about extraordinary Black voices. "However, I'm still thin, I'm cis-passing, I am light skinned and my hair texture is at the preference level of what a lot of people prefer to see when it comes to black hair. Representation of marginalised people shouldn't only begin and centre around the most privileged *looking* of us, because then we are only re-perpetuating white supremacist values."[52] In a roundtable on colorism, Moore cites *white woman cunt*—"a phrase in the ballroom scene that is commending somebody that is beautiful"—as proof that decolonization of queer bodies is ongoing, painful, and powerful even in our own spaces.[53] *Black femme cunt, Black femme penis* as standards of excellence, they know, are "holy afro futuristic" dreams yet to be realized.

MISS MAJOR GRIFFIN-GRACY

On March 31, 2019, for International Transgender Day of Visibility, Indya Moore posted a video of Miss Major speaking to her "guys and girls" about the annual event. "Hi! This is Miss Major," she begins in the reassuring voice reserved for her children, then furrows her brow as she continues, "I don't really understand why we need a day of visibility, since for most of us, especially Black girls, we are as visible as we need to be. Our visibility is getting us killed." Her voice speeds up as she challenges, "The people who care about us, who are involved in our lives, and who know us, they're the people who need to become more visible. . . . Visibilize this shit: 'I like transgender people!'"[54] A fighter who threw her shoe and spit in a policeman's face during the 1969 Stonewall riots, Miss Major became a prison-justice activist after numerous incarcerations and served as founding executive director of the Transgender, Gender Variant, and Intersex Justice Project until her retirement in 2015. "A veteran of the historic Stonewall Rebellion and a survivor of Attica State Prison, a former sex worker, a human rights activist, and simply 'Mama' to many in her community," her Monthly Fundraising Circle describes her. "At the center of her activism from the 1960s to today is her fierce advocacy for her girls, trans women of color who have survived police brutality and incarceration."[55] In addition to biological sons Christopher and Asiah, Miss Major mothers and grandmothers countless trans people of color whom she loves just because they're themselves. Never one to withhold love from her children, she's also never one to hold her tongue about anything. "We get to call her things like sage, right. Wise. Even though she's spitting tacks and cussing folks out," daughter Valerie Spencer appreciates, and Melenie Eleneke adds, "Mama, she's a dirty little vixen. She really is!"[56]

It's no secret Mama likes to talk about penises—but not (always) the way you think. She doesn't mince words when she breaks down how myths of the almighty phallus contribute to transmisogyny. "This unspoken separation between trans women and trans men. . . . It comes down to dick and pussy. You got a dick, the world is: 'Yay! Work that thing, it spits cum, how wonderful.' But you have a pussy, and the world is, 'Well, that's OK,'" she states in conversation with fellow prison abolitionist CeCe McDonald. "So going through all that shit, what winds up happening to the trans person: if you were born male, and you want to be female, or look like a female, you're a sick, demented, twisted loser. But, if you were born with a vagina and you want to have a dick, how wonderful of you to recognize the power of the penis."[57] She also doesn't mince words talking about her own penis—not as a source of the patriarchal power she's spent her life fighting, but as a beloved font of sexual pleasure. While *Pose*'s trans characters object to lovers touching them between the legs, Miss Major doesn't imagine anyone rubbing, sucking, or otherwise enjoying her penis makes her any less a woman. "Having a dick ain't got nothing to do with my womanhood! Bitch, get over it!"[58] Asked if she considered vaginoplasty when she moved to New York in the 1960s, she explained, "What New York did for me was it um, woke me up and let me know I don't really need to have a sex change if I use what I have with the right people, I can keep what I got! And still be the prettiest thing in a pair of heels. So they knocked my dick in the dirt, honey, I was the happiest bitch for a long time."[59] One of her favorite things to do was pull her skirt up over her breasts while getting blow jobs in the Forty-Second Street movie theaters. Because sometimes a femme penis can't be kept covered up in #MyCalvins.

GOLDEN PUSS AWARDS

"Just so you know, I don't think you should have snagged grand prize, but I do want to congratulate you on your surgery. I'm happy for you," Angel tells her former housemother Elektra (Dominique Jackson) as they leave the Mother's Day ball where Patty lies in wait.[60] Elektra's decision to undergo vaginoplasty despite an ultimatum from her longtime "gentleman friend" was central to the character's first-season story arc, and Mock's writing around the surgery was particularly meaningful for transfeminine viewers. "I never thought I would see positive discussion centered around a trans woman's vagina on a popular TV show, but it happened on last night's episode of *Pose*," trans Latinx writer Mey Rude appreciated. Episode 3, "Giving and Receiving," finds Elektra in a doctor's office, resplendent in a sheer chocolate-brown grid blouse and matching brown leather skirt and boots. Waiting in the exam room, her eyes are drawn to a pamphlet on "Sex Re-assignment Surgery," and the camera fixes on a close-up of the pamphlet as she turns its pages. "We see detailed and graphic illustrations of the steps of vaginoplasty. We see a penis being turned into a vagina—and no one laughs, groans, or grimaces in disgust," Rude continues. "There's a lot of power in being told that your body isn't wrong, and the importance of the ways media portrays trans surgeries cannot be overstated. By hiring Janet Mock and Our Lady J to write for his latest show, Murphy has helped trans women gain the representation we've been hoping for."[61] The story line was also important to Jackson, who has been vocal about how lifesaving vaginoplasty was for her. "I love the way Janet wrote the scene," she explains. "It was tender and yet it was still a woman fighting for her own independence. It was about trans women realizing that they can achieve full-blown gender operation surgery and they should go towards that no matter what's possible. It has to be up to them."[62]

Representing *Pose* on the red carpet that season, Moore chose their dresses to create a different kind of narrative arc around nonbinary vaginas. Consciously politicizing their fashion statements, they attended awards shows in a series of transfemme-inist naked dresses paired with transfemme-inist Instagram captions. *Naked dress*, you may remember, is a phrase from a *Sex and the City* episode where the main character chooses a skin-colored slip dress for a first date. "It's the naked dress. You're obviously going to have sex with him tonight," one friend disapproves, but another counters, "She's not gonna have sex. She's just gonna look like sex."[63] With its infamous transmisogynoir slurs in an episode featuring Black trans sex workers, that series (which characters cast shade on in the *Pose* series finale) was narcissistically uninterested in imagining a dress that *looks like sex* for trans folk—but Moore is interested, invested, and creative in looking like nonbinary sex. They arrived at the Peabody Awards in a sheer LaQuan Smith sheath dress glinting with a mosaic of metallic beads, black panties and bare breasts showing through the dress's beaded windows. Their burgundy lips remained closed as they posed for the cameras and reminded, "Femmes & Women Don't need to smile. When you see us on the red carpet and beyond don't ask us to if we choose not to!"[64] At the Paley Center for Media's 2019 PaleyFest they wore a beige, see-through, netted dress by favorite designer Altuzarra, tagging #bus sitdownthotiana in homage to Blueface's song in praise of "thots, sluts, whores." And at the Golden Globes they stunned in a see-through, futuristic, bronze Louis Vuitton mini with outsized shoulders, telling *Vogue*, "I feel like a superhero"—"like a cyber-Afro-warrior," stylist Ian Bradley clarified the look.[65] Posed nude in a chair with the dress hanging behind them on Instagram, they served, "Golden Puss Awards. 'AND THE GOLDEN KITTY GOES TO: @louisvuitton' 'Trans bodies are always under scrutiny especially when we show skin.' —@undocuqueer. This photo takes over that power dymanic."[66]

Vaginoplasty is commonly represented as the technological apex of male-to-female medical transition, but Moore's series of naked dresses presents another technology for creating nonbinary vaginas: fashion. Fashion has always been intertwined with technology in its traditional, physical sense, and the week Moore's Calvin Klein ads came out, CB Insights declared, "Tech is transforming fashion at a faster pace than ever. From robots that sew and cut fabric, to AI algorithms that predict style trends, to VR mirrors in dressing rooms, technology is automating, personalizing, and speeding up every aspect of fashion."[67] Fashion also participates in the web of social technologies that feminist theorist Teresa de

Lauretis calls "technologies of gender," or "social technologies, such as cinema . . . institutionalized discourses, epistemologies, and critical practices, as well as practices of daily life," that produce and process the binary gender system we know.[68] Sporting a gravity-defying dress suspended by beads and declaring it the winner of a "Golden Puss Award," Moore engineers a nonbinary fashion technology that's both physical and social: one that approaches "fashion as social, processual sculpture at the interface of technology and of art, and [enables] it to manifest political, social and aesthetic forms."[69] "Fashion should be conforming to body types, not body types conforming to fashion. Clothes didn't come first and then humans, humans came and said we need clothes to fit our bodies," Moore told Hari Ziyad of *Afropunk* in 2017.[70] Two years later, they were instrumentalizing their heightened media presence to show the world what kind of clothes fit and look like a wild nonbinary vagina.

A wild nonbinary vagina (dress), I've learned from Moore's red-carpet technology, has lots of holes: hundreds of parallelogram-shaped holes in Louis Vuitton, nearly a thousand parabolic holes in LaQuan Smith. Why so many? Reflecting on Angel's story lines, Eva Reign lays out, "Cis men's curiosity for transfeminine bodies subjects trans women to intense objectification. Instead of becoming a significant other, trans women are treated as cis men's easily dispensable toys. . . . Trans women looking for love are trying to exist in a world fraught with labelling them hypersexual."[71] Moore themself comments, "Cis-people's perception of trans people coupled with the commoditisation of femininity is what I think has created this hyper-visible, hyper-attacked and hyper everything to do with transwomen and trans-femmes."[72] Moore's hyperholey vagina dresses take over the power dynamic of transmisogynoir hypersexualization, wearing it as a work of art. Posing with a carefully cultivated look that's unclassy, unlady, and proud of it, they are *not* there to be anyone's plaything—their fashion art including "a face that did not come to play with you hoes," as Moore describes at the Time 100 gala.[73] That's the first intervention I see through Moore's dresses; but as I look longer, I see other challenges in the patterns those holes form on their body. If straight has an "opposite," these curving lines of beads—whose purpose is to join so many openings, rather than divide, as lines sometimes do—might be it. Their LaQuan Smith holes bend and connect to form fractals, ovals within larger ovals. And fractals, Jeanne Vaccaro imagines, are a way of spatializing the multiplying, inter-related possibilities for understanding the sexualized body that transness materializes. "Transgender is a shape," she posits, "and, in the conjoining of feelings beside fractals, an alternative dimension of shapes . . . can co-exist to proliferate an abundance of shapely possibilities for transgender life."[74] Moore's naked dresses win the nonbinary Golden Puss Award not because they look like any kind of biological organ we already know but because they glitteringly offer "a sensory way to look, feel, and inhabit dimensions that exceed the grids, rectangles, and straight networks that organize the built architecture of our lives."[75]

A decolonized nonbinary vagina (dress), I've also learned from Moore, comes *only* in shades of brown. Pink may be the color of pussyhats and va-gina pants, but Moore's beige-to-mahogany spectrum of naked dresses join their red-carpet preference for Bantu knots, braids, and African diaspora designers as a fashion technology of unapologetic Blackness. "Sometimes I have to remind people I'm black and that makes me feel less black, But yeah! I'm black and I'm trans and I'm here," they proclaim.[76] As a light-skinned person of Puerto Rican, Haitian, and Dominican descent, Moore aligns with Blackness as an act of resistance to both colorism and racism. "One of the things I experience as an Afro-Latino is that once men find out that I'm Dominican they overstep their boundaries with their com-ments about Black people," they explain. "I see this all the time . . . with people asking folks to change their African hair texture and everything. So I make a point to identify with my blackness and my transness and to be aware of my roots and be conscious of everything trying to erase them or make me feel less than for them. This is my art. My art form is existing."[77] One of the only times I've seen Moore in pink on the red carpet was at the 2018 Ebony Power 100 gala, where they appeared in a ruffled, diaphanous Celestino Couture gown paired with matching pink blush, pale-blue eye-shadow, and a white line bisecting their chin to embody the colors of the trans pride flag. There, they explained to interviewer Mike Hill why trans pride has *always* been Black. "I think we've gotten so far down this dark hole that colonialism put us all in that gender variant people don't exist," they answered Hill's question about why it was important to attend this event. "Before colonialism all the tribes that we all belonged to and that we have ancestry a part of acknowledged gender variance and there wasn't any such thing as a gender binary. You know, colonialism came through and fucked everything up—excuse my language!" The African and Taino browns of their nonbinary vagina wardrobe are reflections of their belief "that my ancestors loved me. And that I am my ancestors' dreams."[78]

While penile-inversion vaginoplasty—the kind demonstrated in the pamphlet Elektra reads—may be the gold standard for MtF medical transition, trans folk *becoming their ancestors' dreams* might be the gold standard for Black femme flight: a flight that confounds Western categories of male/female, penis/vagina, goddess/whore, colonizer/colonized, Indix/ Negrx, past/present. And, pursuing this flight through artistic rather than medical technologies, Moore also erodes the standard pre-op/post-op binary that marks transition. What if (their naked dresses push us to ask) you've operated to create a vagina out of cloth—or clay, or paint, or your mind's eye—instead of flesh? "So often the only people who get to speak for the trans community are those who have pursued transition," Moore tweets. "It's important for us trans people who have medically transitioned to include and legitimize trans people who cannot or do not pursue medical transition." This is especially important for trans women of color, since, as Moore's costar Dominique Jackson lays out, "A lot of trans women of color have felt that approaching surgery was something they could never possibly achieve. Not only financially but from a mental perspective."[79] You can transition with a pink pussy, a brown one, a flesh one, a fabric one, or none at all, Moore's fashion technology declares; all can be wild, decolonized, nonbinary, and flawless.

JANET MOCK

Never. That, Janet Mock has made perfectly clear, is when trans women and trans femmes should be expected to talk about their vaginas. "I don't talk about my kitty cat with my friends. It never seems to come up when we're gabbing about *The Real Housewives* or gagging over Beyoncé's 'Partition' music video," she wrote for *Elle* in 2014, reflecting on journalists' insistence on asking trans women about their before-and-after genitalia. "But I—an unapologetic trans woman and writer—have been asked about my vagina (by people I do not know, mind you) more times than I can even recall."[80] Mock made clear the hypersexualizing and transmisogynist underpinnings to these questions when, later that year, she accepted journalist Alicia Menendez's invitation to flip the usual trans interview script and have Mock ask Menendez the kind of questions Mock is usually peppered with. "Do you have a vagina?" "When was the moment you first felt your breasts budding?" "Do you use tampons?" were among her pointed questions for Menendez, who tripped over her answers and dodged questions (despite having seen them in advance). "As illustrated, this experience was beyond uncomfortable—and we were only involved in a mock interview (pun intended)—but I hope our demonstration sheds light on the ongoing, longstanding problem in our media culture of inquisition when it comes to framing trans people's stories," Mock wrote of the exchange, which quickly went viral. "I also hope it serves as a teaching moment for us all about self-determination and self-definition, about what remains public and what's private."[81] Trans vaginas are vaginas, period, and pussies aren't available as topics of public conversation unless their owners want them to be.

And sometimes, they do want them to be. Sometimes, like Elektra in the doctor's waiting room, trans women create safe(r) spaces to access and share information about vaginas in ways that are supportive, nonbinary, and nonexclusionary. In her first autobiography, *Redefining Realness: My Path to Womanhood, Identity, Love and So Much More*, Mock describes the importance of learning post-op care from other trans women after her vaginoplasty in Bangkok. And in her second, *Surpassing Certainty: What My Twenties Taught Me*, she includes a short, powerful reflection on the importance of learning about the infinite variety of vaginas from cis and trans women at the strip club where she worked stealth. I referenced the beginning of the passage earlier but now want to call attention to how it continues: "Dancing in the club gave me greater confidence in my body, particularly enabling me to appreciate the aesthetics of my vagina. I had long feared that mine did not look 'normal,' as if there were a standard look for all vaginas, and in my mind, I thought normal equated to the picturesque pink blossoms that were neatly folded and delicately layered." Where, after all, would a girl get her first look at vaginas in the pre-Pornhub '90s? "These were the polished pussies of *Playboy*—smooth, without layers or complication." The corrective to the insecurity brought on by these "vaginas birthed from male fantasies" was not found in support groups, activist circles, or classes at the University of Hawai'i, where Mock was an undergraduate at the time. Instead, she found it in the strip club where she worked to pay the bills: "It was at Club Nu that I was exposed to vaginas from all walks of life. Some were juicy, flappy, slim, fat, thick, slack, compact, and variations in between. No two were identical, yet all belonged to women."[82]

Passages like this give readers a controlled glimpse of what Mock means when she speaks of her experiences with sex work offering "a sense of community, of sisterhood, resiliency, resources, strength . . . it was like our underground railroad."[83] Mock's insistence on sex workers' rights as femme-inism was pivotal to her work on the 2017 Women's March on Washington, even after a key line she wrote for its vision statement—"We stand in solidarity with sex workers' rights movements"—was excised. When it was, she reaffirmed her stance on Tumblr. "It is not a statement that is controversial to me because as a trans woman of color who grew up in low-income communities and who advocates, resists, dreams and writes alongside these communities, I know that underground economies are essential parts of the lived realities of women," she wrote. "I know sex work to be work. . . . It's not a radical statement. It's a fact. My feminism rejects respectability politics, whore-phobia, slut-shaming and the misconception that sex workers, or folks engaged in the sex trades by choice or circumstance, need to be saved."[84]

Of course, Mock was one of many Black feminists who wrote back to the politics of the Women's March and its aftermath. Another was Crunk Feminist Collective cofounder Brittney Cooper, who on January 23, 2017, published a piece titled "Pussy Don't Fail Me Now: The Place of Vaginas in Black Feminist Theory and Organizing." Reflecting on the pushback against the pussyhat (which Mock chose not to wear) as ciscentric, she writes, "When I think about what it would mean to build a Black feminist framework which decenters the pussy, it gives me pause. The call is of course to decenter cisgender Black women from Black feminist frameworks. Again, this move, and the ways in which, in far left social justice spaces, such moves are assumed to be a clear mandate, a clearly desirable end of our politics, gives me pause."[85] Mock's beautiful reflections on the luscious garden of Club Nu pussies suggests that in some ways Cooper is right: the time to stop correcting harmful mythologies about the vagina has not yet come. But instead of imagining that conversation led by and primarily benefitting Black cis women, as Cooper does ("For cisgender Black women and girls, our vaginas constitute the material locus of our cisness," she stipulates), what if Black trans folk—women, men, and nonbinary folk alike—who have vaginas, flesh and blood and otherwise, orchestrate those conversations? Mock and Menendez got it right: it's time to flip the pussy script so that trans women and femmes are in control. And yes, that reference to Mock's namesake Janet Jackson is absolutely on purpose.

WAP FACTORY

On August 7, 2020, rappers Cardi B and Megan Thee Stallion broke the internet with the release of their video "WAP" (Wet-Ass Pussy), a celebration of "the complex, messy, sticky, and even joyous negotiations" of two Black women's pussy power[86]—and of "punani [so] Dasani" you need "a bucket and a mop . . . your boots and your coat" to enjoy it.[87] Set in a sprawling pink playhouse replete with arches leading into breast-shaped fountains, dancers flexing in cat prints, and Cardi and Megan splashing together in water, "'WAP' is an unadulterated feast of fantasy costuming, twerking wall fixtures, and dance moves akin to a pliability and flexibility test," Rhea Cartwright celebrates. "The pinnacle, however, is the openness in which female sexual pleasure is discussed and presented without the all-assuming male gaze."[88] Debuting at number one on the *Billboard* Hot 100 and finishing as 2020's most acclaimed song, "WAP" drew immediate, self-righteous backlash from conservatives, including Republican congressional candidate James P. Bradley, who inveighed, "Cardi B & Megan Thee Stallion are what happens when children are raised without God and without a strong father figure. . . . I feel sorry for future girls if this is their role model!"[89] Black fem(me)inist social media gleefully ripped critiques like Bradley's to shreds. "Folks are really mad about Cardi and Meg owning their sexuality, but it just reveals the sad state of our culture. Imagine if more folks put their energy into ending people being violated and assaulted instead of denouncing when people embrace their bodies," Black transfeminist media strategist Raquel Willis demanded pointedly. "Imagine if women and other folks could love their selves on their own terms without being concerned with the white cis-hetero patriarchal gaze. Imagine if folks weren't more accepting of voting a guy to office who brags about taking advantage of women than women saying how much they enjoy sex. We just might have a better, more pleasurable world for all. In other words, love on your #WAP, boos."[90]

On October 1, self-described "Cuntess" Indya Moore added their own contribution to the flurry of WAP-generated "pussy theorizing."[91] "WAP FACTORY," they captioned a red-carpet photo from the Savage X Fenty Show Vol. 2, posing in a black Savage Not Sorry glissinette teddy, open robe, and thigh-high patterned stockings.[92] Moore joined Rihanna's 2020 lingerie show along with a carefully curated team of gender-nonconforming talent, including drag stars Shea Coulée, Gigi Goode, and Jaida Essence Hall and nonbinary models Memphis Murphy and Jazzelle Zanaughtti. Modeling a black bodysuit "with dreamy, holographic lace, Xtra-enticing cuts and surreal designs" (as Savage X Fenty describes it), fishnet stockings, latex gloves, and peep-toe stilettos, Moore and five backup dancers perform a cameo of floor work to the soundtrack of N.E.R.D.'s "She Wants to Move."[93] Floor work, Tente notes, stands out from other elements of vogue femme because "apart from the general rule of keeping the moves clear and precise, which applies to all vogue femme elements, in the floor performance there are no other rules and the body is free to do whatever it desires and to employ other dance styles, more theatrical elements, even acrobatics. This limitless potentiality makes the floor performance a surprising and unpredictable element in the vogue femme performance." If vogue femme is a mode of storytelling, Tente concludes, "floor performance is the plot twist, the scene that everyone anticipates but no one really knows when, where and how it will develop."[94] "She makes me think of lightning in skies / (Her name) She's sexy," the soundtrack plays as Moore performs their Savage plot twist. Much as they conjure Aphrodite rising from the sea on the Time 100 red carpet, Moore at Savage X Fenty, body rolling from a one-legged crouch into a backbend to the lyric "lightning in skies," conjures another Greek deity for me: Astraea, the winged "Star Goddess" who carries a blazing torch and lightning bolts at her sides.[95]

Launching a WAP Factory, Moore-as-Astraea's caption tells us, is part of their Star Goddess justice mission. Not about vaginas, female penises, or other pendulous flesh, WAP Factory is about commitment to a world where *every* body can "love their selves on their own terms without being concerned with the white cis-hetero patriarchal gaze"; about being open to seeing in *any* body the same "limitless potentiality [that] makes the floor performance a surprising and unpredictable element." And of course, about creating a Savage Not Sorry space to recognize Moore's truth: "Human beings actively enjoy sex. It is an important part of our lives, our mental health, self-esteem and recreational life. . . . We have a sexy ass culture, we love sex and that's ok. We can move in really beautiful ways by acknowledging that."[96] WAP: Women Accessing Power; Workers Applying Pressure; Woke As Panthers; We're All Pussy, loves. "How else is God supposed to write / (Her name) She's sexy," the soundtrack asks as the Star Goddess concludes their cameo twerking on all fours. "Do things my own way darling," Moore captions their straddle-legged pose and identifies their location, simply and aptly, with the eternal Black femme question: What Is Pussy?[97]

PART TWO

Hymns for Crazy Black Femmes

"Doctors want President Trump's head examined," Jen Christensen's CNN headline caveated the results of POTUS's physical on January 16, 2018.[1] The week before, after a tweetstorm in which Trump declared himself a "very stable genius" whose "two greatest assets have been mental stability and being, like, really smart,"[2] over seventy medical and mental health professionals cited his "declining faculties for complex thought, rambling speech, difficulty completing a thought," and "suspect judgment, planning, problem solving and impulse control" in a request that the president's physician evaluate the seventy-one-year-old's cognitive and mental health functions.[3] Their letter continued a wave of challenges to Trump's psychiatric fitness that began with California representative Karen Bass's "#DiagnoseTrump," a 2016 petition urging "the Republican party to insist that their nominee has an evaluation to determine his mental fitness for the job," and declared it "our patriotic duty to raise the question of his mental stability to be the commander in chief and leader of the free world."[4] The group Duty to Warn, founded by psychotherapist John Gartner after Trump's inauguration, amplified Bass's efforts by gathering over seventy thousand signatures to remove Trump from office because of "serious mental illness that renders him psychologically incapable of competently discharging the duties of President of the United States."[5] The group's efforts were widely publicized by the *New York Times* ("Mental Health Professionals Warn about Trump," "An Eminent Psychiatrist Demurs on Trump's Mental State," "Is It Time to Call Trump Mentally Ill?") and yielded two books as well as the documentary

#Unfit: The Psychology of Donald Trump. "Is Donald Trump fit to serve as president and commander in chief?" psychiatrist Justin Frank sums up the film's inquiry, then answers categorically, "No. Trump is a sociopath, a sadist, a con artist, a racist, a misogynist, a sexist in general, and I think it is a problem."[6]

But "racism, xenophobia, Islamophobia, and misogyny" aren't mental illnesses, queer disability justice agitator s.e. smith objects. "They are learned behaviors. Donald Trump is the way he is because of who he is—a powerful, privileged man who's gotten everything he wanted in life in a culture where these behaviors are tolerated and sometimes actively rewarded." Smith points out the potential material consequences of psych ableism that equates disability with violence, bigotry, and "unfitness to serve": "When I hear that Donald Trump is crazy and that means he can't be president, I hear that people think the crazy people are 'incompetent'—a medicolegal term that's used to deprive mentally ill people of their autonomy, placing them in conservatorships. People under guardianship can't own property, make their own decisions (including marrying), or even vote."[7] Dan Schindel asks in his underwhelmed review of *#Unfit,* "What if all the shitty, glib discourse about Trump's mental state actually functions less like attacks on him and more like attacks on people with confirmed mental illnesses? You know, people who aren't in positions of considerable power, who are far more likely than Trump to be harmed by furthering the stigma around their conditions."[8] The rhetoric around #DiagnoseTrump and Duty to Warn barrels forward with the assumption that mental health professionals have the responsibility to protect the "sane" from the "insane." But what if, instead, like radical madvocate Greg Procknow, we assume that "if Trump is 'mentally ill,'" medical professionals "should be supportive of the President seeking and receiving treatment, rather than pathologizing his politics"?[9] Throughout his campaigns and presidency, Trump repeatedly referred to the neurodivergent as "sickos" and called for their institutionalization. Instead of pointing the finger back at him to accuse, *"You're* the sicko!" what if activists countered Trump by imagining disability in relationship to *expanded access* rather than expanded prohibitions?

In fact, as the Trump era dawned, self-described "crazy" and "crip" activists were defending *everyone* from the self-described stable genius's policies. Even as Duty to Warn pathologized (Trump's) disability as an impediment to democracy, organizers were applying sufficient pressure to the Trumpocracy for the Center for American Progress to declare 2017 the "Year the Disability Community Reshaped Progressive Politics." Citing "ongoing pushes for community-based mental health care [that] have demonstrated the ability of people with mental health conditions to contribute to society" and the efforts of the grassroots disability rights group ADAPT to defend the Affordable Care Act and Medicaid, the center concluded, "In an age in which President Donald Trump and his conservative allies have operated a virtual whack-a-mole game rotating attacks on marginalized communities, much can be garnered in the way of promising practices, solidarity, and perseverance in the work of the disability rights movement."[10] The solidarity evoked here begins with activists' recognition of disability as a socially constructed category entangled with race, class, gender, sexuality, migration status, and other politicized identities that, engaged together, undermine the fiction that reality as usual is the only reality worth living. The messy, unpredictable, oversaturated, underexposed, electric entanglements of disability justice rewire perception in ways that render disability "more than the deficit of diagnosis," queer disabled dancer and choreographer Alice Sheppard writes in her manifesto.[11] Surviving in and through a "fugitive relationship to rationality,"[12] as disabled filmmaker Tourmaline describes neurodivergence, psychiatric disability can be a "process, aesthetic, culture, politic, and identity" in turns and at once.[13] Not unfit, it *unfits* socially constructed lines between myth and reality, magic and science, history and fantasy to create spaces for disabled self-definition.

These are spaces capable of holding disabled body-minds, yes, but also of holding disability as "an aesthetic, a series of intersecting cultures, and a creative force."[14] In her evening-length duet *Descent*, Sheppard creates radically accessible space by choreographing on an "architectural ramp installation with hills, curves and peaks" that provides literal support for "obliterating assumptions of what dance, beauty, and disability can be."[15] Visualizing radical accessibility for neurodivergence, though—given how its invisibility, in Tourmaline's words, plays into the ways "ableism figures psychiatric disability as not 'real' disability"—involves even more figurative turns.[16] For Tourmaline and Kelsey Lu, the head—as in *get your head examined, sick in the head, head case, headshrinker*—first needs to be *unfit* from pathologizing metaphors, then reimagined in its own crazy Black femme fullness. In their performances, music videos, and photo shoots, Lu works with hair artist Nena Soul Fly to create intricate, gravity-defying sculptural hairstyles that concretize the twists and turns, weight, and resilience of living with depression. Training her viewers' eyes on something "higher" than the physical head, Tourmaline covers Black trans protagonists' heads in brilliantly colored scarves, crowns, and hoods that visualize psychiatric disability as a Black femme aesthetic. Even as some dump-Trumpers challenged "Forty-Five" with red MAGA-parody hats shouting MAKE AMERICA SANE AGAIN, Lu, Tourmaline, and other Black femmes resisted ableist antics in *pynk* headgear—with soft, femme-inist, Afrocentric, neurodivergent-loving crowns instead of strident, scarlet trucker hats. *Yes*, these Black femmes' art challenges us to go ahead and examine our heads: see how "disability, impairment, and psychiatric illness," as Tourmaline reflects, can be "a form of surplus" rather than lack—how "not having it all together can be its own form of beauty and power."[17] "Black femme, fluid, and boundless bodies embarrassed by their magic," as neurodivergent artist Bria Royal calls her disabled sistren, are the future that "very stable geniuses" will never be ready for.[18]

Kelsey Lu

Braids, Twists, and the Shapes of Black Femme Depression

(For Ann, with all the public feelings,
femme vulnerabilities, and cat companionship)

"Dear friends: I wish I were in a circle with all of you, if only to have a visible reminder of the wide-ranging networks that I have at UT," my fire-red-haired, collaborative-minded, unapologetically vulnerable femme mentor Ann Cvetkovich emailed queer and feminist colleagues the week after 11/9. "I would love to create some kind of public feelings gathering, as some of us did in the wake of 9/11."[1] Ann began public feelings gatherings at the University of Texas and nationally to bring colleagues together for something traditional academics might dismiss as soft, subjective, and girly: sharing feelings about current events, bearing witness to one another's "'political depression,' the sense that customary forms of political response, including direct action and critical analysis, are no longer working either to change the world or make us feel better," with the intent "to depathologize negative feelings so that they can be seen as a possible resource for political action rather than as its antithesis."[2] On December 1, 2016, I attended the second of two post-election public feelings groups in a newly constructed building named for a Texas oil tycoon. Never had I seen the half dozen colleagues there— including several femmes—so baldly honest as that morning, stream-of-consciously narrating anxiety, fatigue, anger, obsessive thoughts, and family conflict while Ann timed their two minutes. I felt guilty and defiant that I wasn't, like others, ruminating in sadness—that I was still stunned, punchy, in denial.

She never said so, but I imagine Ann called these gatherings partly out of worry for junior queer of color colleagues who were, she acknowledged, mired in "already difficult atmospheres of campus carry, persistent racism, and sexual violence" at the University of Texas.[3] And she was right to worry: because paramount to mobilizing "negative emotions . . . as a possible resource for political action" is to never underestimate the danger of depression, the leading disability in 2016—also the year suicide became the second-leading cause of death among Americans ages ten to thirty-four. "Sometimes, I think of the past three years as 'the femme suicide years,'" Sri Lankan disabled femme Leah Lakshmi Piepzna-Samarasinha observes, remembering four femmes who committed suicide within months of each other. "[It] seemed to be a year where the ancestors were being called home rapidly, maybe to get the fuck out when they still could to avoid the Trump hell that was coming, or maybe to help guide us. Maybe both."[4] Before reading Piepzna-Samarasinha's account, I'd known queer AFAB folks' rates of depression were twice those of straight cis women. I learned from Vickie Mays, Susan Cochran, and Michele Roeder that Black queer women's rates of depression not only "greatly exceeded population norms for African American women" but also exceeded those of queer white AFAB and Black AMAB folk.[5] But Care Work was the first text I saw address "the specific factors for femmes . . . when femmes are dealing with suicide or in mental health crisis." The ways so many "femmes do so much emotional labor and care-taking in community and are the ones that show up for everybody," then are publicly lauded for the animal prints and winged eyeliner we show up in; the ways this "femme worship can kill you if you are not also loved in your mess."[6] Where, Piepzna-Samarasinha asks, is the "hymn to femmes who are fucked up and failing, not available, driving everyone nuts, including ourselves," the testimony we're "loved by our communities when we're unable to accomplish the high femme aesthetics that are all many people know how to name as femme?"[7]

By the time Trump declared a "new chapter of American greatness" in his first State of the Union address, reality had set in enough for me to worry about my own wellness. Depression—clinical, subclinical, major, low-grade, situational, persistent—runs in my family, and I did everything I could to outpace it in Trump's first year in office: I wrote a book from start to finish, began teaching yoga and leading yoga workshops, applied for jobs above the Mason-Dixon Line. I felt like I was running on fire—burning nonstop without knowing where my fuel was coming from or how long it would last. That fire fueled me through the publication of two books and a visiting professorship at Harvard in 2018, carried me through job interviews until Matt and I accepted positions at the University of California, Santa Barbara. On July 30, 2019, I returned to California—a state I'd never stopped calling home—and crashed on its impossibly beautiful coast. Finally slowing down, I felt depression catching up. Ann (who also left the University of Texas that year for her native Canada) tells us that sometimes the work of a politics of depression is "to let depression linger, to explore the feeling of remaining or resting in sadness without insisting that it be transformed or reconceived," and to know "there are no magic bullet solutions, whether medical or political, just the slow steady work of resilient survival."[8] Or, as Geoffrey Jacques puts it in a poem about the Trump presidency, waking up mornings with the feeling "I can't breathe / I can't move," then repeating the simple acts "breathe, move, breathe, move."[9] I dragged out my reserve of antidepressive tools: literally ran again with our dog, Zora, practiced yoga first thing in the morning and last thing at night, collected supplements and essential oils, curated playlists.

While packing for California I compiled "Due West," a playlist whose eponymous first track was by up-and-coming, Los Angeles–based Black queer musician Kelsey Lu. Meditating on depression once I got there, I created "Shades of Blue," anchored in another Lu song the artist describes as "written during a time of deep depression, and later . . . realized as a conversation with it."[10] Lu—who prefers their androgynous second name and they/them pronouns—also felt political depression mount during Trump's presidency, culminating in "wariness" at responses to police violence in summer 2020: "There's this arising happening, but also a scrambling," they observed, urging listeners to be "suspicious" of the "hurry up and do something" approach to centuries' old maladies of "white, cis, male hetero-patriarchy."[11] Lu is also open about their recurrent psychological depression, which started as a heavily restricted teen, continued at art school, and reemerged while living in New York. They admit music is "something that has at times healed me; in moments of deep depression, and despair and dark thoughts, it's been able to be a catalyst of hope."[12] Trained as a classical cellist but drawn to alternative music scenes in Charlotte and LA, Lu elaborated their musical conversation with depression into a style they call *Luthereal*. "Luthereal stems from the word Ethereal ... which means, extremely delicate and light in a way that seems to be not of this world," they tell *Teen Vogue*'s Jessica Andrews. "My music is delicate and I, at times, can be delicate as well, but I would not say it is light."[13]

Their sartorial "style is just as eclectic" as their music, Andrews observes. "It's not uncommon to find the Charlotte, North Carolina native in a floral tunic paired with an oversize 'church hat' one day, and a red Gucci suit replete with a pussybow blouse the next—each look punctuated by colorful makeup [they do themself]."[14] And each look is topped by creative natural hairstyles their collaborator Tanya Melendez dubs "Crowns for Southern Queens and the Elevation of Ori."[15] The reference to the Yoruba concept *ori*—literally *head* but also indicating higher consciousness—nods to Lu's ancestral roots in Nigeria, where, according to art critic Babatunde Lawal, "Yoruba women regard hairdressing as a mark of honor to the inner head."[16] On the flip side, Ayana Bird and Lori Tharps note in their classic *Hair Story*, "In Nigeria, if a woman left her hair undone, it was a signal that something was wrong. The woman was either bereaved, depressed, or 'habitually dirty.'"[17] As I watched Lu's videos and scrolled their Instagram, I found myself focusing on their ever-changing hair as much as—honestly, more than—their understated, dreamlike lyrics, fascinated by how their "funky, sexy, playful, punk and out of this world" coiffures (to borrow the description of their stylist, Oluwabukola Becky Akinyode) queered Nigerian traditions and understandings of hair art.[18] Instead of "undone" hair, elaborate hairstyles—bloodred bangs and teal brows, silver-laced box braids twisted like octopus tentacles, asymmetrical space buns—externalize an "inner head" that tends to be "depressed or 'habitually dirty,'" as in *dirty queer*: visualizing how the color changes, dramatic twists, and half-controlled messiness of living as a depressed Black queer can become its own art form. Watching their videos while I sat with Zora after runs, I got something from Lu's expressive braids, twists, and naturals neither Ann nor Leah could give me: a vision of what's particularly *Black* about how we, Black femmes, move through depression.

This chapter isn't about the much-discussed tensions between natural and protective styles "versus" weaves and perms (though these tensions make appearances). Neither is it about the woman-and-femme-centered, communal, often therapeutic, and frequently expensive space of the Black hair salon—a subject many have addressed beautifully and evocatively. While I initially thought this chapter would take me into the beauty shop often, I realized (after months of reading and watching) how persistently Black femmes weave their depressive hair stories into larger pictures of isolation and alienation; how persistently hairstyles are evoked as something Black femmes *feel alone while wearing*, no matter how many people these styles took to create. So I came to explore how Lu's elaborate, sculptural hairstyles—as well as the radically simple hairstyles of other Black femmes—are engineered to express depressive *feelings* that are complex, nuanced, and culturally specific. Circling through Lu's music, hair stories from other Black femmes, and the edges of my own depression, I write this chapter as the praise song Piepzna-Samarasinha longs for: as "a hymn to femmes who are fucked up and failing, not available, driving everyone nuts, including ourselves."

Feeling shades of blue, blue. Like Lu's song, this chapter of *The Color Pynk* circles through shades of the color William Gass lyricizes as the hue of "afflictions of the spirit—dumps, mopes, Mondays—all that's dismal— low-down gloomy music . . . the shaded slopes of clouds and mountains, and so the constantly increasing absentness of Heaven (*ins Blaue hinein*, the Germans say), consequently the color of everything that's empty: blue bottles, bank accounts, and compliments, for instance, or, when the sky's turned turtle, the blue-green bleat of ocean."[19] The color blue, Lu's work visualizes, is not the "opposite" of pink. Their shades of blue are also shades of pynk: liminal, muddied, and fluid, their ruminating, dissociating, self-liberating nonbinary femme characters color themselves in ways that circumvent gender binaries as well as binaries between disability (depressive "blues") and "wellness" (being "in the pink"). In recognition, I write this praise song as a *pynk blues*: an exploration of how, as Andi Schwarz writes of her visual art series *Low Femme*, "depression and anxiety need not necessarily be fixed or avoided or be considered unproductive, but should rather be considered alternative routes that undercut standards of success and happiness we never agreed to" and so "challenge femme identity to open up, to see if new understandings of femme can be forged" through the unexpected twists and turns of blue femmes' depressive hair, moods, and imaginations.[20]

WITH "STRAIGHT" HAIR

"Had the blues all day. Wrote letters until one thirty and then told my fortune (with cards), which made me bluer than ever," Alice Dunbar-Nelson brooded May 18, 1931, then picked up in her next journal entry: "Made engagement to have my hair waved at a beauty parlor. . . . Didn't know whether I'd 'get by' [not be challenged because of her race], but evidently did. Nice wave. Nice place. Nice girls. Beauty problem solved."[21] When the prominent Harlem Renaissance writer, activist, and educator started journaling at age forty-six, she recorded days knotted in family obligations, speaking engagements, financial worries, household chores, boredom, perimenopausal discomfort, and recurrent depression. Gloria Hull notes in her introduction to Dunbar-Nelson's diaries, "Too much of the time, Dunbar-Nelson's mental health was . . . as she put it, 'profoundly in the D's—discouraged, depressed, disheartened, disgusted.'"[22] Her persistent self-doubt was intensified by living in the shadow of her famous writer husbands Paul Laurence Dunbar and Robert Nelson, despite her own accomplishments—her 1895 *Violets and Other Tales* was the first short story collection published by an African American woman—and her decades of relationships with women. The happiest days her diary records are those spent visiting lover Fay Jackson Robinson in California in 1930. As she left by train she daydreamed from San Francisco to Omaha "of the eight perfect days—of the romance, the beauty, the loveliness—and register anew a vow to return to California to end my days. . . . Too much emotional upheaval those two days on the train—thinking of California, and Fay.

Consequent depression."[23] Dunbar-Nelson nursed depressive episodes with small, embodied daily acts of self-care: sunbathing, stargazing, flower gathering, card games, new hats, haircuts.

This light-skinned Louisiana Creole clubwoman lived a complicated relationship to Black hairstyling. After one speaking engagement she derided women there as "brown huzzies, with Walkerized hair elaborately coiffed,"[24] and she—hair loosely curled enough not to need Madam C. J. Walker's chemical straightener—patronized white salons to press her natural curl into waves. But far from flaunting "good hair," Dunbar-Nelson's public writing describes struggles to accept her curls. Her essay "Brass Ankles Speaks" evokes "miserable" memories of a color-conscious New Orleans childhood: "Bitter recollections of hair ribbons jerked off and trampled in the mud. Painful memories of curls yanked back into the ink bottle of the desk behind me. . . . How I hated those curls!" Even as an adult, Dunbar-Nelson continued, she was forced into light-skinned company because darker sistren rejected her as a "light nigger, with straight hair." "We were literally thrown upon each other, whether we liked or not," she claimed. "But when we began going about together and spending our time in each other's society, a howl went up. We were organizing a 'blue vein' society. We were mistresses of white men. We were Lesbians."[25] Dunbar-Nelson was part of "an active Black lesbian network" of clubwomen who "were prominent and professional, and most had husbands and children," Hull notes, but they contrived to "carry on these relationships in what most surely must have been an extremely repressive context."[26] Reading Dunbar-Nelson's self-distancing from both elaborately coiffed huzzies and light-skinned lesbians, I wonder: Would her depression have run as deep if she'd been able to love the parts of herself she saw reflected in these women? If she weren't known as much for her "regard for reputation, manners, and the proprieties" as for her imposing appearance as a "tall, attractive, auburn-haired woman"?[27] If she'd been literally and figuratively able to let her hair down, to love the deep, uneven waves just as they grew out of her head?

But I wonder too: Why do I want to attribute this Black femme's recurrent depression to the ways she lived Black queerness differently than I choose to? How have I internalized psych ableism even as I criticize Dunbar-Nelson (not unfairly, I still think) for her internalized racism and homophobia? Do I really think "good politics" heals depression, and if so, what part of this thought is born of my own shame?

SHADES OF PROTECTION

On July 24, 2014, twenty-one-year-old Lu shared their whimsical, layered, blue-striped personal style on the "What's Underneath Project," "a series of docu-style video portraits where people of all ages, races, body types, genders, and sexualities remove layers of clothing while sharing stories related to style, self-image, and identity" (in the words of mother-daughter creators Elisa Goodkind and Lily Mandelbaum).[28] Perched on a stool against a brick wall, Lu begins their video interview in a feather-topped fedora, cropped button-down shirt, chunky necklaces, fringed wrap, striped shorts, and thigh-high gartered socks. Their hat is the first piece of clothing they remove, spilling a halo of tightly curled hair indented from the ears up. Unruly, minimally styled curls exposed, Lu shares teary memories of growing up Jehovah's Witness as they shed accessories: of teen years when their clothing was strictly monitored, church and cello lessons were their only out-of-house activities, and the decision to attend the University of North Carolina School of the Arts earned them a beating and expulsion from their family home. But they brighten when they shed their blue robe and answer a question about their favorite body part. "My hair," they offer thoughtfully, elaborating, "I feel a lot of strength in my hair. I grew up trying to make it straight. I begged my mom to give me a perm because I wanted to fit in with everyone else. . . . Kids would be chanting at me, 'Your hair is frizzy and nappy.' And now! I wish I would have been like, 'Fuck you!'"[29]

Embracing sometimes-unkempt, sometimes elaborately styled hair, eclectic fashion, and an unconventional fusion of classical cello and neo soul, Lu continually issues *fuck yous* to childhood constrictions and insecurities. The cellist left their home state in 2012 to follow a lover to Brooklyn, where they recorded their first EP, *Church*, in 2016. But when the relationship became increasingly abusive, Lu extricated themself by squatting in a leather factory in Hoboken. "Shades of Blue" ("SOB") was composed in the fertile depression of that squat. "I was really depressed at the time, and my life had flip-flopped in many ways—musically, financially, romantically and, really, soulfully. Yet, I was writing a lot more than I had been and this song is a manifestation of that point in my life," they explain. "For me, it was a glimpse of hopefulness and peace from within that depression, and I can only hope it will bring a similar moment of peace to the listener."[30] Reviews appreciated Lu's musical arrangements, stylistic range, use of landscape, and vulnerability. *Refinery29*'s Kathryn Lindsay eye-catchingly titled her review "Kelsey Lu's 'Shades of Blue' Music Video Might Be the Next 'Lemonade'" and justified, "I would never belittle Beyoncé's *Lemonade* visual album by tossing out comparisons willy-nilly, which is why I hope you know I mean it when I say that artist Kelsey Lu has made [their] own version of that masterpiece." Lindsay lauded the *Lemonade*-esque way the video "takes a freeform approach to storytelling, weaving in the song with intense visuals, pauses for ambient noise, and spoken word."[31]

Blue-lit and melancholy with panoramic beach shots, the similarities of "SOB" to *Lemonade*—particularly the latter's "Love Drought," with its beaches of Black women soulfully posed in ocean water and white dresses—may flow from these Black southern feminists' citation of a common visual foremother, Julie Dash's *Daughters of the Dust*. While Beyoncé's homage to *Daughters* is vivid, Lu's plays more ethereally. Dressed in a flowing white shirt, full-length white skirt, and royal-blue ribbon that ties their tight cornrows and trails their back, Lu opens the video descending a path to a marshy coast, where they doggedly shovel frozen mud into a pail. Their appearance evokes *Daughters*' narrator, the Unborn Child who runs and plays on a beach in a loose-fitting white dress and braids tied with a royal-blue ribbon.[32] The Unborn Child graces *Daughters* as a vision of hope for women who manifest Black-girl-magic futures despite violence, exploitation, and loss; but Lu's Femme Child, mired in mud that sucks them deeper as they try to dig themself out, haunts me. What happens when those of us who are supposed to be our ancestors' wildest dreams—children born into Black, women's, queer civil rights—find ourselves mired in depression as unmovable as Lu's mud? Stalled in this scene for four minutes, the song proper begins after Lu drops their pail and sinks to their knees. The marsh disappears, replaced by shots of Lu struggling through holistic remedies for depression: tai chi, cold-water swimming, running, spending time in nature. Their physical motion is slow and constant, their lyrics sparse and repetitive, their path from sadness to "glimpses of hope-fulness and peace" twisting, lonely, lovely, unfinished. "SOB" is as "patient with the moods and temporalities of depression, not moving too quickly to recuperate them or put them to good use," as Ann wishes, holding space to "let depression linger, to explore the feeling of remaining or resting in sadness without insisting that it be transformed."[33]

Linked to traditional Chinese medicine, 1960s US white-male-centered fitness culture, and a Eurocentric turn-of-the-millennium ecotherapy movement, Lu's therapeutic activities are Black-femme-inized by their protective hairstyles. A fishtail braid sways as they do tai chi, goddess braids wrap their crown as they run, box braids flip past their waist as they emerge from the water. Protective styles—named because they tuck in ends to shield the shaft's oldest, most fragile part—traditionally "include braids, twists, cornrows," lists natural hair blogger Yolanda Renee, and "recently naturalistas have also been rocking natural hair inspired protected styles such as poetic justice braids, box braids, marley twists, faux locs."[34] Lu's "SOB" protective styles were created by Tanya Melen-dez, "who is guided herself by the ancestors" and whose intricate braids Lu describes as "an ode to my ancestry and heritage. I am part African, specifically Nigerian, and if you look at original hair styles of different tribes throughout, you will see adornments and power within all of it."[35] Like martial arts, running, or hiking, Melendez's protective styles require sustained physical effort. Some of the video's (at least) eight styles took hours, others days to complete: time for hair to be washed, conditioned, detangled again and again, tufts parted and pulled in opposing directions, strands braided, rebraided, and sewn together, edges done and braids wrapped in cotton, all while braider and braided soothe aching neck, scalp, shoulders, fingers, backs. Committing to make art out of textured hair—particularly for femmes who (like Lu) grew up curl shamed—also requires sustained work and self-study. Poet TJ Bryan reflects on hair talk with Black sister-femmes: "We've talked that hair shit to DEATH! Wanting to love it, color it, cut it, fry it, locks it, grow it, hide it, politicize it, ignore it, or just plain pull it out from the roots in big, kinky handfullz! Notions of blackness and womanly beauty converge on top of my head."[36]

Laboriously, lovingly, collaboratively elaborated between stylist and client, protective styles become a concrete expression of how the wearer moves through the world. "This hair marks me as . . . not just black, queer, female," Bryan says of her locs, but as "eternal, twisting, undulating, dread, dark, dangerous, and true";[37] "My hair styles definitely hold power," Lu professes.[38] One of the many powers Black hairstyles can hold: a Black femme who's learned to be patient, tender with themselves through their hair's twists and turns—to work with, instead of against, the kinks that make their hair both fragile and versatile—has learned styles of self-care that can serve them as profoundly through their depression as other "natural" therapeutic activities. Their hair is a source of the kind of creativity Ann sees intertwined with depression. "Defined in relation to notions of blockage or impasse" that mark depression, she explains, "creativity can be thought of as a form of movement, movement that maneuvers the mind inside or around an impasse, even if that movement sometimes seems backward or like a form of retreat."[39] In her experience, depressive creativity is a psychological movement that often begins with bodily movement—with "efforts to keep it moving, whether through exercise, such as yoga or swimming, or through ordinary daily activities ranging from washing the dishes to sitting at a desk"—and "is embedded in everyday life, not something that belongs only to artists or to transcendent forms of experience."[40] What if we think about moving through depression as one psychological equivalent of wearing a protective hairstyle: a sustained physical and emotional commitment to protecting our fragile ends, a culturally specific art form we embody while moving through our daily lives?

The first protective style Lu wears after surrendering to the frozen mud is a four-strand, upward-climbing sculpture of wrapped braids tied in thick cotton ropes. Called *irun kiko,* sculptural styles like these were developed by Yoruba artists in the 1960s to shape hair "using a black thread to tie strands of hair into filaments that are then gathered to form intricate designs . . . high rising coils and arches that evoke the social mood and landscapes of the period" and were named for Nigerian bridges, skyscrapers, stadiums, and theaters.[41] While these styles evoked built environments, Lu's *irun kiko* mirror organic forms—and as I watch "SOB" I name them accordingly. *Bloomless branches* I call this style, which Lu wears with a high-collared, floor-length dress of ombré blues. In one wide shot Lu kneels in a field of bare wintry bushes and casts their face earthward so their four asymmetrical plaits are on level with the brown branches whose color, shape, and angles they blend with. Downcast and literally covered in shades of blue, Lu is alone but not disconnected: they're part of a natural world, still, caught in cycles of retreat like those that strip winter branches. The first verse is rhythmed by Lu sinking their protectively styled head to the ground over and over, at once slumping into depression and planting themself for growth. But the second witnesses them unfurling in different directions—pushing forward into a run, rocking side to side by the water, floating upward in a grove of pine trees. Yes, upward: swathed in a free-flowing blue dress, Lu hovers "suspended in the air, [their] heart chakra pointing toward the sky, head back, arms dangling toward the earth," then comes to rest facing outward on a tall pine-tree branch.[42] *Carolina pine,* I call their protective style here, six plaits sewn into a crown that flares broadly at the top like a longleaf pine cone. "I'm letting myself just fall and float and be," Lu explains their styling in the scene. "But then there was another layer underneath that you can't really see, but that is supporting me and the harness that was around my body, so it was like, *Okay, I need something that's enveloping me to protect me, but also something around that that's loose and allowing me to be free.*"[43]

The thread wrapping their *irun kiko* is a physical something that envelops and allows movement, providing (in the words of Yoruba stylist Busayo Olupona) "an infrastructure that can be manipulated into any shape." Arresting hair's breakage and lengthening its curl, *irun kiko* also promotes rapid growth. Olupona explains, "The hair style was a double edged sword—on the one hand it was ridiculously painful, but this style makes your hair grow like weeds."[44] Depression, some biologists suggest, performs a similar psychic function. Painful as it is, the condition forces humans enmeshed in complex social problems to slow down, analyze, and rest to prepare for necessary change and growth. "Depression is nature's way of telling you that you've got complex social problems that the mind is intent on solving," Paul Andrews and Anderson Thomson Jr. opine.[45] Many African diaspora healers agree. Yoruba diviner Day Dream Alston reflects that depression "is actually a brilliant time because . . . it's forcing you to meditate. . . . Depression is telling you something is off, something is not right, you're not in the right job, you're not in the right relationship, you're living in the wrong place, living with the wrong people, you're doing the wrong things. It's all just a reminder, a nudge to you to get it together . . . a push in the right direction."[46] And for Lu in "SOB," this means a push in the direction of a pine tree: an evergreen whose pollen herbalists promote as a natural antidepressant and whose needles conjurers claim help restore mental wellness.

While it doesn't magically lift them out of depression, Lu's pine interlude does mark a transitional moment in "SOB." "I'm not over you, not over you / But I'm over feeling shades of blue," they sing twice in the first chorus, vocalizing the second "blue" over several rising, melancholy beats. The second chorus begins and ends with Lu singing these lines suspended from the tree, crooning several beats a cappella and changing the lines' endings. "I'm not over you, no . . ." it begins, and it ends with Lu replacing the final "blue" with a skyward turn of their head and wide-open spread of their arms. Instrumentation rushes in to fill the evaporated "blue," led by Lu's swelling cello. Accompanying shots include the artist dancing in an orange, yellow, and red paper jumpsuit crowned by their final *irun kiko*, one I call *dancing arms*: two plaits kiss in the center of their head, mirroring the wavelike motion of their arms and the branches behind them. Shades of blue haven't permanently lifted; the color returns in the next shots' lighting and costumes, leaving the video open-ended and refusing to "either perform depression or perform overcoming depression," as #DepressedWhileBlack creator Imade Nibokun puts it.[47] Depressive self-care and self-love in "SOB" is a process, not a product: one that, like protective styling, will be repeated again and again.

Repetition of lines and melisma—drawing out a single syllable over several notes—are formal elements "SOB" shares with African American hymns and spirituals. They're also elements that concretize how depression can feel: the over-and-over-and-over-again of taking care of yourself through shades of blue; the on-and-on-and-on of a condition that runs on without running its course. "SOB" sings the experience of "femmes who are fucked up and failing, not available, driving everyone nuts, including ourselves" in ways that *sound like* a hymn, and also visualize, lyricize, and are tender with ways depression moans, stutters, and trembles like a hymn. "No reference is linear; none is supposed to be," Lynette Nylander describes Lu's songwriting in a spring 2020 cover story for *AnOther*. "Deeply spiritual, emotive, powerful and disarming. To listen to Lu's music is to go along with an artist in the very midst of their journey—[they are] inviting you along for the ride."[48]

AND OUR HAIR CARE TOO

In her headshot on the sidebar of *Wear Your Voice* magazine, managing editor Sherronda J. Brown faces the camera with a severely raised right eyebrow, perfectly traced black lipstick, and a sleek braided bob magnified into a three-pane, mirror-effect image. Alongside Black asexuality, antiracist body positivity, racist BDSM practices, child-free-by-choice feminism, Black girls' sexual abuse, queer POC mental health, and zombies, Brown's posts regularly engage the politics of Black womxn's and femmes' hair care—in ways that build on and push against natural-hair-positive blogs. Her hairstyling choices, she owns, are protective in more ways than one: low-manipulation styles like hers can represent radical self-care for Black womxn living with depression, anxiety, and other mental illness. "With mental illnesses like depression, it's difficult to motivate yourself to do basic tasks or take care of yourself, and that includes hair care," she lays out in a post

titled "Nothing about Being Black Is Easy, Including Our Hair Care."
"I have experienced a lot of breakage and damage in the past because
I simply could not find the strength to tackle my hair. . . . The crying
fits. The panic attacks. Breaking combs and throwing hair brushes.
The sheer rage at having to dedicate so much time and energy and
money to our hair in order to look 'presentable,' 'professional,' and
'acceptable.'"[49] In radical Black political circles, natural hairstyles—
Afros, twist outs, Bantu knots, dreadlocs—are validated as badges of
self-love and racial pride. But does anyone care about the hours it takes
to wash, condition, detangle, dry, twist, untwist, and pick out these
natural styles, "about the amount of labor Black womxn especially
have to do to or what kind of daily barriers we have to traverse in order
to maintain our hair"?[50]

Expecting Black women and femmes to do the most with our
hair to prove our wokeness is sexist, yes, and ableist too. What would
it look like if the politics of Black women's hairstyles were evaluated
not by their Afrocentricity but by how much they empower womxn
and femmes as we move through days where depression, anxiety, and
fatigue trail us? "I know many people who have opted to simply shave
their heads because of the emotional stress of maintaining their hair,"
Brown tells us. "I know many who almost exclusively wear weaves and/
or wigs because it reduces that stress and allows them to dedicate their
time to other things in their life"—work, family, socializing, exercise,
spiritual practice—that support their wellness.[51] And the wokeness of
that choice deserves recognition too.

MESSY LOVE

After leaving Hoboken, Lu spent two years crossing between New York,
London, and Hollywood before settling in Los Angeles, where, they tell the
Los Angeles Times, their "'creative health' spiked" after "getting tuned into
the black arts community and finding [their] tribe."[52] On November 9,

2018, they released "Due West," a single and video NPR hailed as "an ethe-real chronicle of [their] move to LA"[53] and the press release described as "a continuation of the evolution of self. A continuous questioning of the romanticism of 'home.'"[54] "California, California, California," Lu hypnot-ically evokes their new home—but, as Marc Hogan's review intuits, "in the goosebump-inducing turns of Lu's voice lies a sense that, even as [they have] come all this way, [they] can't escape [themself]."[55] Lu's next short film literalizes the inability to escape themself: a synth-driven remake of 10cc's 1975 chart-topper "I'm Not in Love" that places two versions of the singer side by side in a picture window, one playing the piano while the other presses a bloody hand to the glass. Lu codirected the grainy, eerie video with sibling Black arts "tribe" member Alima Lee, a Los Angeles–based femme filmmaker, DJ, and cofounder of Akashic Records. Lee first collaborated with Lu on *La Fleur Noir* (2017), a documentary on Black women in professional dance directed by Lee and scored by Lu. Their com-mon interest in Black femme-ininity, depression, and creativity reaches back further, though: while Lu wrote "Shades of Blue" Lee was filming "Garden," a short that offers an "unfiltered window on the daily life of a black woman, as she goes along with her daily rituals in order to overcome anxiety & depression."[56] Together the alternative-Black-arts femmes take a soft-rock song one critic describes as a "big, billowing, pink cloud of sound"[57] and "wrap the original in lace, gauze, and cobwebs . . . amping out the remoteness and detachment" in unnerving, queer ways.[58]

Melendez returns as Lu's hair artist, crafting thick, past-the-ankle, single braids—lengthened with extensions that self-consciously jut out at bends—and metonymizing the heavy, frayed, twisting Black femme-ininity Lu explores here. "Kelsey Lu's Floor-Sweeping Braid Steals the Spotlight in [Their] New 'I'm Not in Love' Video" Lauren Valenti titles her *Vogue* review, elaborating, "You can't—nor will you want to—look away from the erotic-horror short, even at its most intentionally gruesome mo-ments. And that is due in no small part to Lu's mesmerizing serpentine braid, woven by hairstylist Tanya Melendez in a number of ornate itera-tions, inspiring awe and curiosity throughout the video."[59] We first see Lu's braid with their back turned to the camera and the plait looped over their shoulder, masking its length and curving to mirror the f-holes tattooed on their back. The braid's next appearance—a wide shot of Lu in a sheer robe running so hard up a hill their shoes fly off and their plait swings around their ankles—reveals the entirety of the hairstyle Valenti calls the video's "breakout star."[60] When Lu appears in the white-curtained window beside their white pajama-ed twin, their braids' pink and blue ribbons punctuate the split-screen shot. They swing heavily as first the blue twin, then the pink dance in slow motion at the window during the second and third verses. But the braid has its own choreography in the bridge, when Lu stands on their bed naked and motionless except for the plait they lasso overhead, then trust-falls back as their cascading hair breaks their fall. Dark, grainy shots of bloody limbs wrapped in plastic follow: "A bloodied, motionless body is seen being dragged across the floor, and although the body is never fully seen," photographer Sarah Sunday notices, "the brown legs match Lu's own."[61] The trail leads to the video's final shot: Lu's bluntly hacked-off braid snaking across a bloody bathroom floor, their unsmiling face framed by a cloud of newly freed curls.

What's happened in this floor-to-ceiling-windowed house of twin Lus? Unlike press releases for "SOB" and "Due West," Lu's introduction to "I'm Not in Love" never clarifies the video's content. "This is dedicated to the ones who have ever felt misunderstood in the name of Love, in the name of Self," they offer cryptically. Who "want to Kill the Confusion all while finding beauty in the abstract of growth and humor that surrounds the horrors both within and around us."[62] While Lu never names these horrors within, "I'm Not in Love" looks like Lu's and Lee's earlier visions of depression. Reprising the shots of downcast Lu in "SOB" through a plate window, "I'm Not in Love" experiments with the superimposed images, dissolves, and grainy shots that also visualize depression's blurry feeling in Lee's "Garden." But shooting through glass and underexposing shots are also trademarks of horror cinematography—visual cues that anticipate the murderous-suicidal shots of Lu-like legs dragged through blood. Why has the drama of "SOB" and "Garden" morphed into horror? On the one hand, horror dramatizes the depressive feeling that *something bad* could overtake us at any time: a feeling that seeps into the "frequent thoughts of doing harm to someone else" and "frequent suicidal thoughts" that Mays, Cochran, and Roeder relate to depressive distress in Black queer women.[63]

On the other, film scholar Shelley Stamp points out that "horror, more than any other film genre, deals openly with questions of gender, sexuality, and the body," bringing "to the fore issues that are otherwise unspoken in patriarchal culture."[64] And as part of its window on depression, "I'm Not in Love"—a cover that deliberately keeps the original's masculine markers, such as the whispered hook "big boys don't cry"—insinuates the horrors of binary gender for nonbinary Black femmes. A 2018 study linked high rates of depression (62 percent) in transmasculine AFAB teens to distress caused by gender norms;[65] but Lu's video visualizes how nonbinary femmes' dis-ease with normative femininity morphs into its own depressive distress.

The snakelike, lace-choked braid circles the video as a symbol of the tightly wound heterofemininity that stalks the Lu twins. It performs its own incarnation of *hair horror*, an early twenty-first-century Japanese subgenre featuring *yukei*, glossed by Colette Balmain as "[female] vengeful ghosts" whose "long and luxuriant dark hair, which partially or fully obscures the ghost's features" embodies "male fears around female empowerment, sexuality, and the breakdown of the family unit."[66] Working with and against this trope, Lu's hyper-restrained, tightly pulled coiffure suggests what's horrific to *Black femmes* about conventional scripts of femininity—starting with the anti-Blackness of a feminine ideal epitomized by long, straight, "spastically flicked hair." "For sistas in search of ideal Femme(ininity), it's all about THA HAIR," Bryan lays out. "What you do with it. If you've got it. Or can scrape together the green to buy someone else's."[67] Lu has clearly done just that for this video. Jutting out again and again down the length of the braid, their extensions are noticeably straighter than their natural hair; deliberately not blended in, their impossible length and straightness frays Lu's look, showing them unravel in proximity to white (hair) ideals. The grotesque effects of standards of femininity that, as my colleague Ingrid Banks puts it, imagine "long, flowing hair as representative of femininity" and close-cropped natural hair as "unfeminine, unattractive, masculine, [butch] lesbian" are visualized in a shot of white-robed Lu dancing next to a harp wearing a silky, wavy, brown wig.[68] Why would a harp need a straight-haired wig that in no way enhances the beauty it's capable of? Well, why would a Black femme?

Alternatively bound in tentacle-like baby-blue and pastel-pink ribbon, Lu's braids also visualize how suffocating being tethered to binary gender can feel. Nonbinary Black femme Hunter Shackelford describes the eeriness of embodying a gender that remains invisible to queer and straight acquaintances alike: "Nonbinary femme DFAB black bodies are often read as not real and erased. The mindfuck of proving to the world you're not a girl and proving to yourself that your nonbinary gender is valid and not a performance is exhausting. It's living at war with . . . yourself, your body and the world every day."[69] Lu knows this burden of proof well. Describing themself as gender "open," they're continually called on to communicate why their creatively feminine wardrobe—which, *Vogue* opines, "can usually best be described as frothy: [they] can pull off mounds of Molly Goddard tulle or a baroque No Sesso gown with a sense of casual ease"[70]—doesn't mean their gender is uncomplicated. Speaking with *Pitchfork*'s Alex Frank, Lu reroutes a conversation about whether they consider themself cis by mentioning "ghost dick dreams": "very vivid dreams where I've had a penis. Once, I had a dream where I had sex with a girl and was fucking her from behind. I remember it all like it was yesterday. I had really long hair. . . . I was looking at her looking out the window and then I just leaned my head back and . . . my spirit went out of my body and I saw myself."[71] "I'm Not in Love" materializes Lu as simultaneously their long-haired dream self and their window-gazing dream lover, both struggling to circumvent gender binaries. Cutting away from the girlish, gauze-and-lace-draped twins of the first verses, the hook alternates between Lu standing motionless in a mechanic's jumpsuit and work boots and doing bicep curls and push-ups topless, shadows flickering on the wall behind them. The echoing hook—"big boys don't cry"—intimates that now-boyish, still-braided Lu wants to do just that, cry: that muscling from feminine- to masculine-of-center has induced its own depressive distress.

The visual trajectory of the "I'm Not In Love" video's multiple Lus resonates with a story nonbinary femme Latonya Pennington tells the Black Youth Project, about "how femmephobia and the gender binary caused me to hate myself." Uncomfortable with the pink-puffy-dress femininity her parents wished on her, Pennington cut her hair and moved through high school as "a thick-bodied, t-shirt wearing, awkward Black girl who also happened to be suffering from depression." But coming out—and discovering the gender-complex stylings of Black queer artists like Janelle Monáe and Angel Haze—opened windows to gender possibilities beyond heteronormative femininity and its tomboyish "opposite." "By exposing myself to a fuller array of gender and self-expression, I was able to redefine femininity on my own terms and confront my femmephobia," she reflects. "I felt part of me identifying with gender bending and gender queer Black girls and part of me identifying with feminine cisgender Black girls."[72] Lu's parallel decision to redefine femininity on their own Black, nonbinary terms is dramatized in the video's final image of their braid motionless on the bloody bathroom floor, its literal and figurative straightness giving way to the twists, bends, and corkscrews of their natural hair. A face-framing length shorter than the flowing cascades Banks identifies with heterofeminine ideals but longer than the close crop her informants associate with butchness, Lu's uneven, big-chopped locks end the video as unapologetically messy as they are unapologetically Black. And in doing so, "I'm Not in Love" answers Leah Lakshmi Piepzna-Samarasinha's call for spaces where depressed femmes "can be messy, in pain, hurting, imperfect, and . . . really know that our genders are still seen"; where "we rebuild how femme is seen, understood, cherished."[73]

Debuting as a single in January 2019, "I'm Not in Love" caught the attention of Jen Malone, music supervisor of the HBO drama *Euphoria*, who featured the song in season 1's penultimate episode, "The Trials and Tribulations of Trying to Pee While Depressed." "Trials and Tribulations" follows protagonist Rue and her transfemme love interest Jules as both struggle through depressive episodes—Rue locked in her room, Jules fleeing to a friend who promises to medicate her with drugs and clubbing. The friend also introduces her to Anna, a blue-lipsticked, nonbinary Black femme who does Jules's makeup while the two discuss their common fantasy of "obliterating" conventional femininity and moving "on to the next level and the next and the next" of queerness. "I'm Not in Love" seeps into the episode as the friends enter the club and a very high Jules—her hands embracing her new crush's wildly curly, rhinestone-clipped hair—moves into her first femme-femme sexual experience, laughing that Anna is "kind of a mess" as she caresses her face.[74] Here, as in its own video, "I'm

Not in Love" plays as the soundtrack for a view of depression that treats "crazy femme"—femme wrapped in messiness, (self) destruction, creativity, shadow chasing, boundary pushing—as a gender presentation as deserving of love, sexiness, pleasure, and tenderness as any other. "Oooh, you'll wait a long time for me," Lu sings as Jules relaxes into Anna's touch while fantasizing about Rue, spiraling toward orgasm under pink and blue lights. Messy, beautiful, and femme, living "to die another day and in the end be hopeful of whatever there is to come or not come at all, and ultimately make love while doing it."[75]

FREEDOM HAIR

Even though Clarkisha Kent's name tells you she's a superhero in disguise, her cultural commentary makes clear this Nigerian, Bi, Black, Fat critic isn't here to save you. In a series of *Entertainment Weekly* articles about *Euphoria*, Kent champions Jules's "trope-burning" femininity and clarifies that though Rue may look to her for salvation, Jules "is not here to save anyone but herself—and she shouldn't have to."[76] Kent knows all about expectations that nonnormative femininity should sparkle, inspire, and entertain to prove its worth. Growing up deflecting fatphobic, colorist judgments that still "trigger my depression," Kent deployed eye-catching hairstyles as her go-to shield. "Dealing with anti-Blackness that has been dealt to me via the cards of Eurocentric beauty standards, fat Black folx have to make negotiations and concessions about which part of us . . . is gonna take the brunt of a societal beat-down every day," she explains. "My negotiation specifically has to do with my hair. As in, to be clear, I have used the eclectic, versatile, and ever-changing state of my hair to absorb the heavier blows of fat-phobia." Growing up, Kent endured scalp-burning perms, touch-ups, and roll-outs to keep a length "considered 'feminine,'" until in college, "combinations of that and the potential money I would sink trying to uphold it drove me straight to 'the big chop.'" Unlike many naturalistas' liberating big-chop stories, Kent's new Afro didn't feel like freedom—or "have quite the same effect [as] my respectable hair." She found herself playing the role of the funny fat friend, "stared at in public while eating . . . or having my space violated because, by virtue of being fat, people assume that you are already taking up enough space." But when the sight of a pink-haired Black woman inspired her purchase of an electric-blue wig, her professor, crush, and friends suddenly gushed about "how 'good' I looked—with me taking silent notes that I had never received said compliments when my hair was natural. What's more is that once my hair had undergone this change, I didn't feel the need to do the same old disarming shticks I did to distract from being fat because there was no need. My hair was technically doing all the disarming for me."[77]

Kent's hair story is a messy one that's never literally or figuratively tied up in a bow. She doesn't overcome depression, doesn't magically rise above the fatphobia, colorism, and texturism that affect her moods and mental health. And she doesn't find the perfect hairstyle— but she does stop trying to please other folks with her hair. "Whether that plays out in purposely wearing my hair shorter and nappier in certain 'professional' spaces or bringing hair color into spaces that are all but devoid of such—all on this fat body of mine—is just another necessary list of things that I have added to my daily negotiations with society as a fat Black femme."[78] And she does continue to have hair goals, not so much in the form of a style as in an attitude—one embodied by Beyoncé's oldest daughter, Blue Ivy. Clapping back at criticism of Blue's natural hair, Kent admits she gets "mad emotional on the rare occasion that we are graced with Blue Ivy's presence and she so much as blinks," because her curls, baby hairs, and Afros offer an image of a Black girl "taught to love all aspects of herself (including her hair and face) without having to go through the wringer of hair breakage, perm burns, bad straightening jobs, bad roller jobs, and so much more." The "confident, effervescent, brilliant, and most importantly, carefree Blue Ivy" she projects onto images of Beyoncé's daughter is, Kent knows, a fiction.[79] But if it can be healing to create and disseminate myths of Black girls whose hair is magic—whose curls spread the message Janet Mock learned from Beyoncé's "ever-changing looks," that "ours was freedom hair . . . we had the freedom to do with it what we wanted"—why wouldn't we do more of it?[80]

With a gesture of self-love and vulnerability, my own "true story," a hymn to Black femme depressive messiness lived: that's how I *wanted* to end this chapter. But after starting and stopping, writing and erasing, looping and stalling, all I've come up with is one truncated verse—a hair story that's not mine, even, but my daughter's. When we landed in Santa Barbara, Nia arrived with back-grazing Senegalese box braids she'd gotten in Boston. Three days later, she sat on the floor of our empty house as I took those braids out and created pillows of discarded extensions at her feet. Released into ocean water and desert air, her hair refused to respond to products we'd lugged cross-country and curled in closer to itself, spontaneously dredding. By the time I found an Ivoirienne braider, Nia's hair was jagged from locs I'd cut out while detangling. She wore her royal-blue-highlighted braids for six weeks, shrugging off classmates' questions about whether her hair was "real" and suggestions she wear it "like that" for Coachella. When Nia decided to return to her signature curly ponytail, I gathered suggestions from a Black cheer teammate and was ready with a hairdresser and Santa Barbara–made hair products. In those late summer months, when I was unpacking, finding my way around, and limping one step ahead of depression, I didn't appreciate the challenge of figuring out Nia's new hair regimen. That daily task—that changed daily—rehearsed skills I needed as I came home to a California that wasn't home, I'm sure. But I'm still not sure why we couldn't have come by those skills in a less painful way. I don't like the way depression sends me messages, at all, descending with heavy hands on *my* tender *ori*.

As I return to this conclusion in January 2021—writing days after white supremacists stormed the Capitol, sitting virtually homebound (except for daily runs with my Zora) as Southern California emerges as the epicenter of a second COVID-19 outbreak—I have no good reason why

I'm not depressed. But today, I'm not. I can trace moments that buoyed me up in the last year; when Nia's all-girl-of-color team qualified for the All Star Cheer world championships; when a lecture I planned with the luminous Tourmaline flew past seemingly unbreachable bureaucratic obstacles to introduce me to freedom dreaming; when I brought home new kittens Mango and Amara. ("Omi and her zoo," Ingrid affectionately calls our household.) But these aren't reasons *why* I'm not currently depressed; they're experiences I can be more present for *because* I'm not depressed. I wish I could write that hymn for myself, because maybe one day Nia will need it, and probably I will too. But also, I suspect my internalized ableism wants me to prove, *somehow,* my family history of depression can be useful, meaningful, beautiful. It's so difficult to take my own scholarly call—that "instead of drowning it out, wishing it away, or smothering it in shame, we hear depression out as part of black femme experience"—*to heart.* As I keep trying, I meditate on Lu's discussion of their lyrics in *Church.* "It's okay to say you are not okay. . . . It's okay to be angry, there is a lot to be angry about. It's okay to be sad, there is a lot to be sad about. The world is whirlwinding out of control, and I am trying my best to keep up," they reflect. "When I wrote this . . . I was going through a tornado of emotions coming from all sides, both personal and worldly. I got through it—temporarily because nothing is permanent—and will continue to get through it because I will not lose faith, especially not in myself. There is no time to, what I am doing is beyond just me."[81]

Tourmaline

Head Scarves and
Freedom Dreams

(For my beloved mentor Kewal,
who *is* peacock blue, unicorns, and Cancer season)

'm writing this in Cancer season. Cancer, the first water sign of the zodiac, opens its season on the summer solstice—the day when sunlight stretches latest into night—but is ruled by the moon, that cosmic high-femme "ever-glowing luminary" and "heavenly portal between the conscious and unconscious."[1] The world-turning year 2020 unfurled its Cancer season under a new moon and solar eclipse, followed by a full-moon lunar eclipse July 4. "So much blooming, followed by periods of deep rest, maintained by consistent, abundant watering. Benefits are beautiful boundaries, passion, power, pleasure, & dream work," queer Boricua astrologer Ari Felix describes the promise of the season.[2] For me, the quintessence of Cancer season splashed on my screen July 2 when I opened a *Vogue* feature by filmmaker Tourmaline illustrated with a photo of the artist on Riis Beach at sunset, sea-foam-green hair dripping and face pensive. Clad in a strapless fuchsia top and a skirt whose train kisses her bare feet, she gathers the ocean's sunset pink and intensifies it pynker against her skin. At her chest she cradles an abundance of stargazer lilies, calla lilies, and pink roses, these last looking up at the tattoo of Marsha P. Johnson stretching from her collarbone to the top of her right breast. On time for the full-moon eclipse, the article offers "how to freedom dream." "Freedom dreams," Tourmaline muses, "are born when we face harsh conditions not with despair, but with the deep knowledge that these conditions will change—that a world filled with softness and beauty and care is not only possible, but inevitable." Freedom dreaming reaches for "the big things—the huge world changes that we are manifesting in our movements, like police and prison abolition, free universal health care, and gender self-determination for all." But it also conjures freedom from small, everyday things: "What seem like the small things, but really are the big things! The everyday acts of liberatory glamour, care, and openness that keep us alive."[3]

"I freedom dream every single day. When I dye my hair blue at home in my bathtub, reclaiming the color from its capture by racist police—and then do my eyeshadow to match—I'm freedom dreaming. I am allowing my very existence to be an aesthetic resistance," Tourmaline offers. "When I take a walk down my block, and slow down to touch and smell the bloom-ing flowers, bursting with vitality, I'm freedom dreaming. I am allowing myself to live in a world where nature is a teacher and friend. When I stay in bed all day, luxuriating in rest, moving in and out of cat naps, I'm freedom dreaming. I am living in the knowledge that I don't have to be productive in the ways capitalism demands of us in order to deserve relaxation and recuperation."[4] Tourmaline came to freedom dreaming while working as a community organizer for Black, trans, queer, and disabled communities in New York. Born (a Cancer, of course) and raised in Roxbury, Massachu-setts, she graduated from Columbia, then stayed in New York to work with the Sylvia Rivera Law Project, Queers for Economic Justice, and LGBTQ youth organization FIERCE. In the course of this work, she began collect-ing, archiving, and aestheticizing stories of trans elders who inspired her freedom dreams. Of Stonewall veterans Johnson and Rivera, she owns, "Much of what exists in the public realm about Marsha and Sylvia I put online. Whether it was the Y'all Better Quiet Down speech that I digitized and uploaded or hand written interviews I found in archives typed and put on Tumblr, so much of what I shared spread like beautiful, virtual wildfire."[5] Her films—*The Personal Things* (2016), *Atlantic Is a Sea of Bones* (2017), *Happy Birthday, Marsha!* (2018), and *Salacia* (2019)—draw on these self-created archives to reimagine, rescore, and bedazzle ancestors' stories: bathing them in colored lights, throwing them birthday parties, framing their pain, marking their grief, celebrating the everyday art they made in flights from a realism too small to hold their genders or their generosity.

In March 2019, Tourmaline was featured in an *Out* cover story honoring "mothers and daughters of the movement." Asked the biggest obstacle to her work, she replied, "Different levels of ableism that are really easy to be internalized, about what productivity can look like and what making a difference can look like, and just different ableist models of what activism should look like."[6] Implicitly and explicitly, Tourmaline's freedom dreams are *always* dreams of radical accessibility. As antipolicing protests spread through New York in May 2020, she laid out, "If you're Black and disabled and feel like you're missing the revolution cuz you can't be in the streets, just remember it's not revolution if it doesn't include us!"[7] Marsha and Sylvia, the freedom-dreaming ancestors whose work Tourmaline lovingly, literally carries on her own body, were disabled revolutionaries. "Marsha P. Johnson would sometimes get picked up by the police for walking naked down the street, talking incoherently about her father and Neptune, and be 'taken away' for a few months. She would return implanted with Thorazine and 'would be like a zombie' for a month or so before returning to 'the old Marsha,'" Anole Halper notes in a careful consideration of these foremothers' "mental health challenges." "Sylvia Rivera, according to her, had 'a drinking problem,' used heroin, and attempted suicide at least twice in low periods. Even though these facts are well-documented, they seem omitted from the mythology that is emerging about these remarkable people."[8] Tourmaline's films are jewel-toned exceptions to this pattern of omission. Visualizing transfemme ancestors' neurodivergence as a "privileged relationship to the immaterial,"[9] *Happy Birthday, Marsha!* and *Salacia* take seriously Marsha's proclamation, "I may be crazy, but that don't make me wrong."[10]

In Tourmaline's films, Marsha's and Sylvia's disabilities are neither hidden nor romanticized. Her characters wear "crazy" neither as a cloak of shame nor as a crown of glory, but in the everyday, intimate, creative ways Black women wear headscarves. By *headscarf*, I mean the rectangular pieces of cloth Black women in the Americas fasten around our heads to cover our hair and emphasize our facial features. Sometimes we wear headscarves protectively, to tuck ends away from sweat, sleep, and unappreciative eyes; sometimes we wear them flamboyantly, multicolored, sculpted, knotted, and adorned as "an Afrocentric aesthetic celebration."[11] But "the headwrap wasn't intended to be an expression of black resistance or beauty," Khanya Mtshali reminds. "Like an offensive slur birthed in racism and white supremacy, it was appropriated by the very black people whose humanity it sought to undermine."[12] Slavery-era edicts mandated women of African descent "wear their hair bound in a kerchief," and slave owners handed out squares of cloth to be worn as a stigma—a badge of enslavement and "a powerful shorthand for the kind of beauty that has been pitted as the antithesis of white femininity."[13] But of course, wearers turned headcloths into material to freedom dream with: tucking flowers at their ears, tying patterns whose folds spoke codes to other Black women, styling turbans for river baptisms and Vodun ceremonies. In the same spirit, Tourmaline's films recuperate what Leah Lakshmi Piepzna-Samarasinha calls "the deep and complicated stigma of crazy—the reality that even in radical communities . . . crazy femmes are not loved or respected in queer community or the world."[14] And Tourmaline's characters re-present neurodivergence as another, underloved Black femme source from which to craft "beautiful, transformative tools for healing and justice."[15]

I'm writing this in Cancer season, literally, figuratively, and always. In his essay "They Diagnosed Me a Schizophrenic When I Was Just a Gemini," Black British disability activist Colin King argues for the importance of self-determination and self-advocacy for the putatively "mentally ill." "I am using the metaphor of my own zodiac sign, being a Gemini, as a challenge to the label of schizophrenia," King explains. "I could simply be Colin with multi-identities, with the liberty to walk the streets without white people feeling like they have to cross over, or hold onto their handbag because of the fear of black men."[16] To invite us to read Tourmaline's films through the metaphor of Cancer season is to make a similar point from a Black femme-inist point of view. "Ruled by the Moon, the planet of women and motherhood," Cancer has seen "the same stereotypes that were designed to break down women and put them in their place . . . pushed onto Cancer in astrology circles today—weak, histrionic, irrational, unstable, not in control of their emotions."[17] Much as in queer communities, "femmes are stereotyped across the board as 'too much': too loud, too crazy, too emotional, too demanding, too many accessories," Piepzna-Samarasinha observes, and "Black and brown femmes, trans femmes, and disabled femmes are stereotyped even more as 'too much'— automatically seen as angry, crazy, harsh, hysterical."[18] But another way to understand Cancer—and femme, and neurodivergence—is as a state in which "creative life force is in absolute *abundance*."[19] An abundance like the armfuls of flowers Tourmaline holds in *Vogue*: heavy, beautiful, overpowering, inspiring, colorful, wilting, overflowing, by turns and all at once. Flowers in so many overlapping pinks refracting the ruffled pink of Tourmaline's dress and mood, shades of rose like summer and rosebudding, rosé and *la vie en rose*, mania and delusion, Ezili Freda and rosaries: rose, the most Cancerian shade of the color pynk.

LADY JAVA'S TIGNONS

Viewing the world through rose-tinted glasses shaped like butterfly wings, edged in rhinestones, and fringed with hanging beads, Sir Lady Java identifies herself to interviewer Pasqual Bettio in 2016: "We're called transsexuals, basically, because I'm in a trance about my sex."[20] Born in New Orleans in 1940, Java—who transitioned with family support at a young age—was a mainstay of Los Angeles's nightclub scene in the 1960s and '70s. Billed as the "World's Loveliest Female Impersonator," she "appeared in shows all over the West Coast with such personalities as Nancy Wilson, Redd Foxx, Lena Horne, Louis Jordan, James Brown, Isaac Hayes, Joe Tex, Ray Charles, B.B. King, and Quincy Jones," according to the brochure "Who Is Java?" As she rose to prominence, she became a target for police harassment.[21] In 1967, the LAPD raided the Redd Foxx Club to arrest her for violating Rule No. 9, an ordinance that prohibited trans women from appearing in public with less than three articles of male clothing. But when Java—performing in a bikini, bow tie, slim men's wristwatch, and tiny socks—proved unarrestable, police threatened to revoke the club's license or to imprison Foxx himself. Java understood this police harassment as racialized: "We didn't know of any establishment that was white that they [the LAPD] were stopping [from employing impersonators], but they were definitely targeting me, because I was queen of the Black ones and they feel that they had more trouble out of the Black ones."[22] Java responded by picketing the Redd Foxx Club (which dropped her act) and hiring the ACLU to mount a lawsuit against the LAPD.

Lady Java's stage career continued brilliantly through the '70s and '80s, garnering positive press from *Jet, Ebony, Sepia,* and *L.A. Advocate.* Her career highlight, she tells Bettio, was performing for Lena Horne at a 1978 birthday party that Horne hosted for her "sister Cancerian, Gertrude Gibson," where Horne enthused to *Jet* about her interaction with Java: "I had the feeling I was talking to a friend I had known for a long while. . . . I feel sort of . . . protective [of Java]. I don't know, because that's my sign—Cancer—always trying to be somebody's mama!"[23] To impress Ms. Horne, Java wore a spangled bikini and towering beaded headpiece whose curving contours—like many of the dramatically draped cloth, carefully sculpted tulle, and angel-wing feather wraps she crowned herself with—recall the tulip-shaped tignons (cloth turbans) made famous by her sister Louisiana Creoles. In an attempt to curb their social and sexual power, in 1786 Louisiana governor Esteban Miró decreed all women of African descent must cover their hair with knotted cloth and refrain from "excessive attention to dress." But as Carolyn Long notes, "Instead of being considered a badge of dishonor, the tignon became a fashion statement. The bright reds, blues, and yellows of the scarves, and the imaginative wrapping techniques employed by their wearers, are said to have enhanced the beauty of women of color."[24] When Java turned her three articles of "male" clothing into high-femme sexiness, she followed in the footsteps of these foremothers' fashion warfare.

Transforming the accessories meant to shame Black women into sex-lessness into pure sexiness, Java declares, she chose "to wear beautiful outfits so a woman can be proud of me when she sees me. I don't dress for men; I dress for women."[25]

By the 1990s Java was "enjoying a quieter life, retiring and, sadly, undergoing some serious health challenges," according to Transas City.[26] These challenges include a stroke from which, Java tells Bettio, "I lost a portion of my brain." During her 2016 interviews with Bettio, her memories and historical records part ways: sometimes in small ways, as when she remembers performing for Horne at the Memory Lane supper club rather than the Pied Piper; sometimes in more sig-nificant ways, as when she proudly recalls winning her lawsuit against the LAPD. "I went to court on it, and I won LAPD. I won the right for Java to work, meaning other impersonators could work also," she recounts—though in fact her case was thrown out on a technicality.[27] It would be easy to indulge the incoherence of her memories as post-stroke cognitive impairment. But it would also be easy to honor that incoherence as its own kind of freedom dream—an alternative his-tory that translates the sinuous, undocumentable ways that change can happen. After the publicity of her case, she reports, "They [other female impersonators] say: We're able to go to work, and we're all go-ing [to] work the next day, and we're going to put on the three male articles [of clothing], and they did the same thing I did: socks and the wristwatch and the bowtie if they wore bikinis . . . little bowties, some of them were jeweled."[28] Isn't a flock of jeweled bow ties bouncing light off foremothers' jeweled tignons another kind of win—another something to celebrate? How do we count and commemorate ways rewired and differently wired Black femme senses make a true story truer, more plentiful, more splendored?

> When I walk naked from my bedroom to my kitchen, adorned
> in nothing but lipstick, I'm freedom dreaming. I am communing
> with Marsha P. Johnson, anti-police activist and sex worker, and
> her naked walks down Christopher Street five decades ago.
>
> **Tourmaline**, "Filmmaker and Activist Tourmaline
> on How to Freedom Dream"

Cowritten and codirected with Sasha Wortzel, Tourmaline's *Happy Birthday, Marsha!* imagines Marsha P. Johnson's life in the hours leading up to the 1969 Stonewall riots. After a day spent drawing invitations, decorating, and preening for a birthday party no one shows up to, the film's fictional Marsha (Mya Taylor) walks her birthday cake to the Stonewall Inn to meet Sylvia Rivera (Eve Linley). When police raid the bar, Marsha throws a shot glass—the legendary "shot glass heard round the world"—to set off the riots. "We initially thought Marsha's birthday was on the date of the Stonewall riots, which would've made her a Cancer," Tourmaline and Wortzel explain. But even after uncovering a birth certificate that recorded Marsha as a Virgo, they kept the original theme. "A birthday is all about putting the focus on someone, and depicting Marsha's birthday felt like an intentional choice for us: *Happy Birthday, Marsha!* is about celebrating Marsha," they reflect. "Her birthday wound up being this beautiful metaphor; so many people talk about Stonewall as the birth of the gay liberation movement, and in a way, we wanted to trouble that, because there have always been moments of disruption, rupture, riots, and fighting back."[29] From 2012 on, Tourmaline had been curating written and visual archives of Johnson's life and work, shared publicly to her blog. *Happy Birthday, Marsha!* draws on these archives by interspersing scripted scenes of Taylor-as-Marsha with black-and-white VHS footage of a 1991 interview with flesh-and-blood Marsha. Narrative scenes are further split between two optics: traditional camera shots that depict the material world (Marsha carrying her birthday cake to the Stonewall alone, for example) and kaleidoscope-edged shots that picture the world seen through Marsha's privileged relationship to the immaterial (like a vision of her riding to the bar in a convertible full of laughing friends).

Shot through soft-focus and tinted lenses with an abundance of loving close-ups, period details, and jewel-toned costumes, *Happy Birthday, Marsha!* is a study in "everyday acts of liberatory glamour."[30] Jeannine Tang notes the filmmakers set out "to make a luscious film as a form of aesthetic resistance" and to conjure "glamour [as] a set of operations upon forms of life and living," an "aesthetics of allure, mutability, gorgeousness, and fascination" that "quotes and reworks the street queens' own grammar of flamboyant femininity, wordplay, and camp, which constituted their liberation aesthetics."[31] Marsha described her Black femme fabulousness humbly: "I've never ever done drag seriously. I always just do drag. I never do it seriously. Because I don't have the money to do serious drag. Years ago I'd have to get some of my stuff out of the trash can and bring it home and wash it. . . . I've always had to get my dresses donated or I've had to get them at a thrift store or something."[32] But her fashion artistry via discarded materials—unsold flowers, Christmas lights, trashed clothing—remains legendary. She was always "over the top with the jewelry, flowers in her hair, very creative looking, very commanding of attention," Ron Jones remembers, and other friends appreciate: "She walked around decked in flowers a lot, remember? She always had flowers in her hair. She put Christmas lights in and they lit up!"[33] Marsha crowned her glamour with spectacular head adornments: a pink beret with EASTER in gold glitter, accented with a red bow and baby's breath; a rainbow-colored Afro wig festooned with Christmas tinsel; a heart-shaped red velvet top to a box of Valentine's chocolates perched atop a red wig with a spray of cloth flowers and a looping pearl necklace. *Happy Birthday, Marsha!* costumes Taylor in homage to Johnson's millinery flair—in a band of red cloth flowers flounced with netting, a wreath of pink gardenias dripping pearls, a fabulous floral crown bedazzled with plastic jewels and ribbons.

One scene, though, finds Taylor's Marsha without a crown: an interior sequence following the birthday queen as she prepares her apartment for a party. Shot through the unkaleidoscoped lens that marks "objective" reality in the film, Marsha's home is a freedom-dreamt departure from historical record. For most of the '60s and '70s, Marsha was, the *New York Times* noted in her obituary, "effectively homeless."[34] James Gallagher remembers her sleeping in hotel rooms, a shared apartment in Brooklyn, the baths, Forty-Second Street movie theaters: "It really was amazing how [she] was able to survive and get through life without having a place to really call home."[35] But in this film, we see Taylor's Marsha—who just skinned her knee escaping a police officer—caring for herself in an *apartment of her own*, soaking in an enamel claw-foot tub she emerges from only to answer her cat's meow. (Like me, Tourmaline lives with a cat companion; when Jean and Nunu made their way on-screen during our public Zoom conversation, she called this a *glimpse into the scaffolding that makes our lives possible*.) Marsha's apartment is painted entirely ballet-slipper pink: its walls adorned with a mirror, framed prints, a hat, and cooking utensils; its floors strewn with a record player, 45s, and a phone; its windowsills holding green plants and a singing bowl; its drop-leaf table celebratory with cake ingredients and crystal goblets. Initially, the background details of Marsha's apartment remain blurry as she lifts herself out of the bath and into a close-up shot from the back. In this frame, she wears only a simple, colorful plaid headwrap tied at the center of her hairline. She pulls on a bathrobe that drapes loosely as she hangs streamers on her lace-curtained windows, frosts her pink cake, and licks her finger. At once healing from an attack and preparing for a celebration, this sequence foregrounds the un-self-conscious glamour Ari Felix calls "style as the genius that comes from just being without pretending to make something marvelous out of the inescapable pain in the ass it is to exist."[36]

As Taylor's Marsha emerges from the bath, a voice-over of archival Marsha intones, "I think every day's my last one." The scene cuts to a black-and-white wide shot of Marsha in a chair by a small round table, wearing a dark dress and sparkling headband adorned with baby's breath and pearls as she continues, "After the party's over I'll be gone, back across the river Jordan." The film cuts back to Taylor's Marsha frosting her cake, then breaks to a close-up of archival Marsha peering into a compact mirror and admitting, "I mean, I don't never know what to do, Andy, you know I'm always getting confused, my computer gets all tangled up." "But you always seem to have it together," the interviewer contradicts, and Marsha replies, "I try." The interviewer presses, "I don't know how you do it. Every time I see you at the 20/20 you're there, you're just the most together person, you're

just there and you're so together." Marsha's volume elevates: "It's expected!"
she shouts in a voice momentarily tightened by frustration and anger, then
pulls back into a fragile laugh. The interviewer's seemingly well-intentioned
comments enact a kind of microaggression Rhoda Olkin finds overwhelmingly directed to feminine-of-center disabled folk: not only are "women
with hidden disabilities . . . more likely to experience denial of disability,"
her study finds, but "the person's disability was denied due to how she appeared. As one woman reported she was told, 'you are too attractive to be
disabled.'"[37] The agitation with which black-and-white Marsha responds to
this casual ableism erupts in contrast to the calm of Taylor's Marsha in
her apartment: a space that fills the screen as a colorful, carefully dreamt
vision of radical accessibility. Taylor's Marsha bathes and bakes in the kind
of messy and beautiful and expansive disabled femme space Tourmaline
conjures as somewhere "it's easy to relax in your own house. . . . It's easy to
be soft. It's easy to remember your power. . . . It's easy to not have to work.
It's easy to be in bed all day. It's easy to be free. It's easy to be alive."[38]

The fictionalized Marsha has everything she needs, everywhere she
needs it. Music and telephone rest together on the floor, keeping creativity and communication in close proximity; cake ingredients and goblets
marry nourishment and beauty on the table; lace and leaves on windows
offer both openness and shielding. Marsha's apartment incorporates
astrologer Mecca Woods's decorating tips for home-centered Cancers
(beautifying bath space, adding crystal or mirrored surfaces to reflect
light, decorating in soft pinks),[39] as well as design suggestions for neuro-
divergence-supportive spaces (plants and other natural elements, strategic
use of color and art, varied interior landscape).[40] But Tourmaline designs
a space for her ancestor that "imagines access [as] far more . . . than a
checklist of accessibility needs," as Piepzna-Samarasinha insists: a living
space where "the daily practice of loving self is intertwined with any safe
room."[41] Marsha's radically accessible space is sacred space, literally as
well as figuratively. After she places her cake at the window, Taylor's Marsha sits down at a mirrored dressing table that doubles as an altar. Alongside curlers and powder sit a clear glass figurine of the Virgin Mary and a
pink seven-day candle with a blue outline of Our Lady of Sorrows, a sprig
of baby's breath balanced between the two. The twin virgins and wrapped

back of Marsha's head split center screen, and the colors of the altar—white, pale green, rose, baby blue—are mirrored in the colors of Marsha's headscarf. In this frame, Tourmaline envisions a radically accessible space where Marsha can both be her most fully human, disabled Black femme self *and* see that self as a reflection of the divine.

So pink, so flowered, so wish piled on wish, so lost in the music, so imagined beyond the possible. Marsha's pink candle and its image of the Mater Dolorosa—like the white flowers, pink cake, mirrors, and lace that grace her apartment—are hallmarks of an altar to Ezili Freda, "agile and elegant goddess of love and of sex, beauty, jewelry, flowers, luxury, wealth, dance, femininity . . . the loa of ideality in Haitian Voodoo."[42] As soon as Ezili Freda enters a ceremony, she embarks on a toilette much like Marsha's: she bathes in an enamel basin, seats herself at a mirror, and arranges a rose-colored scarf around her hair. When people write and talk about Ezili Freda—and I've done my share of both—we usually foreground her divine glamour, love of love, spectacular femininity, boundless imagination. In the process, we background stories in which she maps and mirrors *crazy, confused, tangled computer* as part of her divinity. When Ezili Freda arrives at a ceremony she's "here for the party," as Marsha describes herself—she comes laughing, dancing, flirting, drinking champagne, and eating cake. But at some point, she crosses "an invisible threshold where even the most willing reason and the most ready reality cannot follow," in Maya Deren's words.[43] Mambo Vye Zo Komande LaMenfo explains, "A visit from Erzulie is never fully satisfying to the Lwa. In the end she always begins to weep. The party is not fun enough, the food is not fresh enough, there was not enough champagne. The potential of the event has not fulfilled her desire."[44] In this moment, Ezili Freda "can degenerate into compulsion, obsession, or delusion. This bipolar analogy is the place that Erzulie straddles."[45] When Ezili Freda's candle and Marsha's wrapped head split the screen, they do so as twin "models that encompass falling apart and reforming not as a failure but as a life pathway. Ones punctuated with whirlwinds and whirlpools, that Coatlicue/Kali/Oya energy that dismembers. And gifts."[46]

After Taylor's Marsha—now glamorous in a red dress, platinum wig, and flower headband—leaves her dressing table/altar, she lives her own failed party that spins into a series of kaleidoscope-filmed "delusions" (to reprise Mambo Vye Zo). These kaleidoscope moments may be what psychiatry calls reactive delusions—dives into the immaterial in response to a day of devastating events, including police violence and friends' abandonment—but they're also generative, allowing Marsha to make her way to the Stonewall to instigate the riots. Marsha's unattended party opens to a night of *falling apart and reforming* that, unintentionally, becomes historic. Once she gives up on guests' arrival, Marsha calls Sylvia, who cajoles her into meeting at the Stonewall. Walking there with her pink cake, Marsha hears a siren and starts to run—then passes through the kaleidoscope into a vision of flower seller Junior inviting her to ride to the Stonewall in his convertible. "I made you something," he offers, presenting a pink flower crown flounced with red netting. Now safe from police and crowned in a token of friends' love, Marsha makes it to the Stonewall. There an even more dazzling kaleidoscope ushers her through two pink curtains onto a tinsel-draped stage, where her headdress grows into a two-tiered, pink-and-white-flowered, plastic-bead-draped, feather-topped crown as she performs a poem. "I'm not saying it's easy, to shine, to love, to twirl / I'm not saying it don't hurt to be awake in this world," the poem admits (falling apart), then re-forms: "But the river keeps on flowing, the water's cool, deep and blue / That river keeps on flowing, shining light right back at you." "Earth to your majesty," the bartender interrupts just before police raid the bar. A minute-by-minute, precarious, unforeseeable process of continually falling apart and re-forming, dismembering, and gifting, Marsha's disability isn't romanticized as a visionary power that directs her to throw the shot glass. Like her friendships, love of flowers, and headdresses for every occasion, it's part of a complicated, beautiful, painful pathway that brings her to that moment.

"When we think about disability, impairment, and psychiatric illness, we tend to think in an ableist way that instability and incoherence are deficits, a form of lack. This film asks, 'What if those things are actually a form of surplus?'" Tourmaline and Wortzel reflect. "There's a kind of inconsistency in having two different Marshas," they recognize. "We are offering that as a form of disabled beauty, an aesthetic of movie magic that pushes back against an idea that you have to keep it all together. Because we know that Marsha didn't have it all together a lot of the time, and actually that was a part of her beauty. You don't have to have it all together to have tremendous impact on the world. In part, what we learn from Marsha is that not having it all together can be its own form of beauty and power."[47] The untogether, untoward power of the tangled computer—the dirty computer—whose crossed, sparking, liquifying wires produce meltdowns, yes, and ignite possibilities for a "Black femme digital love practice" that, Jessica Marie Johnson promises, "blazes so brightly, it indexes something institutions . . . can't plan for or reconcile because we are the ghost in the machine."[48] "Who is crazy enough / to create and wear a flower crown every day when she has no house / to throw the first brick in a cops face / defy Reason / demand the unreasonable / start every moment of queer liberation that has allowed my life?" Piepzna-Samarasinha meditates on *Happy Birthday, Marsha!*, imagining, "Marsha would say *I wouldn't have made the revolution / if I wasn't Crazy / Love the Crazy queens in your midst / Listen to them / Love yourself.*"[49]

HEADWRAPS FOR POWER NAPS

A brass bowl overflowing with pink and red carnations blooms between Clara Mejia's thighs as she leans back, smiling, her pink peignoir open to a sheer camisole and her pink silk headwrap adorned with baby's breath and a carnation.[50] Her image announces *Siestas Negras / Black Power Naps*, an interactive installation by Afro-Latinx femme artists Fannie Sosa and Navild Acosta with iterations in Madrid, New York, and Miami in 2018 and 2019. The installation "invites people of color to break with constant fatigue by slowing down, resting, and interacting with soft, comfortable surfaces" in "healing stations": the Atlantic Reconciliation Station, a waterbed vibrating with a subwoofer playing om underneath; the Black Bean Bed, a pit of uncooked beans to submerge tired bodies in; or the Polycrastination Station, a lush, canopied bed four times the size of a full mattress, reflected by an illuminated ceiling mirror.[51] "Research has found that Black Americans experience significantly less slow-wave sleep—the kind required for actual, rejuvenating rest—than white Americans. The lack of slow-wave sleep can cause serious mental and physical health issues," Janine Francois reflects. "Just as sleep deprivation was used as a means to control slaves, the modern-day sleep gap continues to weigh down many Black people, like me, today. . . . This may be the true power of racism—its force encompasses everything, seeping into our dreams at night and deflating our capacity to envision a better future."[52] Mejias, a Black trans artist living in Venezuela, describes nightly dreams like these: nightmares of being chased and drowned she calls "a manifestation of growing up black and trans in a society which tells me, at every step, that it doesn't have a place for me. My dreams were a place where my deepest fear crystalised and manifested." She asks, "What must it feel like to want to dream? Being sure that sleeping you'll see your joys and pleasures instead of the oppression of your fear?"[53]

Black Power Naps is a radically accessible space designed by and for Black femmes like Mejia. Its healing stations are engineered to hold the bodyminds of Black folk wired and rewired in all the ways: the Atlantic Reconciliation Station to "permit people whose African ancestors were forcibly trafficked across the ocean to make peace with the Atlantic,"[54] the Black Bean Bed to soothe panic attacks, the Polycrastination Station to slow time in ways that support PTSD. The installation holds pain, flashbacks, and exhaustion the way the pink silk headwrap holds Mejia's head: recognizing how Black headspace deserves and creates care, softness, and beauty. This recognition, Acosta and Sosa are clear, resists much of what Black folk are taught is upstanding, strong, or productive. "Black Sleep requires total divestment from what is largely expected of a Negro," they write. "To successfully sleep, a Negro must unlearn all that drives our inclination to please and appease others. Black Sleep is the full acceptance that you will disappoint simply by saying 'NO' and taking a nap instead."[55] Pushing back against capitalist common sense "that disabled, tired bodies that spend too much time in bed are useless," Piepzna-Samarasinha jokes,

"My bed, heaped with cushions, is my office, my world headquarters. My life is arranged around my bed. There is good art to look at, a window, my vibrator plugged in, a stack of books within easy reach. I lie in it thinking of all my other crip poet friends who spend most of their days in bed too. Draped in pillows, red and plum sheets . . . curtained by plum sari fabric. This is my place of power, the fulcrum, the place everything emerges from."[56] *Black Power Naps* takes the "useless" space of the tired femme's bed and makes it lushly accessible for public use. And as Acosta and Sosa drape their sleep stations in velvet and chiffon, they literally "make room for the other dreams, the ones that are fertile ground for creating the versions of ourselves that thrive and live long lives."[57]

> When I write to an incarcerated loved one, on colorful paper, enclosing exuberant childhood photos, I'm freedom dreaming. I am reaching through the walls designed to prevent connection and delight, and announcing that they have failed in their intent.
>
> **Tourmaline**, "Filmmaker and Activist Tourmaline on How to Freedom Dream"

Salacia (2019)—Tourmaline's self-described "16-millimeter, experimental, freedom dream of a film"—imagines a day in the life of Mary Jones, a Black trans woman, sex worker, and outlaw who "made a wayward way out of no way" in 1830s New York.[58] Sensationalized in tabloids as the "Man-Monster" during her 1836 trial, Jones spent five years in prison for grand larceny and five months for cross-dressing before abruptly disappearing from historical records. *Salacia* raises Mary from the murky waters of official history where her story dissolved. In the precredit sequence, the camera moves upward from an enamel basin, past a yellow dress and diaphanous robe, to Mary's expressive face as she water scries and a voice-over conjures history left out of formal records. "They say the people could fly. That long ago in Africa, some of the people knew magic. They would walk up on the air like climbin up on a gate. They flew like blackbirds over the fields. Black shiny wings flapping against the blue up there," we hear the first page of Virginia Hamilton's *The People Could Fly*, a retelling of Sea Islands lore about enslaved folk who flew across the Atlantic. One of many stories Tourmaline "was raised on about the power and possibility of Black life . . . [a]nd our ability to access magic in moments of extremely violent conditions," the myth is cast by historians as a rememory of captive Igbo people's 1803 mass suicide by drowning on St. Simons Island.[59] "Flying African folklore demonstrates the power of cultural memory to reshape past tragedies, transforming stories of suicide into stories of strength and propelling them into the future," Terri Snyder reflects.[60] In the same spirit, Tourmaline reshapes slim historical records of Jones—whose yellow dress mirrors the flying Black woman's in Hamilton's book—into a story of multiple possibilities and realities. "Split screens; montages that flow from the documentary grain of archival video to the lush purples and oranges of period narrative; layered images of waterscapes, the face of the moon, and the sun's flashes" visualize this multiplicity, Thomas Jean Lax notes. "Incommensurable textures and asymmetrical scales rub up against one another to create a sense of friction that reanimates the past in the present."[61]

Just as she rehomes Marsha from a shared hotel room to her own apartment, Tourmaline transports Mary from Soho (her documented residence) to Seneca Village, a nineteenth-century community of Black landowners razed to build Central Park in 1857. After its title, *Salacia* enters Seneca Village through a split screen that imagines fragments of everyday life for its women and girls. At one moment, Black women in pearls and cameo brooches, plumed hats, and headwraps laugh and fan themselves on the left, while children play ring games around a fire pit on the right. Mary (Rowin Amone) flits on both sides of the screen, serving tea, chatting, flirting—and stealing a white man's wallet. She reemerges at night in the community's shared space, passing through hanging laundry, clad in an orange dress covered by a black, hooded cloak. Concealing her updo and shielding her face, Mary's cloak serves the "very practical function" Lisa Ze Winters ascribes to the tignon in nineteenth-century New Orleans: "to cover the hair completely" and so "render the black female subject mysterious . . . and unknowable."[62] When she passes a wanted poster for the "Man-Monster," the hooded cape—an article of clothing that disguises the race (Josiah Henson) or gender (Ellen Craft) of folk crossing to freedom in slave narratives—promises but fails to shield Mary from police, who quickly apprehend her.[63] As the black cloak flaps at her back the night of her arrest, the garment recalls the "black shiny wings flapping against the blue up there" of the opening voice-over. Will Mary escape imprisonment by committing suicide like the Igbo who inspired the legend—a plausible explanation for her disappearance from historical records? Or will Tourmaline's Mary fly free another way?

Mary is incarcerated in a dank, dirt-floored cell at Castle Williams, where a shot of her curled up on a mat by a puddle is superimposed on an image of the Upper Bay outside the prison walls. As she contemplates her shackles and the sticks and rocks in her grasp, the ring of a Tibetan singing bowl vibrates from the puddle. Mary huddles over the muddy water, reaching her hand toward its hum as a voice-over of Sylvia Rivera breaks into the prison. The Upper Bay slides into archival footage of the banks of the Hudson where Sylvia lived in a homeless encampment on the Christopher Street Piers. "Every time I look at that damn river and sit there and meditate on the river . . . you got to keep fighting, girly, cause it's not time for you to cross the river Jordan," Sylvia reaches back in time to tell Mary. She points to the river washing between the piers and adds, "This is the river Jordan, the Hudson River." This clip comes from an hour-and-forty-five-minute interview with activist Randy Wicker in 1995 that explores how disability inflects the experiences of residents of Shady Brook Lane—the section of the "gay" homeless encampment where Sylvia lived.[64] The words Mary hears are excerpted from Sylvia's memories of her suicide attempts, the last an interrupted drowning—"I went down to the river to meditate . . . when I was drinking I was thinking how with Marsha gone there was no one left. I thought it might be time to take a little swim"—that led to psychiatric hospitalization.[65] Mary's puddle vision also includes silent images of Sylvia talking to neighbors John and Miss Janice, whose interviews document AIDS-related mental and physical disabilities in Shady Brook's tight-knit community. In this moment of Salacia, the video artifacts of Sylvia's homelessness simultaneously reach backward (to Mary) and forward (to us) to offer what Piepza-Samarasinha calls "crip wealth": a virtuosic web of survival skills disabled folk curate as an "encyclopedia of knowledge and resources . . . ways that we have brought ourselves and each other to the other side and the other side and the other side again . . . the seed bank, the promise, the gift that we give to each other."[66]

Sylvia's time-traveling crip wealth is the turning point that enables Mary to transform her cloak into wings. The transfer of wealth begins when Mary answers Sylvia's call to understand her cell beyond the confines of the visible, following the sound of a singing bowl to (what continues to appear on-screen as) a muddy puddle and hearing Sylvia's voice emerge. One of the gifts of invisible disability—"a physical, mental or neurological condition that is not visible from the outside, yet can limit or challenge a person's movements, senses, or activities"[67]—is how it "disrupts sight as having exclusive critical purchase over interpretation," Therí Alyce Pickens reflects in *Black Madness :: Mad Blackness*.[68] Sylvia and John impart the most literal version of this when Sylvia informs Randy that John has full-blown AIDS and he flatters, "You look perfectly healthy!" "Yeah, that's a big problem," John answers and explains how failure to perceive beyond the visible limits his care: "A lot of times people think that because you have a little size, you have a little stature, that you are healthy, but they don't realize how weak you feel a lot of times, you know, or how sick or the other things, you know, that you have." But before she introduces Randy to John, Sylvia has already described more metaphysical, Marsha-fueled ways that perceiving beyond the visible colors her life on the piers. Not only the pain of her and John's disabilities, the *invisible* Sylvia deals in is also connection beyond physical presence—"passing knowledge back and forth, beyond the beyond . . . [as] another kind of crip relationship," in Piepzna-Samarasinha's words.[69] The message Sylvia delivers to Mary is in fact a message Marsha delivered to her: "I am a survivor. Marsha's not here to survive with me, Marsha unfortunately—Marsha passed on. But she's with me in spirit and she gives me a lot of hope. Every time I look at that damn river and I sit there and meditate on the river . . . I actually feel her spirit telling me, 'You got to keep fighting, girly, cause it's not time for you to cross the river Jordan.'"

Connecting Mary to Sylvia and Marsha, the future speech that reaches through Castle Williams's walls warps, crips, and reconfigures the fort's penal space: "the prison itself, the architecture of confinement," Nicole

Fleetwood theorizes in *Marking Time: Art in the Age of Mass Incarceration*, but also "the disruption of family relations and domestic space, the imposition on movement and mobility, the restrictive and highly monitored experience of the geographic, material, social, and psychic environments in which the incarcerated are warehoused."[70] And as the future (Marsha's death and Sylvia's life) washes into Mary's present, Sylvia's words interrupt penal time: the ways "penality turn[s] time into a mode of punishment," constituting the years, months, and days of a carceral sentence as its own architecture of confinement.[71] When Sylvia relays to Mary the words Marsha relays to her, she simultaneously speaks as the unborn and the living, while Marsha is invoked as at once the unborn and the dead. The exchange between these three trans women takes place in the time of mad Blackness, which, Pickens tells us, "refuses linear temporality, invaginates space, deposes ocular for sonic knowledge, embraces silence, pursues control, and relinquishes power, all at the same time."[72] But it also takes place in *spirit time*: a phrase African diaspora spiritual practitioners use to explain the liquid time of ceremony, "when from one moment to the next an ancestor can return you to the past—or a lwa can pull you to a more expansive present—or an unborn spirit can give you glimpses of the future."[73] M. Jacqui Alexander describes time's refusal either to be contained or to act as a solid container in Vodou and Santeria: "Time becomes a moment, an instant, experienced in the now, but also a space crammed with moments of wisdom about an event or series of events already having inhabited different moments, or with the intention of inhabiting them, while all occurring simultaneously in this instant, in this space, as well as in other instants and spaces of which we are not immediately aware."[74]

Salacia sends me into my own kind of spirit time. During my first viewing, I screamed when Sylvia's voice broke through; for hours I rewatched the six-minute short on loop. I'm not sure how many viewings it took before I realized Tourmaline casts the film into spirit time at its opening. The opening image of shadows flitting over water Mary uses to scry—seeing into the future, in the past—is followed by the title slide: gilt-framed "SALACIA" against a black background that fades into a sunset-pink, then twilight-blue image of the wave-rippled Upper Bay. When I first encountered the title I assumed *Salacia* was a back-formation of *salacious* (like the scandal surrounding Jones in her lifetime). But the Mississippi Mardi Gras Krewe of Salacia informed me otherwise: "In ancient Roman mythology, Salacia was the female divinity of the sea, worshipped as the goddess of salt water who presided over the depths of the ocean. . . . Salacia was the personification of the calm and sunlit aspect of the sea. Derived from Latin sal, meaning 'salt,' the name Salacia denotes the wide, open sea, and is sometimes literally translated to mean sensational."[75] That a film honoring Sylvia is named for this sea deity made immediate sense to me. Because, of course, Sylvia is a Cancer—a sign Felix honors in a love letter that vows, "I love you as the ocean you are. all the creeks, the rivers, the waterfalls guide me back to you. they teach me about how you seem to be still but are always moving. they teach me about how you seem to be always moving but never really leave. they teach me trust without control . . . thank you for being the water that holds the earth together."[76] But more importantly, because Salacia is the consort of sea deity Neptune. And as Tourmaline reflects, the challenges and gifts of Marsha's disability—her crip wealth—were deeply connected to Neptune: "One of the things that is so specific to Marsha was her imagination and relationship with people and places that no one else could see. Marsha would talk about seeing her dad and Neptune in the Hudson River. She would take off all of her clothes and give them as an offering to the Hudson River and Neptune."[77]

If we understand Neptune as a metonym for crip wealth, can we also view Salacia (and *Salacia*) as a femme-inized form of that wealth? After the archival footage of Sylvia fades out, *Salacia* returns to Mary's cell, where two versions of the protagonist occupy the same frame. In the background, one lies prone by the puddle with her cloak folded over her back; in the foreground, a larger Mary faces the camera in a medium close-up, feathers pinned at her neckline and cloak cascading down her back like open wings. "We can be anything we want to be. We can be anything we want to be. *We can be anything we want to be*," foregrounded Mary repeats as the film closes. "As historical time moves without linear progression, the narrative time of *Salacia* ebbs and flows so that the words with which Jones begins seem to touch her last utterances," Lax notes. He adds, "Just as the magic of narrative enabled our ancestors to flee slavery, and just as the power of self-making has ushered in a moment when a girl can catch the bus to a liberation march in the middle of the day in all of her stuff, our black shiny wings will flap as we become anything we want to be."[78] The weapon that frees Mary from imprisonment is a chain of crip knowledge that breaks neuronormative limits on the possible; that melds the invisible into the tangible, the present into the future, and the cape on her back into wings. If more Black folk followed these trancestors in their fugitive relationship to rationality, how many would find Black femme freedom? "I want *everyone* to have crip knowledge," Piepzna-Samarasinha proclaims, and *Salacia*'s loop between Mary and Sylvia visualizes one reason why: re-wiring the senses to crip perception and crip time opens new possibilities like wings.[79] Asked about *Salacia*'s resonance with the historic events of Cancer season 2020, Tourmaline replied, "In a moment when there is in-creased visibility around the everyday violence that black people face, it's important to also be creating and dreaming. Right now, people are really paying attention to, 'What's the world that we're seeking to create? And who's coming along with us?'"[80] *Salacia* invites us all to come along with Sylvia and Mary, confluxing alternate Black femme pasts, presents, and futures into our now.

HONEE BAE FLIES FREE

"Happy Birthday to The Girl Who Lived," Cherno Biko posted in CeCe McDonald's honor on May 26, 2015. "Thank you for making me realize that #FolksLikeUs are worth fighting for. Wishing you all the best and much success in this next year of your divine life."[81] A col-lage shows the birthday femme smiling in a floral crop top, sleek in a leather jacket, and flashing the shaka sign in a black skullcap embla-zoned with bae. This was her signature cap in 2015, worn while film-ing the documentary *Free CeCe!*, appearing at the National Trans and Gender Non-Conforming Anti-Violence Convening, and speaking at the University of Wisconsin–Madison and the University of Texas at Austin. Black femmes in the Midwest wear skullcaps as cover-ups year-round: to keep out rain in fall, to stave off windchill in winter, to hold hair until salon day in spring. But CeCe wears hers as a declaration—of her nickname, Honee Bae, and her knowledge she's Beautiful And Elegant, Before All Else. The year 2015 was CeCe's first full year of freedom after spending nineteen months in a men's prison for defending herself against a racist, transphobic attack. When her prison writing mobilized activists nationwide under the cry "Free CeCe!," the *Minneapolis Star-Tribune* noted, "Rolling Stone called her a 'folk hero.' Her friends call her 'Katniss,' the persistent protagonist from 'The Hunger Games.' CeCe McDonald describes herself simply as 'the girl who lived.'"[82]

The Girl Who Lived speaks candidly of the ways the assault and its aftermath changed her. "I never knew what PTSD meant," she admits in *Free CeCe!* "I've been through traumatic experiences in my life, of course, but not to this extent, and my PTSD began instantly the night of the incident."[83] Penal space and time—including six months in solitary for "protection"—exacerbated her PTSD. "They keep this constant light on you so you can't really sleep well, so I could never get proper sleep. And it was really starting to weigh down on me mentally. There wasn't any concept of time, either. In jail, if you don't have a clock, you really don't know because there aren't any windows."[84] Years later, CeCe continues to deepen the story of how incarceration produced an invisible disability that renders "just regular human adult things that we're all supposed to have"—a job, a lease, a partner—"accomplishments." Reflecting on how COVID isolation reactivated the trauma of solitary confinement, she offered in 2021, "Studies show how solitary confinement actually changes the makeup of your brain chemistry; show the elevated depression and paranoia, anxiety, and many other mental instabilities that come from solitude and being alone. I'm just using my platform to have those conversations, because I, myself, am dealing with how solitary confinement affected me mentally."[85]

CeCe's Gemini imagination—a quality Felix compares to smoking incense that "moves at an impossible speed in slow motion, the quicksilver movement that fills a room of lungs like butterflies caught in copal [and] amber" and "disrupts illusions of linearity [and] one dimensionality"—sustained her during incarceration.[86] "When I was in prison I would sit in my cell and think about how, if I got struck by lightning, maybe I would gain superpowers so I could start kicking down all these walls," CeCe remembers.[87] After her release, she rendered her invisible superpowers visible through body art. *Free CeCe!* intersperses CeCe's discussion of her PTSD with footage of her designing and sitting for a phoenix tattoo that covers her stomach. She explains, "My idea of the phoenix was of the fire being in the inside. The bird has a crown. It symbolizes the fire that is within me. If you cracked open my phoenix, it would just be like this bright, white liquid fire that is keeping me charged and keeping me going."[88] In Egyptian myth, the one and only phoenix lives for five hundred years before flying far and wide to gather cinnamon and oak branches, nards and myrrh, and set them ablaze, immolating herself so she can rise from her ashes three days later with more strength, wisdom, and power than in her last life. "This creature embodies resilience. It embodies me," CeCe reflects.[89] Now whether she goes out in a black skullcap, fur-lined winter hood, or colorful headscarf, CeCe always wears her phoenix crown. "If the Creator, whoever He-She-They are, wanted me to be a certain way, that's how They would've made me," CeCe told *Rolling Stone*. "But until then, until all this shit is figured out? I'm-a rock this. Till the wheels fall off. Till the wheels . . . fall . . . off! Mmmph! Crop tops and all, trust and believe that!"[90] In her tattoo-baring crop tops, CeCe gifts everyone she encounters a chance to see her phoenix crown—to see how she wears trauma and healing, daily, centrally, and permanently.

Cancer season 2020 was a season for Black trans crip wealth. Creating a public "seed bank" because they knew the state never would, Black trans public figures like Indya Moore and disabled model Aaron Philip mobilized Instagram to boost Black and LGBTQ folk in need of material support. On July 2, Philip shared an emergency mental health fundraiser for a "Black, Fat, Low-Income, Nonbinary, Disabled, Queer Femme" on her birthday; July 3, she forwarded a campaign to raise rent for a Black trans disabled elder; and July 5, she posted a plea from a Black Asian genderqueer femme for help to move out of a homeless shelter and get treatment for bipolar depression and PTSD.[91] Amid this wealth sharing, the *Vogue* image of Tourmaline holding flowers on Riis Beach reappeared on GoFundMe July 3. The campaign: "BIRTHDAY BENZ FOR TOURMALINE." "It's our magical loved one Tourmaline's birthday on July 20. For her birthday, let's harness the power of collective dreaming and redistribution and make this dream car real for our bday girl," the text of the fundraiser (officially organized by her cat companion Jean) rallied. "Many of us are deeply indebted to Tourmaline for her endless contributions to our lives, our trans + queer culture, our magic, our ability to dream. She has reached back into history and helped us to remember our transcestors through her art, her beauty making, her presence. She is the reason so many of us know who Marsha P. Johnson and Sylvia Rivera are. Let's continue to fundraise beyond Black trans angels' survival and basic needs—let's continue to support their EASE, PLUSHNESS, PLEASURE, FRIVOLITY, JOY, + LUXURY."[92]

Ten days later, Tourmaline posted the GoFundMe image to Instagram with the location "Off to the Places Where Dreams Cum True Till U Wake Up!!!!" "Thanks so much for showering roses on me while I'm here," the caption appreciated. "It's so fun to come together and fund it all: Pleasure gardens where prisons once were, playful dreams and healthcare and housing. It's all worth resourcing!" Who says radically accessible space doesn't extend to a convertible as pink as Marsha's freedom-dreamt apartment? No: as *pynk* as Marsha's freedom-dreamt apartment, a rosily abundant aesthetic colored by deep faith that neuro-wealthy Black femmes, too, *deserve nice things.* "BOOST because Black folx shouldn't have to say why they ask for money. I hope it's a candy pink with shimmery paint," one comment affirmed, and the next declared, "This is inherently radical. Rooting for you and this fresh whip."[93] Radical, the idea Black disabled femmes "shouldn't only have to ask for the things we need to survive. People like me need to be safe, and housed, and loved, and protected—and we also need to have fun, to take risks, to laugh, to feel beautiful, to be playful. There is enough to go around. There is enough for us to flourish.

And we don't have to have done big things to be deserving of this pleasure."[94] Radical, the idea Black disabled femmes should be able to wear neurodivergence the easy, beautiful, transparent way Tourmaline wears a headwrap of woven flowers in James Falciano's drawing to illustrate her quote, "Our glamour is not superfluous to changing the current order, it is instrumental."[95] Happy birthday, Tourmaline. Never afraid to be *too much*, she wishes, "I want a world where we are invited to bring the most. The most full cup. The most full version of ourself. The most turned up. I believe when we do that we are giving gifts to behold."[96] Who else but a Cancer gives gifts on her own birthday?

And yes, Tourmaline's birthday wish came true. *Of course.* On August 9, she posted a picture of the interior of her convertible Benz parked at the beach, a metallic Telfar handbag propped up in the passenger seat like a promise of eternal Black femme abundance and on-trend crip wealth. "THANK YOU DREAMY COMMUNITY FOR GETTING ME THIS DREAM CAR! OVERWHELMED WITH LOVE AND APPRECIATION!! CAR CONTENT CUMMING SOON!" she captioned her image, leaving us all with so much to look forward to in the long, heated days of Leo season.[97]

PART THREE

Black Femme Environmentalism for the Futa

At midday on September 20, 2019—my daughter's tenth birthday, her first in California—a stream of placard-waving high school students marched down our block on their way to a rally in Girsh Park, chanting, "Hey hey, ho ho, climate change has got to go!" "Local teens participated as part of a nationwide protest in conjunction with Swedish environmental activist Greta Thunberg, 16, who went on a weekly strike on Fridays and began skipping school to demand the adoption of renewable energy by the Swedish parliament," *Noozhawk*'s Brooke Holland reported that afternoon. "Dubbed the Global Climate Strike, the youth-led activism movement to protest and call out governments for their lack of action on climate change has spread into a worldwide phenomenon since Thunberg began demonstrating alone in August 2018."[1] The photo under the article's title centered a fresh-faced, blond teen in cutoffs and a tank top yelling into a megaphone while another blond marches behind her with a sign declaring, "I'm the Lorax, I speak for the trees." The over-representation of white students in *Noozhawk*'s coverage—Santa Barbara High is 57 percent Latinx, 36 percent white—as well as its centering of the formidable Thunberg, mirror the optics of a slew of articles on environmental activism published in the weeks leading up to the 2019 United Nations Climate Summit. "You probably know who Greta Thunberg is. But you've probably heard much less about young people like Mari Copeny, otherwise known as Little Miss Flint, who has been bringing attention to the Flint water crisis since she was eight years old. . . . You probably aren't tuned in on the Brown and Black kids and youth around the globe, from Myanmar to Brazil, who were out striking along with Greta," Haitian American journalist Jude Casimir guessed that November. "If you didn't know about these activists and groups, it isn't your fault. There's a reason why these groups haven't been given as great a platform as Greta, and that has to do with the media's consistent whitewashing of climate activism and White Environmentalism being framed as the only answer."[2]

Ancestrally European as she is, Greta Thunberg isn't a white environmentalist; I hope the teens pictured in *Noozhawk* aren't either. Not a function of proponents' race, white environmentalism is distinguished by its platforms' willful blindness to how race impacts environmental injustice. "Like white feminist organizations, white environmental organizations refuse to recognize the intersectional implications of the problems they claim to want to solve," Naomi Thompkins explains.[3] Long before white teens here declared they "speak for the trees," Santa Barbara earned its reputation as an influential activist and academic hub of white environmentalism. In 1968, University of California, Santa Barbara, professor of human ecology Garrett Hardin published his watershed article "The Tragedy of the Commons." "It's hard to overstate Hardin's impact on modern environmentalism. His views are taught across ecology, economics, political science and environmental studies. His essay remains an academic blockbuster, with almost 40,000 citations," Matto Mildenberger explains in *Scientific American*. "But here are some inconvenient truths: Hardin was a racist, eugenicist, nativist and Islamophobe. . . . His writings and political activism helped inspire the anti-immigrant hatred spilling across America today. And he promoted an idea he called 'lifeboat ethics': since global resources are finite, Hardin believed the rich should throw poor people overboard to keep their boat above water."[4] No wonder contemporary mainstream environmentalists' proposed "solutions"—"pleading for people to drink oat milk, shop at Whole Foods, buy $25 reusable water bottles, and purchase electric cars," Thompkins quips[5]—"routinely overlook those of us who live at the intersection of multiple oppressions: race, class, gender, disability, and sexual orientation, to name a few," queer disabled Haitian Japanese artist Patty Berne critiques.[6]

While it may not be readers' fault mainstream media overreports white environmentalism, Casimir stresses, it's everyone's responsibility to expand the lens through which we view climate justice. "If you call yourself an environmentalist, if you take yourself seriously as an activist, you better be working on recognizing your complicity in white supremacy and listening to all the youth climate activists involved," she writes. "If you truly think the climate crisis is an important issue, you need to uplift the voices of Black and Brown youth as much as you do the already megaphoned white ones."[7] Not because anyone is doing organizers of color any favors by including them, understand, but because these activists' positions at intersections and shorelines are crucial vantage points from which to resist planetary change. Speaking of her disabled queer of color Bay Area communities, Berne lays out, "At this moment of climate chaos, we're saying: Welcome to our world. We have some things to teach you if you'll listen, so that we can all survive." So many lifesaving examples of queer of color climate activism never make it to headlines, she stresses. "During the fires and floods of 2017, queer disabled organizers in the Bay Area shared masks and air filters with one another, while in Puerto Rico, communities banded together to share generators to refrigerate insulin," Berne informs. "At the 2018 Solidarity to Solutions grassroots summit, held alongside the government-organized Global Climate Action Summit, trans Latinx organizers affected by the North Bay fires led a healing justice workshop for queer and trans people of color environmental justice activists from around the world to connect and learn from one another. This burgeoning movement may be invisible, but it should not be surprising."[8]

News outlets let us all know what white environmentalism looks like: it eats locally grown kale and drinks from Hydro Flasks, wears Patagonia hemp clothing and vegan lip gloss. I'm not mad at any of these things; I do some of them. But environmentalism can look other ways too. The green movement can be as pynk as Juneteenth watermelon or cruelty-free Fenty Petal Poppin blush. It can wear shiny Lycra in the saturated colors of the Everglades, like Miami artist collective (F)empower at their interactive fashion show envisioning postapocalyptic South Florida. It can rock blue #SHOCKVALUE lipstick, like artist Juliana Huxtable spectacularizing and weaponizing the words that pass through her clenched vegan teeth. Black femme environmentalism advocates for the conservation of rainforests and animal species, the restoration of clean drinking water and healthy oceans, of course. But Black femme environmentalism also imagines the creation of "a world where queer Black feminine folks are living their most abundant, expressed, and loving lives," as Alexis Pauline Gumbs so beautifully writes, which will emerge as both cause and effect of a truly inclusive environmental justice movement.[9] Almost certainly, I'll never see a march of Black femme environmentalists go past my door here in Santa Barbara. But I can create one in these next pages, as a gesture of love and hope for my daughter's next decade.

(F)empower

Swimwear, Wade-Ins, and Trashy Ecofeminism

(For Jafari, Black queer love letters, and
shoreline meetings still in future tense)

Pisces sun and Pisces rising, daughter of two waters and Ezili's love child, I was raised by the Pacific: *by* as in next to, *by* as in guided to adulthood with the constant westward blue as my compass. So where else would Nia and I go our first days in Santa Barbara, except the beach and the beach and the beach? Goleta, Ellwood, Mesa Lane, Haskell, Arroyo Burro, East, Carpinteria: every day we went to a new stretch of coast. August spilled into September and October and afternoons still broke warm enough for Nia to play in the surf; still the "weather felt like summer, that's the fall in California," Saweetie sang on my "Due West" playlist.[1] But by November, something in the still-balmy air and rainless skies felt *off*. On runs, Zora and I saw people in their front yards watching the hills for smoke, tracking small blazes and wondering out loud if flames were moving our way. Then on November 24, they were: fanned by high winds, the Cave Fire tore through four thousand acres of dry brush in the foothills as fire trucks rushed in, helicopters dropped water at night, and the blaze resisted containment until freezing rain and snow (in Southern California?) arrived November 28. "Life in Southern California, once as mild and predictable as the weather, is being transformed as the climate grows hotter, drier and in some regions windier, fueling more intense wildfires, deadly mudslides and prolonged extreme drought," Scott Wilson reported in the *Washington Post* that December. The sunny waters Nia and I had been enjoying were part of a warming trend that literally fueled this fire. "The warming waters offshore are beginning to resemble tropical oceans that, according to local fishermen and farmers, are intensifying the dry winds that cascade down the steep coastal range and deepen the effects of drought. . . . That results in less coastal moisture, and more risk of fire."[2] Feverish, riotous, and hurt, the Pacific I lived by now wasn't the cool, deep blue I thought I knew.

"How can we ally with this Brown, queer, disabled, femme planet to support her survival, and the survival of all who depend on her?" Patty Berne asked in an op-ed published the day after I moved to Santa Barbara.[3] I read her piece over and over that winter; with a fire lit underneath me, almost literally, I floundered through digital and social media to learn from other queer of color climate justice activists. Relaxing at my mother's house on New Year's Day I stumbled on the Instagram of (F)empower, an "artist collective and community raising queer feminist consciousness in South Florida."[4] Double Pisces that I am, I immediately connected with its unapologetically imaginative, Ezili-bright, riotously femme-centric messages; I also connected with the profile of founder Helen Peña. Like me (but younger), Helen moved away from her native coast only to come back years later to a climate-changed shoreline that unsettled her. That unsettling became the vantage point from which she imagined ways to change the most climate-vulnerable city on the continent. Her work and insights met me as an Atlantic example of Berne's claim that "queer and trans communities of color are already preparing for the survival of their communities through oncoming disasters, teaching each other skills in resilience-based organizing to strategically create the changes that we need for queer and trans futures."[5]

Thigh-deep in sand and thought, kneeling in a honey lavender bikini, rosé shades, and a riot of windblown curls, Peña captioned her August 17, 2017, Instagram beach pic, "Reading an article about climate change and if artists can make a difference & it got me thinking . . . what if this is all underwater in 20 years? What're we gonna do about it!! Anyway, here's a pic of me enjoying the beach while we still can."[6] For months, I found as I scrolled, Peña's social media had been preparing for the end of the world as she knows it—conjuring Black and brown femme-centric ways "to make sense of the world burning and living in the Trumpocalypse."[7] "In 2017, after Trump got elected, I was having an emotional response considering the violence that would continue to be enacted against black and brown bodies and particularly, women," she told *Dazed*'s Nicole Martinez. "I started blogging and created this speculative fictional story, where a black female girl gang led the way to this invisible future. The blog post became a zine, and from there it was like: 'What's next?'"[8] She weaponized Instagram to gather Miami's femme of color artists into a radical collective named for her fictional girl gang, (F)empower. The "feminine energy gang" (as member Rae calls it) took off like California wildfire in "an underground scene in South Florida ready to combust."[9] (F)empower hosted its launch party and art showcase, Femgaze, June 10, then spent the summer giving workshops and curating a body-positive social media campaign, #FuckSwimWeek, that bathed pictures of queer, soft, scarred, hairy beach bodies in online love. "In a city so reliant on money from tourists—many of whom are searching for a sexxed up, unrealistic, body-toned taste of the Caribbean—(F)empower's vision feels like an affront to the city's most toxic attitudes and its most reliable revenue streams," *Remezcla*'s Jorge Courtade notes.[10]

(F)empower's headquarters (and Peña's home, the "fembassy") are nestled in Miami's Little Haiti, settled by Haitian migrants in the 1980s and bustling with Haitian-style murals, art galleries, bright-painted homes, the Haitian Heritage Museum, *botánicas*, bakeries, thrift stores, Caribbean Air Mail, and Notre Dame D'Haiti. But climate gentrification is rapidly altering Little Haiti's demographics. "The predominantly low-income neighbourhood, ignored for years, has been thrust into the spotlight of late: as one of the highest-ground areas in Miami, developers have turned their sights onto the neighbourhood as sea levels have risen," Martinez explains.[11] Peña moved to her fembassy in November 2017, two months after evacuating from Hurricane Irma—the largest Atlantic hurricane in recorded history—and returning to downed trees, debris-littered streets, contaminated water, and Black communities kept in power outages. "I just wanted to feel the bliss and warmth of being back home, but I never expected to face piles and piles of trash washed up on the shore," she recounts. "In that moment I just felt all this pain—like the pain of mother Earth. . . . I just want to re-instill the humanity in us all and give back to the OG femme—muva Earth—because without her, nothing would exist."[12] This spirit of giving back led her to join sister (F)empower member Ashley Varela to turn her yard into the Femme Fairy Garden, a "POC & LGBTQ activated community garden bringing environmentalism, activism and herbalism to Lil Haiti."[13] And to support Nicole Thais's formation of the Liberation Book Club, a group that meets weekly to discuss topics ranging from climate change to mass incarceration to polyamory. Peña explains, "Where Fempower started, there's always the idea that the apocalypse is now. It's here. So, how do we navigate through apocalypse? It's by doing things like coming together, and learning things."[14]

A *dream world*, Peña calls the Femme Fairy Garden. She reflects, "While we believe we have to radically change our current system . . . we also know that it may not happen in our lifetime. We don't know. So, what we're trying to do is be in the practice of building those dream worlds right now, and so the garden is that space. It's an alternative way of being."[15] (F)empower's practice embodies what Tina Campt calls "black feminist futurity": "a politics of pre-figuration that involves living the future now— as imperative rather than subjunctive—as a striving for the future you want to see, right now, in the present."[16] Or, more accurately, by "mothering the idea of survival on queer terms,"[17] Femgaze, the Femme Fairy Garden, and the Liberation Book Club dream up Black *femme*-inist futurity: one where Black and brown femmes garden, read, smoke, cry, make art, preen, fuck, swim, heal, and resist together, refusing to cede "OG femme" ground. This, I knew when I saw it, was an eco-femme-inist future where I wanted to live. Instagramming photos of femmes embracing in swimsuits, gardening shirtless, and posing with the V sign at clubs, (F)empower queers feminist futurity by imagining a Miami-to-come where Black women's love for each other is unapologetically embodied, erotic, and effervescent. Calling together femmes who literally live on South Florida's shores, this collective of young, Black, Caribbean, underemployed, queer, trans artists locates itself in the figurative space Alexis Pauline Gumbs calls *the shoreline*: the survival space "for those of us who live on the shifting edge of the world, close or brave or stupid enough to sell the details of the line we walk, to guess the conversation between sea, sand and air . . . for those of us who know the truth of erosion and bet against it."[18]

Facing down Florida's coastal erosion and "enjoying the beach while we still can," (F)empower persistently stylizes its Black femme-inist futurity in the most Miami of all garments: the swimsuit. Since 1920s Miami booster Carl Fisher enacted his plan to "get the prettiest girls we can find and put them in the goddamnedest tightest and shortest bathing suits" in promotional photographs,[19] "consumers throughout the United States and abroad increasingly looked to Miami Beach for the 'very latest and smartest'" swimwear.[20] "Miami, the Magic City . . . grew up as it were, over night, with two flourishes of the fairy's magic wand," journalist Burroughs Perry puzzled in 1929, describing the recently cleared swamp as a "most unconventional" city where everyone "wears as much or as little as one pleases" and it's "nothing unusual to see men and women in bathing suits" or "men with hair long enough to bob and women with hair cut short."[21] This skin-baring, queer-sounding fairyland was whites only, though: starting in the 1920s Black West Indians and African Americans were barred from public beaches. Activist M. Athalie Range recalls, "Signs on beaches said: No Jews, No Dogs, and No Coloreds."[22] When the Negro Service Council staged its first direct action, they targeted the beachfront as their protest site. "On May 9, 1945, two black women and four black men arrived at 'whites only' Haulover Beach Park and took off their street clothes to reveal bathing suits underneath. They were about to boldly swim into the waters that were forbidden to them," Roshan Nebhrajani recounts. "It was a wade-in. And it's what would begin the process of equalizing access to Miami's greatest gem: the water."[23] To avoid tourist-repelling protests the county designated Virginia Key Beach South Florida's first "colored only" waterfront. Black "Miami mermaids" photographed soon after—leaning against palm trees in fashionable swimsuits, riding the carousel in beachwear—embody another kind of magic: a "place where," Range remembers, "we could be free, in a way."[24]

Looking like "a mystical tribe of black and brown femmes emerg[ing] from Miami's sewage-laced shores" in sustainably produced, gender-neutral swimwear, (F)empower orchestrates next-millennial iterations of South Florida's historic wade-in.[25] Their demands: Black femme access to livable futures on Miami's literal and figurative shorelines. Separate-but-equal Virginia Key Beach created possibilities for beach-going Black folk that far outstretched the blow-off-some-steam recreation Dade County intended. "It provided a new gathering place for the black community in a natural setting," historian Gregory Bush notes. "Churches and social groups used it for entertainment, organized recreation, and everyday beachside activities. It was a distinct, defensible, and largely self-policed public space where blacks could be free of white surveillance and control. It was a place that generated solidarity and fueled later civil rights activism in South Florida."[26] On its Instagram, at the fembassy, and in the Femme Fairy Garden, (F)empower looks to do the same. "Welcome to your new local playground: (F)empower, a space for you to connect, collaborate, educate, fight and showcase," the collective's first Instagram post offered on May 7, 2017.[27] When we arrived in Santa Barbara in 2019, I encouraged Nia's fierce Virgo desire to literally wade in to new stretches of the Pacific every day. But by 2021, I was reaching to (F)empower, Berne, and their sibling eco-femme-inists—many of whom cross this chapter—to help me imagine what it means to enable Nia to wade figuratively onto new shorelines, demanding new habitable zones for Black girls of the future.

(F)empower styles their Instagram posts in a signature color palette: unapologetically sex-positive, anticapitalist scarlet and forcefully femme-inist, emblematically Miami neon pink, swirled together as a background against which the "girl gang" announces their events and campaigns. "Bright, brash, and artificial," graphic designer Grace Fussell describes neon pink—a color that hasn't "always been associated with good taste. While muted tones tend to have a more chic and intellectual reputation, neon hues are affiliated with fun, frivolity, and excess . . . nightlife, clubbing, and cities after dark." Sidestepping white environmentalism's bourgeois pretentions and embracing pleasure as a force for change, (F)empower's neon-pynk, eco-femme-inist messaging shouts with thot power, some-times, but also with urgency. "Neon colors can also be associated with warning and danger, due to their use in high-visibility clothing and signage," Fussell continues.[28] Illuminating Black femme bodies too easily overlooked in the scramble to climate gentrification, (F)empower's shades of pynk—like all neons—emit light: illuminating "the future we want to see, while inhabiting its potential foreclosure at the same time."[29] This is how we wade in to the future, femmes—brightest colors flying as we sink below sea level and reemerge, facing the apocalypse in ecosustainable Day-Glo armor.

ZORA NEALE HURSTON'S PALMETTO FRONDS

"In honor of Black herstory month," (F)empower announced February 1, 2020, "for the next 29 days, (F)empower will be highlighting black femmes throughout history who have transformed cultural thought through art, literature and activism."[30] February 6 honored novelist and anthropologist Zora Neale Hurston, "a fixture of the Harlem Renaissance and author of the masterwork *Their Eyes Were Watching God*."[31] Hurston spent her childhood in Eatonville, an all-Black township near Orlando she described as "a city of five lakes, three croquet courts, three hundred brown skins, three hundred good swimmers, plenty guavas, two schools, and no jailhouse."[32] After her mother's death in 1904, Zora shuffled between family members before landing with her brother John in Jacksonville. There she settled in an "environment she could breathe fresh clean air, laugh and smile at leisure, walk bare-foot in the soft white sand," where she made a lifelong best friend and travel companion in "tomboyish" Gerda King.[33] These two "quickly became like sisterly soul mates," longtime Jacksonville resident M. Alene Murrell remembers: "Gerda and Zora traveled and got into a lot of trouble together in and around Jacksonville in the early decades of the 20th century. There were many exciting and unbelievable tales that the two of them would tell."[34] One such tale recalled an afternoon of skinny dipping in Little Pottsburg Creek. When Zora and Gerda emerged from a long, playful swim, the clothes they'd left on the bank had been hijacked by mischievous boys. "They were in a panic, but soon they recalled a story from the Bible, the story of how Adam and Eve covered their nakedness with fig leaves," recounts Murrell. "They had no fig leaves, but they did have plenty of palmetto fronds, which they soon put to good use! Zora and Gerda used the fronds to cover their nakedness and they continued on down the path to go home."[35]

Zora maintained an intimate, reverent relationship with Florida's waterways throughout her life. "I have given myself the pleasure of sunrises blooming out of oceans, and sunsets drenching heaped-up clouds," she lyricizes in her autobiography. "I have found out that my real home is the water, that the earth is only my step-mother. My old man, the Sun, sired me out of the sea."[36] She became an early, powerful chronicler of how capitalist exploitation of these waterways—the drainage of Florida's swamps for sugar and fruit plantations—spiraled into Black death. *Their Eyes Were Watching God* documents the 1928 Okeechobee Hurricane, the second-deadliest tropical cyclone in US history. Seventy-five percent of the storm's 2,500 casualties were Black migrant farmworkers, and Hurston describes the storm from their terrified, awed point of view. "Ten feet higher and far as they could see the muttering wall advanced before the braced-up waters like a road crusher on a cosmic scale. The monstropolous beast had left his bed," she writes. "He seized hold of his dikes and ran forward until he met the quarters; uprooted them like grass and rushed on after his supposed-to-be conquerors, rolling the dikes, rolling the houses, rolling the people in the houses along with other timbers. The sea was walking the earth with a heavy heel."[37] Reflecting on how Hurston's environmental prescience inspires her, Haitian novelist Edwidge Danticat marvels that this "relatively short book . . . covers so much—poverty, migrant work, preservation and respect for Indigenous people. There's even climate change in this novel from the 1930s." She continues, "I remember when Hurricane Katrina came through, and we saw those images of what happens after a flood like that goes through a predominantly poor and black community. I thought it was the book on my screen. She was just prophetic in that sense."[38]

Prophetic, too, in her vision that while climate disasters "magnify black women's traumatic alignments with nature, they also reveal black women's unique ability to sustain life amidst the basest social and environmental oppression" and "clear space for black women to articulate their stories, pose more productive models of ecological stewardship, and exemplify kinship and care."[39] After surviving the hurricane, Hurston's protagonist Janie memorializes her dead lover by planting a garden for him and telling their story to her best friend, Pheoby. Janie and Pheoby mirror the lesson Zora and Gerda learned that day at Little Pottsburg Creek: that when Black women love each other and think together, they can turn the unexpected into a chance to start over again—to imagine themselves as a new Adam and Eve, partnering with the landscape around them to find a way to "continue down the path."

TRASHY ECOFEMINISM

December 6, 2018, broke sunny and clear in South Florida, the skies stormless for the six-continent influx of planes pulling white carbon dioxide contrails toward Miami International Airport. "Today, creatives and collectors alike will be touching down in Miami for Art Basel. The annual four-day festival is known to require an impressive amount of stamina—and an even more impressive suitcase, filled with eye-catching pieces bound to capture both hearts and shutters," *Vogue* advised. "Sparkly sandals (easy to slide into; easier to kick off) and tropical-theme frocks . . . will surely make the cut, as should a carefully curated cosmetics case."[40] Touted as the premier art fair of the Americas, Art Basel Miami Beach—the largest art fair in the United States, with 268 galleries and 32 countries represented that year—annually draws collectors, art advisors, gallerists, curators, and celebrity art enthusiasts like Tessa Thompson, Venus and Serena Williams, Alicia Keys, and Issa Rae. Every attendee traveling commercially from New York, *Art World*'s Naomi Rea estimates, generates about a metric ton of carbon dioxide, while every one-hundred-pound work of art transported from Europe emits .15 metric tons.[41]

Ground travel to the fair and related parties, plus expensive carnivorous dinners and receptions, added to the per-person carbon footprint for that year's eighty-three thousand attendees. Art tourists touched down that weekend in the world's most climate-vulnerable coastal city, where greenhouse-gas-driven sea level rise is projected to reach eight to twelve inches by 2040. "People are flying in on private jets to buy art in a region that is on the frontlines of climate change," chastises Extinction Rebellion's William Skeaping. "It's almost an incredible and artistic self-destructive loop. The more people come to Art Basel Miami Beach, the faster Art Basel Miami Beach disappears. All these people with art collections and new foundations in Miami are actually threatened by the people who come to visit them—the loop is completely unsustainable."[42]

That weekend (F)empower held a parallel art show, *2040*, and invited viewers to enter Miami's catastrophic climate future now. Up to 90 percent of warm-water coral reefs are projected to disappear by 2040. Rising seas could displace 2.5 million Miamians by 2100. Florida will see the most dangerous combination of heat and humidity in the country, with index temperatures at 104 degrees. Indigenous womxn, Black womxn, and womxn living in the Global South are the most heavily impacted by climate crisis. These and other climate predictions shouted in green, all-caps slides on (F)empower's Instagram, counting down to the show's opening. "Miami inhabits the rhythm of both pre and post apocalyptic realities, the in-between worlds and possibilities," the event description warned. "In reaction to the forecast of destruction and climate collapse, (F)empower welcomes you to encounter what is left of our dying world. Through art installations, panels, performances, and multidisciplinary media, *2040* submerges you into the future, that in this moment, has already passed us by. DEC 6 will feature Project Z, a fashion presentation showcasing the last generation in a dying world."[43] Styled by Margo Hannah, Carleen Donawa, and Stephanie Bigot, the neon-splashed, apocalyptic Amazons eschewed sparkly sandals and tropical-themed frocks to imagine a future where fashion is brutally seasonless and unapologetically femme. The models' "eyes are shielded from the scorch of the sun with large dark goggles; their locks twisted into braided crowns to protect their scalps," *Dazed* describes. "Long-sleeved, turtle-necked neoprene suits help them wade smoothly through the water. Ancestral survival wisdom is their sword; their unbreakable bond is their strength."[44] The show was accompanied by a showcase of (F)empower members' artwork, and its first one hundred guests received a door prize: (F)empower survival breathing gear.

Throughout that month, stylist Margo Hannah posted her favorite Project Z looks to social media. "Here's what you missed if you didn't attend @projectz.miami," she captioned photos of a model stunning in orange eye shadow and hair wrapped into horn-shaped *irun kiko*.[45] A medium close-up shows her in a silver string bikini top stretched so wide its triangles barely cover her areola, paired with black lamé pants cropped at the knees and extended with red cellophane trim. Over this cascades a floor-length, woodland-print orange kimono with shoulders cut out and restitched into asymmetrical orange cellophane tufts. "Look inspired by some of your favorite 90s r&b groups," Hannah glosses a photo of swimsuit model Dominique Jeffries in a hot-pink lamé, bikini-esque combo reminiscent of Destiny's Child in "Independent Women."[46] Worn over a black fishnet bodysuit, her spandex top stretches taut over an under-bust cutout while the asymmetrical bottom extends to her right ankle but ends at her left butt cheek (bodysuit cropped to match). Both models wear elbow guards—on right elbows only—and pose on concrete blocks in white Wellington boots. In these and Project Z's other ensembles, Hannah styles (F)empower's Black femme-inist future as a vision of streetwear-cum-swimwear, Black-music-inspired, vibrantly neon-pynk *rasanblaj*. "Rasanblaj is a word from Haitian Kreyòl that envisions an 'assembly, compilation, enlisting, regrouping,'" Larry La Fountain-Stokes describes, citing Haitian scholar-poet Gina Ulysse. "It is an invitation to engage with the multiplicity and complexity of the Caribbean, not in an effort to move away from it, but rather to dirty metropolitan models: to make them engage the radical, communitarian, erotic, decolonial, utopian, profoundly historical present and future of the region."[47] And yes, Project Z came to dirty metropolitan Art Basel: to speak in defense of OG Femme Muva Earth from the point of view of queers, migrants, urban farmers, thots, and radical femme-inists.

In a city famous for skimpy fashions, Project Z showcases a futuristic technology of protective layering—femme armor whose full-length pants

(replacing bikini bottoms) are layered with robes on top, bodysuits underneath, and Wellies below. Technology to shield Black femmes against
climate change, Hannah's designs are striking both for what they shield
and what they expose. The first model lets her danger-orange robe fall
open to bare her torso, her widely stretched bikini displaying the brown
rise and fall of clavicle, ribs, and inner breasts. With hair weaponized
into horns and limbs glowing fiery with cellophane accents, she poses
as a warrior who remains radically vulnerable at her core—embodying
the "fiercely soft-hearted" ethos Monica Uszerowicz ascribes to (F)em-
power activism.[48] In response to Miami's extreme climate vulnerability,
Project Z mobilizes the "unapologetic, ferocious, fiercely fabulous Black
radical vulnerability" that Black Lives Matter Canada cofounder Janaya
Khan sees in movements that imagine futures where "Black transfeminist, queer women" have resources both to protect ourselves from toxic
overexposure and to remain open (hearted) to change. When observers
see only anger behind movements for Black futures, they miss "the heart
of the matter": the radical vulnerability of "demanding that you see us; as
worthy of life, as fully human, as enraged at the injustice of the oppressive
conditions we have been forced to live under."[49] To do so in a context like
Art Basel is to go out on a limb as precarious as the fall branches on this
model's orange robe. "I don't think [they] were ready for something so
powerful that didn't follow the typical Basel agenda," (F)empower member Loka reflected after the event. But since "brown and black bodies are
more vulnerable to the climate crisis . . . we need to be more extreme and
radical about preserving our lives, right now, but, more importantly, for
the future we hope exists."[50]

But Project Z's technology of layering isn't all about heart baring.
R & B–styled model Jeffries keeps her chest covered with superhero-
metallic Lycra whose shine, as Krista Thompson writes, acts "as a shield
or apotropaic, simultaneously reflecting and deflecting the deidealizing gaze on black subjects."[51] Her exposure comes lower, at a left thigh
where Lycra and fishnet suddenly end and the deep cinnamon of flesh
begins. Left, as in the side that energetic healing practices associate with
femininity; thigh, as in the thick seat of sexiness. While the transformation of Jeffries's bikini bottom into a full-length pant leg on the right

represents a "functional" adaptation for predicted sea-level rise, the opening on the left looks like what adrienne maree brown calls *adaptation toward pleasure*. "Pure" adaptation is an inevitable process that "has led to every functional and dysfunctional condition we know," but adapting toward pleasure comes from the "combination of adaptation with intention, wherein the orientation and movement towards life, towards longing, is made graceful in the act of adaptation."[52] Movements for Black futures, brown believes, should prioritize this kind of adaptation: "Facts, guilt, and shame are limited motivations for creating change, even though those are the primary forces we use in our organizing work. I suspect that to really transform our society, we will need to make justice one of the most pleasurable experiences we can have."[53] And what better to evoke the marriage of Black femme-inist justice work and pleasure than '90s R & B girl groups? These were years when, Lyn Mikel Brown and Dana Edell write, "a new generation of bold, sexually confident, politically charged young women of color such as Queen Latifah, Salt-N-Pepa, Lauryn Hill, and Missy Elliot . . . 'carved out a space for black feminist expression and validation.'"[54] Wouldn't the Destiny's Child independent women of the future enjoy "killing you with those legs / better yet those thighs," as Beyoncé sings?[55]

Foundational to Project Z's technology of layering is the deconstruction and upcycling of the kimonos, pants, and bodysuits its models armor themselves with. On her blog *Black and Broke*, Hannah explains how her *rasanblaj* of '90s looks and recycled materials is realized through hours spent in thrift stores. "The best part about thrifting is having an outfit that no one else will have for the lowest price," she lays out, then explains why scissors are her favorite tool: "I've been on a cutting spree since! I love being able to get creative with my outfits. Actually being able to cut and fit clothing to my body, the way I want it is pretty dope."[56] The *way she wants*, is cut and fit to be sexy on her own terms. Her post "Get Off My Areola!" describes, "The top was originally a bit longer but I decided to be a thot, so I whipped out my [*sewing*] machine to nip & tuck this top into a crop."[57] Crop tops, cutoffs, Lycra, fishnets, underwear-as-outerwear: in Project Z, as on her blog, Hannah adapts her designs toward the pleasures of both the recycled and the trashy. *Trashy*, said with love;

trashy, as in unapologetically feminine, explicitly sexualized, and proudly working class. This, too, is pushback against the designer femininity Basel's art jet set invests in: "Unlike her conservative cousin, tasteful, there's nothing subdued about a trashy dresser's appearance. Her motto is: 'I ain't no fake—take me or leave me! I don't give a @#$*!' Trashy dresses like she does because she wants to be seen, and she's proud of the look she's created."[58] If (as I once wrote) Black femmes "are in a position where their history—like their reproductive and other labor—is considered trash,"[59] (F)empower's *2040* imagines that our future is trash/ed too, and that unapologetically wielding any materials and pleasures we can scavenge is as much an artistic practice as anything else at Art Basel.

Adding to Basel's art tourism emissions, the carbon footprint of visitors' *Vogue*-approved fashions shadows Miami's climate future. "One billion new items of clothing are produced every year, and every second, a garbage truck's worth of textiles are put in landfills or burned. If things don't change soon, fashion could drain a quarter of the world's carbon budget by 2050," *National Geographic* warns. "The fashion industry emits more greenhouse gases than ocean shipping and international airline flights combined."[60] In response, the decade preceding *2040* saw the rise of "trashion"—art couture designed from recycled materials. But the budget and audience of high-end trashion shows is decidedly *not* broke and Black: "Due to the specificity of the final product and the lack of most of the properties necessary for comfortable and long-lasting operation, trashion remains more demonstrative and artistic than utilitarian. The designs are mostly created for thematic exhibitions, competitions, fashion shows, and photo sessions," a 2019 eco-fashion market study notes.[61] Well, fine. But why has *trashion* become art while *trashy* remains an insult? Eco-fashion didn't invent the practice of upcycling wearable art; broke fashionistas did. Project Z maps a future runway that valorizes the organic, everyday-use, curve-enhancing way "Black and broke" women remake things, including a sometimes-trashy aesthetic that Little Haiti femmes enjoy while gentrifiers judge. "ThIS planiT IS Ours Now has cum the time for TRsh 2 invadE; THIS IS A CALL TO STRATEGIC pollution = An infection of FILTH Wmn are instinctively programmed to communicate and protect WE MUST USE THIS IN OUR GLOBAL DUMPSTER

DIVE," Elizabeth Broeder proclaims in "TRASHGiRRRRLLLZZ: A Manifesto for Misfit ToYZ."[62] Diving deep into Black Miami's trashy ecofeminist imaginations, Project Z emerges with thought exercises—and thot exercises—on how to invade the future in upcycled armor built for Black femme pleasure.

So this, femmes, thots, and other art lovers, is how (F)empower staged a wade-in at the Western Hemisphere's most elite art fair. On December 6, 2018, *2040* invited viewers to exit champagne-flowing parties and enter postapocalyptic Miami; required them to abandon carefully curated suitcases for a queer *rasanblaj* of layered lamé and fight gear; challenged them to prioritize leading with the heart over maximizing profits; and primed them to recognize that ecofeminism will be trashy, or will not be for all Miamians. After the fashion show, visitors viewed pieces like Mumbi O'Brien's *Memorial to Mother Earth*, a mound of dirt surrounded by two sprouting seedlings and white votives; donned backpacks to watch a film about effects of climate change, shaking as the pack vibrated wildly with each tornado, hurricane, or flood that flashed across the screen; and attended panel discussions on how urban farming techniques can combat food shortages. "We used art as a way to agitate, upset, and awaken people, and to inspire a sense of urgency and paint a picture of what will happen if we don't change," punctuated O'Brien.[63] And captioning her own pose in a deconstructed white swimsuit-cum-life-vest, dubbed this girl gang: "Femme Future Protectors."[64]

"HOW BLACK CAN I GET?"

"Black Spring Break 1999 in Daytona, Florida": two smiling Black women with immaculate updos pose breast-to-breast in sporty, high-waisted bikinis, each with another friend leaning in beside them.[65] "Spotted at our shop earlier today, early/mid 1950s and 1960s *Jet*, *Say* and *Hue* Magazines": including a January 1, 1953, *Jet* promising "1953 Calendar Girls," its cover model wearing a bikini bottom with a placard reading "Happy New Year" across her breasts and the title "why lesbians marry" printed over her left shoulder.[66] These posts come from the Instagram of BLK MKT Vintage, a Bedford-Stuyvesant-based marketplace of vintage clothing, literature, records, art, housewares, furniture, and other collectibles curated by Black femme-butch couple Kiyanna Stewart and Jannah Handy. Lifelong vintage aficionada Stewart credits her mother as the inspiration behind this Black love–fueled market: "As early as I can remember, she was pulling over the car on the side of the road to pick up amazing castaways and taking me to the thrift shop with her on the weekends."[67] Attuned to environmental justice in a wide sense, Stewart curates Black vintage as an ecological practice that simultaneously cares for the earth and tends to Black people's past and future on the planet. "To me, black vintage is about historical and collective memory. It's also a radical statement about black people's survival. When I see cultural artifacts—whether they be books, photographs, vinyl records or personal letters—I am reminded that we've existed in so many iterations," she writes. "I think 'we have journeyed and we have survived, so beautifully.'" She and Handy extend these reflections: "Black vintage is laden with sensory memories and each item takes us back to a particular moment, person, space, feeling, while also moving us forward . . . looking to the black past, present and future to inform our vision."[68]

In August 2019, the couple's home was profiled by *Refinery29*'s Eliza Dumais as "maximalist home décor." She elaborates: "Each square foot of vacant space boasts some antique or rare collectible art piece—everything belongs somewhere. There's a palpable air of intention: Demi-walls and closet doors are cloaked in blocks of loud, eclectic paint. The place falls on an aesthetic spectrum, somewhere between 'home' and 'museum' . . . All of it, riddled with color and history and narrative detail."[69] When Dumais describes this color palette as loud, does she mean trashy? Or is she asking readers to see the couple's aesthetic as I do: as Black queer life that makes its home in *rasanblaj*? *Rasanblaj*, which Gina Ulysse glosses as "assembly, compilation, enlisting, regrouping (of ideas, things, people, spirits). For example, fè yon rasanblaj, do a gathering, a ceremony, a protest"; and goes on to clarify, "You don't pick and choose when you make a rasanblaj, you gather everything."[70] *Rasanblaj* is a maximalist aesthetic that embraces the more, gathering other folks' too much, surplus, garbage into Black queer just enough, beauty, archives. In July 2018 Stewart posted a picture of herself reclined on a Miami beach wearing a black strapless swimsuit and black glossy lipstick, her face tilted skyward and the caption quoting her thoughts: "me at any beach: okay, how black can I get?"[71] Black on Black on Black, yes, no amount of Blackness is ever too much.

QUEER ECOWOMANISM

"Closing in on a quarter of a century and welcoming those unfamiliar with the depths of the ocean . . . my balance has never been better . . . swipe right to see rare footage of a mermaid disappearing into the sunset," Femme Fairy Gardener Ashley Varela captioned her March 3, 2020, Instagram post.[72] This sister Pisces shared three Miami mermaid snaps of herself in a strappy white Chromat Strata swimsuit spun from recycled fishnets: a medium close-up of her deeply shaded, nearly bare back as she gazes at a pink and orange sunset on the water; a full shot leaning against a post on the pier, smiling as she arches her back and reaches arms overhead; and a video swimming out to sea, with a voice-over singing, "Iiiit's her birthday and we love her! Her name is Ashley . . . Yaaas!" On March 4 and 5, she shared more birthday femme images, donning the same Chromat suit at Lakes Okeechobee and Apopka: "Happy Birthday Water Sprite!" and "ChromatBabe fantasy!" comments celebrated.[73] The week of Varela's solar return would usher in a month packed with music festivals, street fairs, and foodie events in South Florida. As Varela posted (often literally) reflective solo shots, Miami Beach's annual queer Winter Party Festival overflowed with a record number of attendees; preparations for Miami's 305 Day Block Party and Calle Ocho street festivals were underway; and the first spring breakers made their way to soon-to-be packed beaches. "We can't stay away to save our lives," Florida native Diane Roberts writes of those beaches—"glorious beaches, with their broad, inviting sands and water that shifts its jewel hues from emerald to turquoise to sapphire"— where Varela disappeared into the sunset, Winter Party festivalgoers danced chest to chest, and students fled soon-to-be closed college campuses. "No wonder" those beaches were about to emerge again as "the crucible of Florida politics" when the World Health Organization declared COVID-19 a pandemic on March 11, 2020.[74]

"Miami-Dade County is under a state of emergency, as we deal with the public health threat of COVID-19," Miami mayor Carlos Gimenez declared the next morning, officially canceling all upcoming large-scale events.[75] But—concerned with the tourist dollars that routinely flood Florida in March, the most prosperous month for the state's $86 billion tourism industry—Governor Ron DeSantis let spring break continue until March 17. He limited the size of gatherings and jauntily declared, "The party is over," on *Fox and Friends*, yet refused to issue a mandate to close beaches statewide.[76] While nationwide pressure mounted, he deferred politically tricky decisions about beach closures to local governments. "Schools are closed. Courts are closed. Bookstores are closed. Disney World is closed. But this is Florida, and beach-going is practically a sacrament, or a constitutional right," Roberts sums up.[77] By early April the state counted over 17,500 coronavirus cases as the epidemic continued to spread. "Gov. Ron DeSantis, a Republican, has blamed travelers from New York, Europe and other places for seeding the virus in the state," the *New York Times* reported. "But the reverse was also true: People got sick in Florida and took the infection back home. The exact number of people who returned from leisure trips to Florida with the coronavirus may never be known."[78] (F)empower implicitly called out DeSantis's protection of the tourism industry over the lives of its patrons in a March 15 post. "In the midst of this global pandemic, we refuse to be overcome by fear; we breathe, feel and fight for each other," red letters against a green background declared, and the caption elaborated: "In this moment, a veil is being lifted, and the horrors of global capitalism are coming to light, affecting us all. . . . After this is all over, capitalists will try to erase our memories and act like it's all business as usual. Do not let them."[79]

As (F)empower anticipated, COVID-19 emerged as a Black femme-inist issue in Miami. "African Americans are 2.2 times more likely to have diabetes, 20 percent more likely to have high blood pressure, 30 percent more likely to be obese, more likely to have HIV, asthma and sickle cell anemia and more likely to live in poverty," Florida State Medical Association president Cheryl Holder outlined April 4. "All of these underlying health conditions put African Americans at a greater risk of death if they contract COVID-19."[80] A week later, the first race-inclusive statistics proved her right: in Miami-Dade, the Florida county with the most confirmed COVID cases, Black patients were dying at rates 50 percent higher than whites. Linked to poverty, pollution, grocery redlining, and medical racism, the comorbidities underlying Black death are symptoms of environmental injustice. Climate researcher Derrick Z. Jackson drives this point home with an analogy: "As much as hurricanes Katrina and Maria upended African American and Latinx families, the landfall of the coronavirus brings a gale of another order. This Category 5 of infectious disease packs the power to level communities already battered from environmental, economic, and health injustice."[81] (F)empower responded with ecofeminist activism homegrown in the Femme Fairy Garden. On March 23, an image of Varela wielding a machete announced Survival Skills 101: "Covid quarantine got you questioning whether you got the skills it takes to survive the end of the world? Have you been daydreaming about growing ur own food and becoming self reliant??? Same sis. SURVIVAL SKILLS 101 is an ig live series made for navigating these times. We start today with tincture making."[82] Sunlit mason jars of cat's claw and Spanish needle tinctures appear on Peña's Instagram after the workshop, alongside a picture of Varela feeding fresh herbs into a salad spinner. White bikini bottoms peek from under her T-shirt as she sits open-legged on the floor, a basket of herbs overflowing by her bare right thigh. "Creating lifelines for each other while the state refuses to," Peña captions the post, which also shows Varela packing produce boxes for food-insecure community members.[83]

The Femme Fairy Garden continued its agricultural activism throughout the COVID spring. On May 1, Varela posted a picture squatting in a garage, preparing food-justice boxes overfull with kale, collards, summer squash, and carrots to distribute in grocery-redlined Little Haiti,

Overtown, and North Miami. On May 13 she posted "elderberry journey in two parts," videos and pictures harvesting and cleaning wild elderberries in a long, loose white sundress like the ceremonial whites of
Afro-Caribbean spiritualists. "The syrups made from these elderberries
will be given to those in our community who are most at risk/affected by
the Covid-19 crisis. If you need some herbal medicine no matter where
you are, send me a message," the caption promised. One photo centers
sprigs of elderberries and a sunflower riding carefully in the passenger
seat of a car. Both elderberries and sunflowers are plants associated with
Oshun: Oshun, the Yoruba mermaid orisha (divine power) of sweet water,
abundance, creativity, femininity, sensuality, and all things that make life
worth living; Oshun, the orisha whose offerings Varela displays on the
beach in August 2018 with the simple caption "Oshun's daughter."[84] "Oshun is a powerful healer known especially for her emotional healing and
for handling matters of the heart. Her healing waters are medicinal and
protective. A lesser known aspect to some is her deep connection to plants
and their medicine," Black queer herbalist Toi Scott notes. "Oshun and
her children are master herbalists."[85] And Oshun's children offer healing
for free: a socialist feminist medicinal practice the Femme Fairy Garden
takes seriously. "This is totally what everyone should be doing, is growing
their own food, tending to the earth, putting in the right plants," Varela
told *Scalawag* when the Fairy Garden broke ground. "All this is such a
benefit and a fuck you to capitalism at the same time." Peña added, "To go
back to our roots, and reconnect with earth is a big radical, healing, act of
resistance."[86]

The roots of (F)empower's medicinal activism pass through chattel
slavery, when enslaved healers cultivated plant-based cures for diseases—
including cholera and measles epidemics—against which Western medicine remained ineffectual. "Gathering and making medicines was holy
work" for these healers, whose "daily medicinal practices," Sharla Fett
describes, "rested on a notion of a spiritually enlivened landscape drawn
from both African cosmologies and African American Christianity": "As
they gathered, administered, and taught about botanical medicines, enslaved African Americans enacted a relationship with the land that was
both practical and spiritual."[87] Varela's Instagram visualizes a parallel

relationship to the landscape. "My most treasured relationship is the one I have with nature, the way it whispers and guides me thru it all is other worldly," she captioned a July 2019 photo in a lily pad–fringed lake. While socially distanced from humans during the COVID spring, Varela soulfully, lovingly, erotically communed with the unbuilt environment. She and her cat sheltered in place for three months in a tree house that, she appreciated, "helped me discover and understand that I had hidden parts of myself away out of fear . . . and allowed me the space and courage to let my full self manifest and heal. I'll always think back to this time so warmly. Thank you nature for being the only one every time."[88] And she publicly proclaimed her love for the "spiritually enlivened landscape" when on May 20—while Miami beaches remained closed by municipal emergency orders—she gifted viewers with "blessings from Yemaya": three pictures reclining on the sand with blue ocean and green palm trees at her back, wearing a wide-brimmed straw hat and a high-cut scrunch-tie swimsuit printed in dark-blue, teal, and green flowers. Viewers who swipe right to the last photo find Varela with her chest curving lovingly toward the sand, her right hip opened skyward to show a generous swathe of pubic hair.[89]

In corona time, when, Leah Schnelbach testifies, "touch starvation" has become "almost like a physical presence" that "takes up its own space,"[90] Varela's loving contact with South Florida lakes, trees, and beaches visualizes the healing possibilities of "tapping into the natural abundance that exists within and between us, and between our species and this planet."[91] These last words are from adrienne maree brown, who makes clear how she continued adaptation toward pleasure as Black femme-inist activist practice during quarantine. "A list of additional recent pleasures i opted to fully experience instead of panicking—washing my hands in warm water, writing, reading, new kinds of orgasm, cooking, painting, slow yoga in the sun, going out in the yard to observe my local ecosystem during the day (which often involves attending to what is usually the periphery—the sound on the edge of hearing, motion on the edge of sight) . . . being topless outside, creating and executing rituals," she offered in an abundant run-on sentence.[92] Varela frames her beachside communion as its own kind of ritual. Where once she laid fruits, flowers, and wine on the beach as offerings to Oshun, now she lays *herself* out as an offering to Yemaya.

Yemaya, orisha of oceans, womb waters, full moons, and dreams; Yemaya, orisha to whom all Oshun's sweet waters flow. While practitioners usually imagine Yemaya and Oshun as sisters, some see the river's rush into the ocean as something else. "I have heard it said that Oshun is a woman in love with women," New York–based practitioner Eduardo Mejia recounts. "There is a story that she and Yemaya love each other."[93] And yes, Oshun's daughter Varela dressed for her date with Yemaya the way you would for a lover: curved her cinnamon-brown thighs into a vintage suit bought for the occasion, offered flower-printed breasts and hips and curls of blooming bush in an embodied bouquet. "That last photo got me feelin some type of way," one viewer admitted, while another appreciated, "Wow Yemaya really do be blessin her children." *Flores, flores, muchas flores para Ochun y Yemaya.*

That Varela posted her embodied offerings to Yemaya at a time when almost all Florida beaches were closed was no small thing. Throughout May, Miami-Dade was dotted with wade-ins where white Miamians protested COVID closures by sitting on beaches with signs reading "We Are Free." Kim Falkenstine, arrested at sit-ins May 10 and May 23, explains them as a declaration that beaches are Floridians' rightful property: "The beach does not belong to the governor, it does not belong to the mayor, it does not belong to anyone but the people."[94] In contrast, Varela's wade-in wordlessly dissolves the capitalist illusion that the beach—whom she greets as a divine femme lover—can be *anyone's* property. With a smile and turn of the hip, this Oshun publicly embraces Yemaya in a display of queer ecowomanism: she flouts the governor's order not because she owns the coast but because she loves it, inviting viewers to "imagine how it might be if we treated the earth as our lover and partner, rather than as a resource to be exploited."[95] An unapologetically Black, Alice Walker–mothered counterpart to ecofeminism, ecowomanism is "the reflective and contemplative study of the ecowisdom that is theorized, constructed, and practiced by women of African descent" and "validates their lives, spiritual values, and activism," writes Melanie Harris in *Ecowomanism: African American Women and Earth-Honoring Faiths.*[96] These spiritual values include the loving relationship Oshun's children cultivate with lakes, turtles, sunflowers, and Yemaya: "According to the ethical mandate of earth justice woven into many African tribes and established in the history of many African American churches (from the hush harbor movement to the present day), the relational condition between the beautiful (earth) and the being (human) is that both are honored in a kind of mutually enhancing relationship—one never exploiting or dominating the other."[97] Or as Varela reflects, "Intentionally envisioning a future where the earth is cared for, we are cared for, animals are cared for . . . collectively rejoicing in our joys and sorrows . . . where pleasures are unbound . . . nature flourishing, powerfully humbling . . . back to our roots, to where we belong."[98]

And this, femmes, herbalists, and other healers, is how the Femme Fairy Garden and its director staged a wade-in while a pandemic gripped the Western Hemisphere. On March 23, to launch its Survival Skills 101 series, the Femme Fairy Garden announced, "In the midst of the Covid-19 crises, we are here to provide the people with the knowledge to heal themselves through the land because they deserve it."[99] They followed up by wading in to the garden to provide healthy food and healing plant medicines to community members free of cost. And throughout, Varela modeled a loving, pleasure-drenched relationship to South Florida lakes, rivers, and oceans that honors ecowomanist "connections between black women's health, spiritualities, and ecological concerns."[100] And queers those connections too: "I love being gay," she captions her May 2, 2020, post of a lily, punctuating her statement with a sunflower graphic for Oshun.[101]

SURF LULLABY

During the long, beachless summer of 2020, Alexis Pauline Gumbs gifted Instagram with a series of waterside photos of small girl Alexis taken by her mother, Pauline McKenzie, in the 1980s. One shows little Alexis in a mixed-print one-piece and white jellies, tiny hip jutting out as she stands on a concrete pier built by her grandfather; in another, she smiles in sunglasses and a yellow bikini where sand meets water; in yet another, she spreads limbs like a starfish as she sinks into the sand wearing a black suit printed with stars and spirals. On July 1, she posted my favorite: an image of herself in the same black star suit submerged at the shoreline, propped up on elbows with legs extended behind her like a tail. The image is supported by a poem titled "surf lullaby #1": "One of my surf lullabies (there are several) about the place where land meets sea meets air. Also known as my favorite place. Also known as everywhere we are as salt water beings." In a gesture she calls "homeschooling my inner child," Gumbs reflects, "Especially in this time of adaptation I am seeking this mermaid. That part of me that wants to be at the edge of elements. I am remembering that I love the actual play of adaptation. How to respond to the waves that come and move me. How to be both moveable and held by shifting sand."[102]

That fall, Alexis published a book in adrienne maree brown's Emergent Strategy series called *Undrowned: Lessons from Marine Mammals*. The slim volume invites humans at the shoreline to "humbly submit to the mentorship of marine mammals," oceanic cousins Gumbs reveres as "queer, fierce, protective of each other, complex, shaped by conflict, and struggling to survive the extractive and militarized conditions our species has imposed on the ocean."[103] A Black eco-femme-inist guidebook for how to survive the Anthropocene, *Undrowned* entreats readers to imagine not (just) that humans can save oceans but that oceans and their mammals can help save us. The book offers nineteen thematic movements "organized around core Black feminist practices like breathing, remembering, collaborating, etc., as they can be informed and transformed by learning from marine mammals (and a couple of sharks)."[104] "This is not a book in which I am trying to garner sympathy for marine mammals because they are so much like us," Gumbs clarifies in the introduction. "Instead, the intimacy, the intentional ambiguity about who is who, speaking to whom and when is about undoing a definition of the human, which is so tangled in separation and domination that it is consistently making our lives incompatible with the planet."[105] Rich, lyrical, and generous with imaginative human-marine connections and flights of fancy across Atlantic, Pacific, and Arctic, Alexis promises, "I wrote this with you in mind, dreamers that live near the shore and wonder about the whale bones you find. I wrote this with you in mind, those of you lobbying at the United Nations about deep ocean ecology. . . . And you, the ones who feel cut off from nature. And you, the people who prioritize nature in your lives. And us, the people who are anxious about climate crisis."[106] Her hope, always, is that we first imagine "a world where queer Black feminine folks are living their most abundant, expressed, and loving lives"; and then treat the planet with the same love and care we hold for Black femmes in that dream world.[107] And so, adapt toward a future where a next generation of little Alexises can play in the surf and compose lullabies.

In summer 2019, Nia and I went to the beach almost daily; in summer 2020, we didn't go once. Caution-taped, police-patrolled shores elicited grief, fear, and outrage from millions of Southern Californians who, like us, could see the Pacific but not touch the waters. "It is telling that many beaches in California had to be shut down during the pandemic because too many people were drawn to them. The beach gives us opportunities to exercise and offers moments of mental peace and relaxation, especially during difficult times," water quality scientist Luke Ginger reflected. Even when beaches reopened with new social-distancing guidelines, he cautioned, beachgoers should keep in mind our temporary loss of beach access is a "glimpse into what our future holds": "We still face the reality that soon there will be less beach for all of us to enjoy," because "depending on our response to sea level rise and our approach to coastal development, Southern California is predicted to lose between 31% and 67% of its beaches" as global warming swells the Pacific. To keep losses close to the minimum 31 percent (since climate change has already made some beach loss inevitable), Ginger urges Southern Californians to support legislation against coastal drilling, to urge state and local governments "to prioritize safety, equity, and access when creating reopening plans for our beaches," and to participate in beach cleanups and education efforts. "Our actions now can ensure we give our disappearing beaches a fair chance at being saved," he hopes.[108] But if the ocean is a queer, disabled, OG femme of color, as Berne and Peña imagine the rest of the blue planet, *fair chances* aren't something that come often or easily for her. Survival will only be the result of wade-in after wade-in, fight after fight, in ways that can never be called fair, just, or equitable.

Matt, Nia, and I also planned two trips to the South Florida coast in 2020, one for Nia to compete in the cheer world championships and the other for Matt and I to give talks at the University of Miami. During our Miami trip, set for late March, I hoped to meet Peña and other (F)em-power members in person. While COVID prevented me from adding that air travel to my carbon footprint, its blossoming online landscape enabled me to attend a (F)empower virtual healing circle, "Heart Space: Medita-tion and Healing Circle for Black Folks," on May 30. Facilitated by Emani Castillo, this virtual "space for us to hold each other through the times" brought together Black femmes from Atlantic and Pacific coasts—Florida, Massachusetts, New York, California, Oregon—to share tangles of feelings many of us hadn't spoken during quarantine. Peña closed the workshop with an excerpt from June Jordan's poem "From Sea to Shining Sea" (1985). "This was not a good time to be a tree / This was not a good time to be a river. . . . This was not a good time to be gay / This was not a good time to be Black / This was not a good time to be a pomegranate or an orange / This was not a good time to be against the natural order," the poem laments the Reagan years' environmental and social violence. But it turns its own formulation around: "This is a good time / This is the best time / This is the only time to come together / Fractious / Kicking / Spilling / Burly / Whirl-ing / Raucous / Messy / Free / Exploding like the seeds of a natural disor-der."[109] The year 2020 was not a good time to be a Black femme, whether you're Muva Earth, Helen, Ashley, Emani, or me; and the year 2020 was a good time, the best time, the only time for Black femmes to come together and demand livable futures. *Who's that young girl dressed in blue? / Wade in the water / Must be the children coming through / God's going to trouble the water.* Wade in, femmes; wade in until the beaches are yours.

Juliana Huxtable

Black Witch-Cunt Lipstick and Kinky Vegan Femme-inism

(For Dara, Black vegan lifelines, and the most fiery Pisces love)

Attention, small animals of the jury: this court is definitely *not* in order. The defendant, "a female albino African clawed frog representing *all animals* or *the animal as such*, stands accused of: being disgusting; making people feel disgusting; cannibalism; and, the murder of everything."[1] Sleek in a pinstripe skirt suit with lipstick glowing mauve under the lights, her attorney sits behind a nameplate emblazoned "Juliana Huxtable, DEFENSE." Welcome to Huxtable and Hannah Black's *Penumbra*, an "Anthropocene daytime procedural" staged at Performance Space New York May 15–16, 2019.[2] A wildly (pun intended) absurdist mash-up of medieval animal trials and contemporary Judge Judy–esque antics, *Penumbra* pits Huxtable and her client—a live frog wheeled to the stand in a glass tank—against prosecutor Black, with a bird, flies, a whale, a spider, and an extraterrestrial as witnesses and an ant colony as judge. "You will hear the defense argue that it is the human who has maintained the division of life into animal and non-animal, between so-called thought and so-called experience, but they are completely wrong," Black warns a jury of shadow animals. "We have tried to hold on to the collective being. But the animal has continually refused to speak to us."[3] After a barrage of questions hurled at squawking, buzzing witnesses—Where were you on 9/11? Is it true you socialize with dolphins? What is your stance on sharks? Can you confirm that you eat shit? Can you confirm that you ruin summer?—the trial ends when Huxtable fastens a dog collar around Black's neck and leads her from the courtroom on all fours. Black's human arrogance is finally brought to its pantsuit-clad knees and *likes* it.

Art critic Charlene Lau sees this surprise ending as "a final gesture of dominance and humanity's eventual submission to the natural world."[4] Erotic dominance between Black women playing with their inner animals: yes, please. But by the end of *Penumbra*'s absurdity, viewers should be clear that any natural world Huxtable demands submission to is a perverse, anti-essentialist, artificially colored version of nature. Huxtable's kinky take on the natural world became public long before she forced Black to her knees in front of a caged frog. In her work as a DJ, performer, model, blogger, poet, novelist, photographer, visual artist, vegan, and witch, Huxtable playfully, provocatively explores possibilities for the kind of "intimacy with the inhuman" that geographer Kathryn Yusoff calls "Black Anthropocenes": visions of the natural world where Black folks' imagined closeness to animals, things, and monsters is "repurposed . . . and formed into a praxis for remaking other selves."[5] These *other selves* may be the robotic-sounding vocals of her electronic club mixes, or the "REAL DOLLS, ANIMATRONICS, FAUX-HUMAN ACCESSORIES" of the cyberspace avatars populating her poetry collection *Mucus in My Pineal Gland*.[6] And Huxtable's inhuman-intimate other selves certainly include self-portraits in her series *Universal Crop Tops for All the Self Canonized Saints of Becoming*: inkjet prints *Vogue* likened to "Internet meme[s] made by aliens," where Huxtable, nude body painted "toxic shades of sage green and violet," styles herself as a "cyborg, cunt, priestess, witch, Nuwaubian princess"—name-checking the Nation of Islam sect Nuwaubian Nation, which (Huxtable says) "believes black people are the descendants of lizard aliens . . . like Animorphs before there were Animorphs."[7]

Who *wouldn't* want to paint themselves into a lineage of Animorphs? Skeptical of politics invested in "over-performing humanness," Huxtable taps into Black near-inhumanity as a renewable source of political possibility, fun, and Afro-zoological resistance.[8] Starting from the premise that "white supremacy is both anti-Black and anti-animal,"[9] Black vegan theorist Aph Ko coins *Afro-zoological resistance* to describe why "black experiences with zoological racism (racism anchored to the human/animal binary) should not be treated as an inconvenience to animal rights theory" but can instead "be used to bolster our understanding of both what 'animal' means and how the category of *Homo sapiens* does not necessarily provide refuge from zoological terrorism."[10] As a Black intersex trans femme, Huxtable extends this politics to call out *zoological transphobia* that aligns transition with animalization. "In a lot of ways, anarchy of identity is something I do believe in," she owns. "Like when [conservatives] say, 'If we allow men to become women, then they might as well just be a bunny . . . ,' well, my mentality is, 'OK, bunny. Go.' Because if you fight back directly you only reproduce the same essentializing forms they are enforcing."[11] Huxtable's frog defense in *Penumbra* plays with this transfemme-inist zoological resistance. Frogs became a focal point of trans-insensitive environmental campaigns after a 2008 study of increasing numbers of "'hermaphrodite' frogs (male frogs with ovaries growing in their testes)" led anti-toxics activists to warn that "the rising incidences of male-to-female gender shifts and intersex conditions observed in the 'lower' species of animals, such as frogs, fish, and salamanders, represents the newest 'canaries in the coalmine' portending an uncertain fate for human maleness and for the future of normal sexual reproduction."[12] Rather than denying that twenty-first-century male frogs *really* are intersex or showing why trans folk *really* aren't animals, Huxtable asks, "What is at work in the anxiety surrounding that?"[13]

Amplifying trans (species) anxiety to a fever pitch, then forcing it to its knees, *Penumbra* debuts at a pivotal point in Huxtable's career. After her work generated buzz at the New Museum Triennial and Art Basel Miami Beach in 2015, she opened her first solo gallery show, *A Split during Laughter at the Rally*, at Reena Spaulings Fine Art in May 2017. Her second show, *Interfertility Industrial Complex: Snatch the Calf Back*, followed at the same gallery in October 2019. Both shows, which combine inkjet prints, videos, and text, explore "a whole concept of human-animal trans-species, inter-species genetic modification, furries, etc. . . . a whole world where I am thinking about the human-animal encounter, which activates lines of inquiry that are really exciting to me right now."[14] Self-described theory head Huxtable styles her zoological inquiries in a very different tone than theorist Ko's measured seriousness, though. "I'd rather my work be intelligent *and* funny," she says, noting her aversion to judginess and self-importance.[15] "BLUE LIP BLACK WITCH-CUNT" (her Tumblr heading) infuses her art with a queer, kinky spin on *conjuring humor*: a practice Glenda Carpio teases out of "the rich tradition of African American humor—from the trickster tales of Brer Rabbit and Brer Fox to the John and Master slave stories and the tradition of signifying, of toasting, of playing the dozens," where, "through gothic, grotesque, and absurdist comedies of the body, through stinging satirical narrative defamiliarization, through hyperbole, burlesque . . . black humorists have enacted oral, discursive, cursive, and corporeal rituals of redress."[16] In its quest to redress the humorlessness of TERFs, transphobic environmentalists, and climate change deniers, Black witch-cunt humor is as merciless, playful, outrageous, and boundary-pushing as a twenty-first-century animal trial.

Capitalized into a feminist pun, the CUNT-ness of Huxtable's BLACK WITCH-CUNT humor casts its own transfemme-inist resistance. Black trans women are outrageously, no-holds-barred funny, straight popular culture often imagines—but only as the butt of transmisogynoir jokes. In the wake of comedian Lil Duval's July 2017 appearance on hip-hop radio show *The Breakfast Club*, where hosts allowed his jokes about killing a transsexual partner and laughed at the deliberate misgendering of Janet Mock, Black trans activist Atlantis Narcisse responded bluntly, "We're considered a joke. They still look at us as men dressing up, playing in women's clothes."[17] For Black trans femmes to weaponize humor for their own creative, perverse, animal-loving, freedom-seeking purposes—for an artist like Huxtable to conjure a reversal spell that will set transmisogynoir "stereotypes in disturbing motion . . . inhabit the images, exaggerate them, and dislocate them from their habitual contexts," as Carpio describes *conjuring humor*—is to invoke a witch-cunt humor that's as uncompromisingly pynk as it is Black.[18] Huxtable's satire is hot-pynk Black witch-cunt humor that laughs at the idea Black people can ever be free without claiming the power to transform ourselves into Animorphs, demigirls, or power bottoms; and luridly questions why we would ever want such a pallid version of freedom.

Huxtable aestheticizes her laughter through the highest of high-femme media: lipstick. Her faux-neutral matte in *Penumbra*—which ends up being not so neutral under the theater's lights—stands in contrast to her signature cyan lipstick: a shade that pops as an iconic signifier of her nightlife persona, the heading on her Tumblr page, and the inspiration for MAC Cosmetics' ultrapigmented #SHOCKVALUE lipstick. "The language and intelligence of how you dress or how you do makeup—questions that can easily be reduced to 'fashion' or 'style'" are art forms for Huxtable, who taps them as "a primary source of developing parts of my practice" and a tool for visualizing anarchy of identity.[19] "Lipstick plays into our confusion of identity. Makeup ads are always asking who the real you is, and how you should let the real you shine through. Put on a lipstick and let the person inside come out. But, who's inside? And why don't I know who they are?" an interviewee asks Jessica Pallingston in *Lipstick: A Celebration of the World's Favorite Cosmetic.* Bouncing off sources who describe how lipstick brings out their inner warriors, princesses, devils, vampires, madwomen, and church ladies, Pallingston offers, "How we dress the mouth reflects what we need it for, use it for, and it lets others know to what extent it is being used as a weapon."[20] Huxtable's Reena Spaulings lipstick imagines how to dress the mouth when we're done "overperforming humanness" and ready to start highlighting our *otherness*: when instead of finding "the person inside" we want to connect to the reptile, farm animal, winged beast, or endangered species within.

An art of self-expression, lipstick application is also technology of transition. When she was in eighth grade and longing to start hormone therapy, Janet Mock remembers, "My most prized possession was my lanyard of Lip Smackers. My mom bought my first one at Long's. . . . I tore it out of the confines of the paper package, which read 'all the flavor of being a girl'. . . In the car, I draped the black lanyard around my neck with a single green plastic balm dangling. I proudly dangled my girlhood in all its fruitiness. It cost only $2.99."[21] "The process of learning to wear lipstick for the first time wasn't 'just for fun,' or an experiment," Jacob Tobia explains in a conversation about their memoir, *Sissy: A Coming-of-Gender Story.* "It represented a lifetime of healing, summoning the trans revolution I so desperately needed. Clothing, makeup, and accessories are so much more political than we ever give them credit for."[22] For Huxtable, too, shocking-blue lipstick became "an important look for the artist that helped to affirm her sense of sexuality and personal identity," Michael Bullock reflects.[23] Of course, the conservatives who (Huxtable imagines) "say, 'If we allow men to become women, then they might as well just be a bunny'" rebuke lipstick technology: one commenter scoffs that nonsurgical transition "is not going to make you a woman any more than putting lipstick on a monkey."[24] But isn't that kind of transphobic, femmephobic, speciesist logic exactly why Huxtable wants to write theories in lipstick in the first place? "Because if you fight back directly you only reproduce the same essentializing forms they are enforcing," she continues, and her interviewer affirms, "Indulge their logic, then push it 'til you blow their mind, yes."[25] Juliana Huxtable DEFENSE weaponizes lipstick, trans-species-ism, and Black witch-cunt humor to flabbergast transphobes and, as Ko puts it, "make better and more compelling arguments on behalf of animals than traditional animal rights activists."[26] Always keeping small-mindedness on a short leash, her defense does *not* rest.

SYLVIA THE CAT

In 2000, Val Shaffer shot a series of black-and-white photos of Sylvia Rivera in front of the homeless encampment where she lived on the Hudson River. In my favorite, Sylvia balances on rocky ground wearing kitten heels, stockings, and a minidress, her windblown hair setting off pencil-thin brows and dark lipstick as she holds a cigarette with one hand and cradles a tuxedo cat to her cheek with the other. Rivera—raised in the Bronx by an abusive, queerphobic grandmother after her mother's suicide—started wearing makeup in fourth grade and ran away at ten to live as a girl in Manhattan. There she met Marsha P. Johnson, who helped her with lipstick and foundation, fed her, and shared strategies for survival on the streets. Houseless on and off for decades, Rivera created family with trans women, queers, and non-human animals who lived on the piers with her. When Randy Wicker interviewed her in the encampment in 1995, she started the tour of her neighborhood by introducing a black-and-white cat cleaning her paw.

"I call her Miss Tacky. And then I got her sister who looks like her and I call her Shady, Shady Brook Lane, and then we got Bruno. I think the other two are sleeping. We're going to give them to . . . an area for the elderly. Because we want them to get good homes. And the moms we're going to keep, it's called Sylvia the Cat," she smiles proudly. "Miss Terry did name her cat after me."[27] Being likened to a black-and-white street cat was no insult to Rivera; she welcomed her namesake as part and parcel of the interracial, intergenerational, interspecies resistance she fomented on the piers.

Mother of two movements that changed the US political landscape—gay rights in the Stonewall era, trans rights at the turn of the millennium—Sylvia Rivera was also a mother cat. "Animal doesn't just mean 'cat' or 'squirrel' or 'cow.' Animal is a label. It's a social construct the dominant class created to mark certain bodies as disposable without even a second thought," Ko remarks. "Animal is a signifier that is always convenient and changing, and any group the dominant class deems unworthy is immediately branded with this label."[28] Sylvia the houseless feline and Sylvia the human were both animals in this sense, the human as resolutely unherdable as the cat. "Sylvia was a very disruptive person who entered movement spaces and demanded to be heard and wasn't afraid to break the rules, make people uncomfortable, and push for things that were unhearable inside some of the white-led gay and lesbian politics that were more dominant," trans activist and law professor Dean Spade remarks.[29] If Sylvia Rivera hadn't been so felinely intractable that she moved out of her grandmother's house rather than give up lipstick, where would all of us queers be?

As a no-holds-barred tuxedo cat lover with (only half-joking) faith in the coming feline revolution, I was touched by always-fiery Sylvia's matter-of-fact, tender, Cancerian care for her feline companions. "We expected nothing better than to be treated like animals—and we were," Rivera described pre-Stonewall police treatment of trans women.[30] Decades later on the piers, she advocated for a community where houseless animals and houseless trans women were once again treated alike: but this time, that meant both treated as innately deserving of shelter, food, care, clean surroundings, love, dignity, and beautiful names. Like Sylvia the cat.

CAN DEMONIC SUCCUBI
SAVE PLANET EARTH?

Hey hey, ho ho, Donald Trump has got to go! We want a LEADER, *not a creepy* TWEETER! *It's* TIME *to* FIGHT, *nasty girls u-nite!* As Huxtable prepared her first solo show in early 2017, Manhattan was careening into political hyperdrive around her. A single week of February witnessed a mock funeral in Washington Square for the US presidency, a demonstration in Times Square against Trump's Muslim immigration ban, a rally at the *New York Times* office for freedom of the press, and a march at the Stonewall Inn protesting a rollback of protections for trans students. "In this time, every week a new hyper dramatic policy happened. Like, 'This week all black babies will be grinded with a meat grinder,' and that's a policy so now we have to go protest that. This happened back to back to back, to the point where I felt like I was intentionally exhausted," Huxtable relates. "When a protest was set up because they were banning gender non-conforming and trans people from going to the bathroom, [my friend] Bailey and I figured we should probably go to the protest. But while we were doing this and holding signs and singing chants, both of us looked at each other and we burst out laughing. It felt like a really productive moment and that jadedness and tragedy, but also comic moment, was a place I wanted to work from."[31] The moment inspired her show's title, *A Split during Laughter at the Rally*, as well as its political critique: "I felt disillusioned not just with the structures of power but also with the formats for political engagement that currently exist. I felt a little bit of absurdity."[32] Huxtable conjures Black witch-cunt humor in *A Split during Laughter at the Rally* as a ritual of redress not only for the "hyper dramatic policies" that ushered in the Trump era but for the incongruity of activist tactics that seemed to be frantically trying to empty the ocean with a spoon.

For the show, Huxtable made paintings loosely based on the style of Black Panther Party (BPP) Minister of Culture Emory Douglas, who illustrated the BPP newspaper and posters with images Amiri Baraka calls "ruthlessly funny, but at the same time functional as the .45 slugs pouring out of [a] weapon."[33] She designed campaign-button-inspired magnets with absurd slogans—CROSSDRESSERS 4 CHRIST, THIS IS WHAT A WIKIPEDIA WARRIOR LOOKS LIKE, MISANDRISTS UNITE—to mount the posters to sheet metal on gallery walls. ("The buttons were also just really fun; I loved making them," she owns.)[34] Rounding out the show were a diagram and a digital video on freestanding walls at the gallery's center. Also titled *A Split during Laughter at the Rally*, the video features Huxtable's rally companion Bailey Stiles and members of her artistic collective House of Ladosha in a hyperbolic reimagining of the protest that inspired the show. Marching with placard-waving comrades half-heartedly chanting, "What do we want? Stand up, fight back!" Bailey turns to a friend and admits, "Girl, I am so over this." "These chants are so lame," her friend commiserates, and when the organizer explodes—"Are you fucking *kidding* me?!"—they turn to each other and laugh. Huxtable appears as the film's omniscient narrator, filmed in an extreme close-up of her blue mouth and matching beauty mark. Her lips appear for the first time after a montage where characters tell their motivations for protesting. "I mean, *somebody* had to. So why not me?" Bailey asks before Huxtable's House of Ladosha sister Christopher Udemezue strokes his hair and offers, "I was an indigo child." The film cuts from this indigo child to Huxtable's glossy indigo lips, parted over white teeth and silent for a beat before curling at the right corner and declaring, "Everything feels impossible right now."[35] As the film proceeds, "a close up of Huxtable's blue-lipped mouth narrates theories about the legacy of rhythm as revolutionary communication within black activism, and how that's been co-opted by superficial leftist activism."[36] The narrator concludes: not until the protesters find "a place from which to posit their actions . . . could they stand in something like protest without laughing."[37]

Literally centered in the gallery—projected larger-than-life onto a freestanding wall—"Huxtable's toothy smile," Brian Droitcoeur imagines, leers as the show's "unifying element."[38] That smile jumps from the screen onto Huxtable's magnets, curling upward in "a black-and-white photo of her face where her mouth is exaggerated, big as the Joker's," or grinning in a screen grab of her indigo (child) mouth. Her video lipstick exactly matches the blue peace sign and "BOOP" (Blown Out of Proportion) spray-painted on protestors' placards, coloring Huxtable's femme meaning making as its own kind of protest. "The mouth is an organ of pleasure and a vulnerable way into the body. But teeth form a gate that can block entry, and they're weapons, like the sharp words that can issue from between them," Droitcoeur reflects on the toothiness of her grin. "The way she twists her face into a grinning mask, and isolates the smile, abstracts the body into something else."[39] With Huxtable's clenched-tooth smile as a weapon, *A Split during Laughter at the Rally* challenges viewers to excavate and examine the shaky foundations of Trump-era activism and move to ground where we can "stand in something like protest without laughing." "That it was difficult to parse a clear-cut message or feel-good takeaway only made it feel more timely," said the *New York Times*, reacting to *Split*'s provocations, and quoted Huxtable: "I like a kind of unstable positioning. With a show, you're entering a world I've crafted, and one of the things that I aspire to as an artist is to create a world that can provoke a set of questions."[40]

True to her description, the posters mounted on the reverse of the video wall—*The War on Proof* and *Herculine's Prophecy*—provoke a tangle of questions. Their bold lines, monochrome palette, and dot shading cite Douglas's graphic-design-inspired style. But where Douglas created art as BPP platforms' "extension and interpretation to the masses in the most simple and obvious form," drawn to "cut through the smoke-screens" and to "educate the people as they go through their daily routine," Huxtable flouts the "simple and obvious."[41] This is especially true of *Herculine's Prophecy*, which, as arts organization Kadist describes uncertainly, "features a kneeling demon-figure on what appears to be a screen-print, placed on a wooden table, which has then been photographed and digitally altered to appear like a book cover, with a title and subtitle across the top, and a poem written across the bottom."[42] The capitalized, scarlet HERCULINE across the top, paired with a transgender vector icon, evokes nineteenth-century French intersex memoirist Herculine Barbin; and the counterbalancing nude figure at the bottom, kneeling with a flat chest and hairless vulva facing viewers, poses as a demonic inverse of full-breasted and penised Greek god Hermaphroditus. Two years earlier Huxtable herself served as muse for a reimagining of Hermaphroditus: Frank Benson's 3-D scanned sculpture *Juliana*, displayed at the New Museum Triennial. "Benson's statue made in her likeness was a post-internet response to the Louvre's classical Grecian sculpture *Sleeping Hermaphroditus*. Like that ancient artwork, Huxtable's naked pose reveals body parts of both sexes," describes Antwaun Sargent. "However, Juliana updates the abashed *Hermaphroditus* with a futuristic metallic sheen, a 'mudra' hand sign, and a bold gaze that challenges the viewer on ideas of femininity and representation."[43] When she modeled for *Juliana*, Huxtable "thought 'Well, I guess probably more good will come out of this than not'"—but ultimately, its display felt fetishizing. Her disembodied "iconic blue lip" in *A Split during Laughter* is one response: "I used the lips because I was tired of using myself, having myself be the center of everything, and so for the first show I was like, 'I don't want to trap myself in a situation where it continues to be about fetishizing me and my body.'"[44]

Herculine's Prophecy offers another response. No one who heard Huxtable describe her "complicated" relationship to *Juliana* would be surprised at her reimagining Hermaphroditus, again, in her first show: but why recast the flying god as a tattered-winged, cloven-footed, long-tailed demon? One answer hovers in the poem at the demon's feet: "Our Holy Mother Gaia [Hypothesis], Mentor of Witches / Who flagrantly tempts good men with your health / Salacious in your craving for the suns virile fertility." "I was thinking about the intersection of Christian evangelicals and ecofeminists who both gender the world and their rhetoric around the apocalypse, or the prevention of the apocalypse, as dependent on a female-gendered notion of the earth," Huxtable explains. "Right-wing evangelicals see the earth as a salacious whore who's ultimately seeking her proper punishment," while "ecofeminists . . . are promoting an idea of the earth as Gaia, this sort of earth-mother being that needs to be protected, that's being raped and pillaged and violated by the unhinged progression of industrial capitalism."[45] Evangelicals and ecofeminists alike build worldviews on sexual dimorphism—hard lines between feminine and masculine, the earth and her oppressors—that leaves nonbinary and intersex folk no ground to stand on. Femmes with no future, women-identified intersex folk like Barbin and Huxtable are cast as "limit-figures that become interred in the ground upon which legitimate, recognizable, and acceptable" political platforms are erected.[46] So does Huxtable respond by manifesting a Hermaphroditus as gloriously natural as the cisfemme-ininities idealized by "Gays for Gaia" (one of her magnets' slogans)? No, *no*, of course not. "Rather than policing or merely mapping the logic of the opposition," Makayla Bailey writes, "Huxtable deftly deploys the imagery and language it fears most, unpacking the fertile absurdity of these arguments by stretching them to their absolute, improbable limit."[47] If traditional ecofeminists and evangelicals both claim earthly paradise, Huxtable wants *somewhere else* to live.

Kneeling in the corner of the poster with legs, wings, mouth, and eyes spectacularly wide open, *Herculine*'s demon—like Barbin herself, who declared, "I soar above all your innumerable miseries, partaking of the nature of the angels. . . . You have the earth, I have boundless space"[48]—bypasses claims to natural (trans)femininity and flies toward *reclaiming monstrosity*. To reclaim monstrosity, intersex theorist Hil Malatino writes, "is nothing short of the embrace of a specifically antihumanist ontology, one with possible decolonial potential. To embrace one's status as a 'made thing' is to reject the fallacies of human autonomy, individualism, and self-sovereignty so central to modern Eurocentric conceptions of human being."[49] When Benson sculpted *Juliana*—a realist, life-size nude literally on a pedestal, replete with fabulous details of purple lipstick, Senegalese twists, and mudra to suggest his model's "human autonomy, individualism, and self-sovereignty"—his intention in re-creating Greco-Roman hermaphrodite sculptures, he clarified in the Triennial catalog, was to update figures that "symbolize the human ideal."[50] But Huxtable's monstrous nude refuses to idealize or futurize the human, a species whose anthropocentrism brought on environmental disaster in the first place. What would environmental justice look like if we imagined the ideal future earth not as a place where humans continue to live on our own, clearly destructive terms, but where "demonic succubae" (as Huxtable calls them in her poem) inherit the earth?

Now, Huxtable's sparse poster doesn't draw this intersex succubus-positive future earth for us. She challenges us to imagine it ourselves, somewhere in the out-of-frame her demon gazes toward. And diving into that out-of-frame in the spirit of Black witch-cunt humor, I'm taking up her challenge with some help from *futanari* erotica. In the 1990s, futanari—intersex characters from Japanese folklore—became popular in anime, generating a pornographic subgenre abbreviated as "futa." Kinky US-based writing team Angel Kitty entered the genre in 2017 with their punning series *FutaWorld!*, about a future world where "the male population has declined rapidly! Luckily some ladies—known as futas—have evolved something 'extra' to compensate, and their big surprises make for some steamy stories!"[51] In one branch of the series, *FutaWorld! Sci-Fi*, "not only are female humans born with something extra, but faster-than-light space travel makes it possible for them to travel to new and exciting worlds."[52] In the other, *FutaWorld! Fantasy*, "the land is populated with seductive witches, sexy monsters, and lusty women of all shapes and sizes who share one thing in common—a huge, naughty futanari surprise!"[53] In 2018, *FutaWorld! Fantasy* offered a four-part *Futa Succubus* series. Blond, buxom protagonist Anya summons a succubus—a demon who has sex with humans in their sleep—to impregnate her when her abusive, alcoholic husband can't. Nevan, the dark-skinned, full-breasted, huge-cocked futa succubus who visits her dreams, falls in love and convinces witch Astrid to give her a mortal form so she can live with Anya and their cambion (half-demon) child. Nevan shows up at Anya's house, wrests her from her husband, and takes her to visit Astrid—who sneaks them a sex potion. *Futa Succubus* climaxes (pun intended) in a threesome where Astrid's clit grows into a penis, inviting ecstatic, pregnant Anya to both penetrate and be penetrated by her. Their futa/future world ends overflowing with gender and sexual possibilities, hybrid (cambion and mixed-race) progeny, magic, and orgasms.

Fun, yes: but what kind of environmental justice could emerge from replacing the earth mother with a futa succubus? Certainly one that resists what Giovanna Di Chiro—in her discussion of panics over "hermaphrodite" frogs, alligators with tiny penises, and other "feminizing" effects of endocrine disruptors—calls *econormativity*, an anti-toxics alarmism that "adopts the potent rhetoric that toxic chemical pollution is responsible for the undermining or perversion of the 'natural': natural biologies/ecologies, natural bodies, natural reproductive processes."[54] Not only does econormativity's horror at "gender trouble" alienate trans, intersex, and queer folk; it "can work to reinforce the dominant social and economic order (the forces actually behind environmental destruction and toxic contamination of all our bodies and environments) by naturalizing the multiple injustices that shore it up."[55] Building on the insights of disabled trans theorist Eli Clare, Di Chiro concludes, "While those bodies, communities, and environments that stray from the 'normate' may be hated, impoverished, and poisoned . . . seeing and knowing from non-normate positions may offer outsider views for imagining new, just, and sustainable ways of living on the earth."[56] Sustainable environmentally, of course, but also sustainable in the holistic way adrienne maree brown means in *Pleasure Activism*: "What feels good is sustainable. When my body feels good, my life feels good, and I want to keep going, and fight for my right to exist and love and grow and evolve."[57] Creating paths for bodies to grow, cum, change, and reproduce in all the ways, futa succubus futures *feel good*—and motivate us to laugh *as* activism even as we may laugh at activism. No wonder the succubus in the corner of *Herculine's Prophecy* cracks an open-mouthed grin, echoing Huxtable's smile on a magnet holding the poster to the wall.

A BOLD LIP

For her contribution to Allure's series "My Beauty Ritual," writer and media strategist Raquel Willis—who identifies as "a proud, unapologetic, queer, black transgender woman from Augusta, Georgia"[58]—posed for her photo gazing directly into the camera and resting her head in one hand, her glossy lips unsmiling and her left eyebrow slightly raised. Her beauty ritual? She gets it from her mama, Willis tells the interviewer. "A lip gloss girl" now, she began her cosmetics life committed to lipstick—a commitment born of watching her mother's Sunday morning toilette. "She always had a bright red rouge and a bold lip, some kind of red or plum. Those are kind of like her go-to colors. I mean the whole nine yards, I mean, it was like, 'Kevyn Aucoin who?' No, that's my mama," she recalls.[59] Another thing she gets from her mama: her relationship to the rich soil of Georgia. This relationship is no more about feminine folks' innate connection to the landscape than a bright-red lip and crisply curled hair is about looking natural. Like the toil of a Black churchgoing woman's Sunday toilette, labor forges her bond to the unbuilt environment of the US South. In June 2020, Willis posted a photo of herself as a baby in her mother's arms, posed in the furrows of her grandfather's cropland in South Carolina. The image is superimposed on a picture of a cotton field she walked through in 2018. "I had never seen a cotton plant up close, only on the sides of the road from a car. I walked out into that field and held a stem in my hand for the first time. It was almost impossible to touch the cloudy fluff of the cotton without feeling the jagged edges of the boll," she recalls. "I couldn't help but wonder how my ancestors endured running their fingers over and over something so rough. . . . My people have spanned South Carolina and Georgia for nearly 200 years. Their pain, anguish, doubt, resilience, and survival is so thoroughly stomped into that soil. That's why I'll never forsake the South that they endured. There's power in that soil, in that air, in all that they produced while having so much taken from them."[60]

"Most of slaves' waking hours were spent in labor on the land, but this labor gave them knowledge of the land that was intimate and precise, and in turn had material, social, and political usefulness," historian Mart Stewart notes. "For African Americans, nature was negotiated, it was kin, and it was community. African American environmentalism comes out of this history, and the responses of current African American environmentalists, especially in the South, are shaped by it."[61] Pushing back against ideas of the South as a backward environment and environmentally backward, Willis remarks, "When I think about the South, I think of some of the most powerful, resilient, forceful, revolutionary folks trying to shift all of what's wrong in this country."[62] When she thinks about the South she sees revolution, but when she dreams about it she smells the gardenia in her family backyard: "I always just reminisce about that scent and being a child, and I don't know how well you can keep a gardenia bush in a New York apartment, but I dream about it sometimes."[63] Because Black Southerners' intimate, precise knowledge of landscape is a byproduct of labor, yes, but can also be its own source of satisfaction and Black femme pleasure.

CAN HUCOW VEGAN FEMINISM FIGHT CLIMATE CHANGE?

In June 2019—flying into dry mornings, triple-digit afternoons, and record overnight heat—Juliana Huxtable traveled to her hometown of Bryan–College Station (BCS), Texas. Home to Texas A&M (Agriculture and Mechanics) University and a thriving Red Brangus cattle industry, BCS, Huxtable quips, is a "psycho, super conservative small town, but with the ability to amplify and perform with the scale and magnitude of a Texas football college," where people "enthusiastically labor to design, for instance, a machine for McDonald's to more efficiently grind meat."[64] That June, BCS's Brazos County Expo hosted the annual Heritage Days Classic Horse and Cattle Show as well as two shows sponsored by junior cattlemen's organizations. "Agriculture was everywhere in Texas," Huxtable recalls. "My class would take a trip to a farm every week with the intention of 'raising an animal.' At the end of the year, this animal would then be sold at the County Livestock Show, and everyone would participate in that."[65] Everywhere, too, were transmisogyny and queerphobia that closed in when Juliana—diagnosed with the intersex condition Klinefelter's syndrome—started growing breasts and hips at eleven: "I grew up in an extremely conservative area of Texas and my mother was very religious, so the sense of scrutiny really began in my home, family and immediate community. School was difficult for a long time because the bullying was constant and extreme in nature—death threats, attempts to assault me, verbal taunting, food throwing, signs being put on me."[66] Huxtable's mother planned to "treat" Juliana with breast-reduction surgery and hormones until her father intervened, pushing a strict regime of bodybuilding instead. Huxtable's 2019 trip home allowed her to reconnect with family, particularly cousins, "about all of the weird body stuff, and I found out things about what other family members thought of me."[67] And it reinforced parallels between the agricultural and gender-norming enterprises that shaped her upbringing and art: "Agriculture has always been about the modification and the projection of ideal traits. We, as humans, do that amongst each other. . . . Some people, no matter what I do, will always think of my work as autobiographical. But I think that it's a way of removing the psychosis of what is happening."[68]

"Texas really came out" (Huxtable says) in her second Reena Spaulings show, *Interfertility Industrial Complex: Snatch the Calf Back*, which opened the fall after her visit to BCS.[69] The exhibition "saw grotesque paintings of Juliana as a bovine-human hybrid jostle for space with hot pink photo portraits of her styled as a sexy bat and posed like a Playboy cover girl," *Hunger* described the show. "Elsewhere, an installation of public-toilet stalls called to mind a history of queer cruising, while walls plastered with tabloid headlines repurposed media shock tactics for a speculative Earth teeming with cow people. Drawing on ideas of genetic modification, fetish, and zoophilia while critiquing industrial farming, the show was irreverent, bold, and not afraid to be funny . . . a reminder that vegans have a sense of humour, too."[70] Cows—livestock that "enveloped our lives" in rural Texas, where, the narrator remembers, "we had boots made of their stripped exteriors, we drank their milks, ate their partitioned flesh, fertilized our fields with their shit, mounted their heads on our walls, and somehow, *still* laid claim to loving them"[71]—are snatched back as avatars of transfemme zoological resistance on the gallery's walls. Her hair twisted into *irun kiko* horns, Huxtable's cartoon-bright, pink-and-purple bovine fursona gazes back at the camera while wallowing in feces and looking over her shoulder seductively in *Cow 1*; sits with spread arms and legs to show off four nipples on her breasts and an udder where her genitals should be in *Cow 2*; and leans over a sawhorse with tubes pumping milk from her teats as she tilts her head back rapturously in *Cow 3*.

At the gallery's center, where *Herculine's Prophecy* and the video *A Split during Laughter at the Rally* stood in Huxtable's first show, three gray bathroom stalls display neon images of Huxtable's cow fursona. Open the door on the right and you find *Ass 1*: a life-sized, rear-facing image of a cow-femme bent forward at the waist, lavender, eggplant-dappled, pink-stiletto-ed legs in the suggestive posture Carol Abrams links to both porn and meat ads. "Rear entry images" of women and livestock, Abrams opines in *The Pornography of Meat*, invoke "sodomy, submissiveness, humiliation, degradation"[72]—objectionably in *The Pornography of Meat*, kinkily and humorously (yes, cheekily) in *Ass 1*. Open the middle door and you find images of another orifice: a video close-up of the fursona's matte pink mouth explaining her interspecies transition. Raised in a BCS-like farming community, the cow-femme remembers through blush-painted lips, she spent "the thirteenth year of my life . . . learning to touch, stimulate, to bring the erogenous zones of our livestock in service of orchestrated agricultural reproduction." As her father taught her to inseminate cattle—to insert fingers into a cow's rectum to see if she's ovulating, stroke her bosom "to let her know she's in goood hands," slide an insemination gun into her vulva—"the heifer looked back at me and made a sound I very clearly understood as 'nneooorrrn' . . . and that's what I would call her until I left home." What the father intended as a "near ancestral rite of passage" into manhood became a passage out of humanness altogether. "Neorn had become something of a teen idol to me, an aspirational mode of being bathed in the jade glow of envy. I secretly longed to be possessed by the farmers of my town as she was: not in the commonplace form of a fourteen-year-old nymph but rather as a heifer myself," the mouth recounts. "I wanted to be bred like Neorn! I actually wanted to *be* Neorn, realized that we were the same since before giving her a name. I wanted the burning desire of the farmer, my sex in service of his empire, to have my swollen teats milked."[73]

You might view Neorn's video as artistically imagined backstory for the kind of characters who romp through HuCow (Human Cow) fetish porn: "videos, often showing women dressed as cows being milked by intricate breast-pumping machines while in bondage gear, or animated hybrid cow-women" who role-play scenes where "the cow exists to submit to (usually) her dominant 'farmer,' who milks her, often forcefully," according to sex columnist Mark Hay.[74] But Neorn's tale presents "just one irresolvable plot complication": "I FELT LIKE I SHOULD BE PAID FOR MY SEXUAL LABOR," the pink mouth concludes emphatically. Neorn's video confessional calls out two forms of sex work that Alex Blanchette attaches to the mass insemination of livestock in *Porkopolis: American Animality, Standardized Life, and the Factory Farm*. Noting that men are overwhelmingly assigned the task of inseminating sows—mounting them to simulate the boar's weight during sex—while women deliver piglets, Blanchette concludes that factory farms' "mass-production of life is underpinned by two forms of sex work: at once the industrial reproduction of piglet bodies mediated by human touch, along with the ardent reproduction of a sex/gender system of binary identity and heterosexuality that is made to extend even across mammalian species."[75] Huxtable's imagined tabloid headlines underscore the perverse logic of these intertwined forms of agricultural sex work. "Sex Slavery and 'Animal Husbandry': The Bestiality Behind Your Beef," the *Daily Argus* exposes, while *Progress* announces, "Activists Unionize Cows Under New Sex Worker Protections," and *Saturday Star* reports, "'Females Are Females!' Zoophile Pornographer Defends Cross-Species Heterosexuality."

Before narrating her bovine transition, Neorn briefly names the other unpaid labor that built Texas's cattle industry. She describes the genesis of her family ranch "from chattel to sharecropping to small-, now quite large-scale, farmers, generations before me, stewards of the land, of its mammal, bird, fish, reptile, and amphibian inhabitants." *Chattel* and *cattle* both come from the Old French *chatel*, moveable property; and in Texas, the state with the highest percentage of Black landowners and largest number of Black cowboys, former chattel often marked emancipation by owning cattle. Some "generous" slave owners, historians Thad Sitton and James Conrad find, sent off newly emancipated workers with milk cows in appreciation of their forced labor.[76] Proving their humanity by establishing themselves as "stewards of the land, of its mammal, bird, fish, reptile, and amphibian inhabitants," freed farmers could let "the livestock, as we were trained to call them, [envelop] our lives" while still disproving their animality; they were cattlemen, not chattel. But, Neorn confesses, "things hit me a little differently than the rest of the lot." While her siblings inherited "arthritis, Alzheimer's, agriculture, passed down from parent to child for over five generations," farmwork drew her to kinks around "desire, discipline, dogma." For Neorn to willingly take her place alongside dairy cows is, in Ko's words, to "abandon our former choreography of resistance, which relies upon stepping on the animal," for Afro-zoological resistance that "requires us, as people of color, to not only note the ways in which we are 'animalized' by the dominant system but also reconsider our own attitudes and behaviors toward literal animals," opening new ways "to work alongside/for nonhuman animals."[77] But Huxtable's Hu-Cow portraits don't "boast the serious, sentimental, and sanctimonious sensibilities found in other texts dedicated to similar ends, including animal rights and environmentalist discourse and art," as Nicole Seymour notes of "animal drag."[78] Pleasurable, perverse, and provocative, Neorn's sex work imagines transspecies encounters that are—to use a phrase from HuCow erotica—full of *creamy surprises.*

Dramatized in a replica of the ultimate, absurd site of Trump-era trans panic—the public bathroom—Neorn's zoological resistance is unapologetically transfemme-inist. If all modifications that "explicitly transform bodily being" are "'trans' practices," as Nikki Sullivan writes, then Neorn's changes from farmer's child to heifer are polymorphously trans.[79] "Neooorrrrn!! rushed from my lips in the mirror, cupping my nipples and dreaming of the day I could surgically complete my journey to quadruped," she recounts. "Nipples multiplied from one to two to then four, my chest expanding like two helium balloons filling. Udders appeared everywhere, teats piercing out from the mounds of my sex organs." Huxtable's tabloids paint such species transitions as sources of controversy and conflict: "Face-Off: Genetically Modified Cow Woman Attacks Trans Activists; 'I May Be Part Cow, But I Am a Biological Female!'" the *Daily Sun* reports, and the *Bulletin* announces, "'Please Stop'—Feminists Plead with Cow-Identified YouTuber to Leave Intersectionality Alone." Just as *Herculine's Prophecy* satirized the trans-exclusionary underpinnings of ecofeminism, these headlines hyperbolize the ciscentrism that routinely circulates in vegan feminism. Genderqueer vegan Lilia Trenkova critiques, "Vegan feminism rests upon the philosophical viewpoint that the animal industry is built on the exploitation of the 'female reproductive system'"—mass production and consumption of milk, eggs, and baby animals—and relies on an idea of *female* they find "hostile to our trans sisters because it places people without uteruses and vaginas into the 'male' category."[80] But Neorn isn't a trans heifer with a vagina *or* a penis: she's an animal without genitals whose femme-ininity overflows hyperbolically from "nipples multiplied from one to two to then four" and udders "everywhere, teats piercing out from the mounds of my sex organs." Postgenital and nonreproductive, Neorn's transspecies, transfeminine resistance to the "order" of the factory farm demands a new breed of vegan feminism.

Huxtable's *Penumbra* collaborator Hannah Black sums up her friend's approach to vegan feminism: "You're both an important militant vegan and super, like, not annoying about it."[81] Yes, Huxtable's Black witch-cunt veganism stems from concern for her health and the health of the planet. She calls industrial agriculture "really dark . . . ethically untenable" and Instagram-rants about defenses of fried chicken as Black folks' "ancestral diet": "GAIA TOLD ME DURING MY LAST DMT TRIP 'MISS ME WITH THE PUS AND PUTREFYING FLESH SIS THAT SHIT IS EVIL AND IS BLOCKING YOUR BLESSINGS' AND I SAID 'SURE THING SIS' AND HERE I AM HAPPY HEALTHY AND NOT TWISTING MY 'ANCESTRAL' TIES TO JUSTIFY INDUSTRIAL AGRICULTURAL GENOCIDE AND THE ACCELERATION OF CLIMATE DISASTER."[82] But—as her reference to a conversation with Gaia during a DMT trip underscores—she never justifies veganism via a relationship to any uncomplicated "natural world." She shoots down Black's joking comment that COVID-19 represents "the triumph of the vegans" and proof "meat is definitely fucked," labeling it pretentious and "annoying"[83]; she owns that her dietary commitment is strengthened because "I like my skin to look good, especially as someone who also likes to do drugs."[84] Hers is decidedly *not* the kind of vegan feminism Rasmus Simonsen ascribes to "[Carol] Adams' discourse," where "the human consumption of meat is . . . rendered not only immoral but also unnatural, while the vegan body comes to resemble something like the spirit of proper, primordial humanity."[85] Proudly improper, drug-enhanced, and interspecies-inclined, Huxtable's vegan feminism commits, like Simonsen, "to challenge, or queer, always and everywhere, the normative demands that are placed upon our genders, sexualities, and diets."[86]

This brings me back, finally, to Neorn's lipstick, which—along with normative divisions between human/nonhuman and male/female—challenges normative demands on makeup. In the extreme close-up of her video confessional, Neorn's lower face is painted the same pale pink from above her lips to the tip of her chin, making her mouth blend into her face instead of stand out; and her ultra-matte lipstick doesn't fully cover her lips, leaving the brown skin visible in the creases to expand as she speaks. Not the color of a "real" cow or a "real" human, Neorn's pink speaking mouth challenges viewers to rethink factory farming practices not because they're "unnatural"—which she is too, always and artistically—but *because they're unjust.* Her chalky lips blur momentarily, warping before she pronounces, "I SHOULD BE PAID FOR MY SEXUAL LABOR." Neorn's protest that cows aren't paid for sexual labor isn't just meant to shock. It's meant to make us think about exploitative conditions *all* workers face on factory farms, where, as Black points out in her conversation with Huxtable, "the abjection of the animal has almost produced this condition of total abjection, so also people who are working there—it's not just like 'oh, it's sad for the animals,' it's also like horrific workplaces, completely fucked work practices."[87] Nonhuman animals (cows) and animalized humans (factory farm workers) both deserve safe, nonexploitative work environments, Neorn would be the first to tell us. Her millennial-pynk mouth directs viewers to a HuCow model of environmental justice for the next millennium, one that demands a safe and healthy working environment for *all* human and nonhuman animals in order to be (to use Huxtable's word for the highest form of rightness) *kewt.*

To flesh out what this millennial-pynk HuCow environmental justice could look like, let me return to erotica. Witness the future earth of Leo Solo's *HuCow Madam*, a series about Ashley Underwood's transformation from New England farm girl to director of the world's most pleasurable HuCow ranch, Milkmaid Resort. Solo begins Ashley's tale by setting the scene in a post–climate crisis world. "A few years before, there had been a global crisis. Cows were just producing way too much methane, and the

UN had gotten together for an emergency resolution," he imagines. "From now on, any organization owning more than 5 cows (in order to let small, third-world farmers still keep their livelihoods) would be sanctioned, and forced to give them up. The meat shortage had been quickly remedied by switching to a more vegetable-heavy diet. . . . The one thing not easily replaced, however, was dairy." German scientists invent a solution: a mix of hormones administered gratis (free medical transition!) to turn women into HuCows. The last hurdle to sustainable milk production proves easy to surmount. "They just needed volunteers for this, but who would want that?" Solo asks. "It turned out, lots of women did! Nothing about your mental state was adversely affected, unless you count a strong desire to be milked and. . . . Well, we'll get to that later. The government and private organizations each paid handsomely for hucows to provide their milk, and everything was taken care of for them, from plush accommodations to delicious meals to custom-made clothing suited for the hucow phy-sique."[88] The most successful HuCow in history, Ashley goes on to raise stud bulls who service Milkmaid Resort workers. (HuCows routinely have sex with each other but crave variety.) HuBulls take classes that "teach the bulls to cook, clean, massage, and in general provide every service that a hucow could desire. They obviously took classes in fucking hucows."[89] Obviously. Welcome to the gloriously unnatural, environmentally sus-tainable, pleasure-saturated future that we all need—and that, like Neorn, we should be unafraid to demand.

TRANSFEMME BIOLUMINESCENCE

In April 2018, self-described trans femme and theory queen Che Gos-sett contributed a guest post to the blog for queer vegan beauty brand We Are Fluide, whose mission is to make cosmetics "joyful and fun—as well as powerful and transformative . . . through providing a platform and amplifying the voices of queer and gender expansive identities and through showcasing queer beauty."[90] In their photo Gossett faces the camera with a thoughtful head tilted left, sporting a black velour shirt

with glitter flecks, vegan-leather collar with a heart-shaped clasp, diamond stud earrings, and deep-purple lipstick. Behind Gossett sits a wa-
tercolor of a small-breasted, generous-bellied Black merfemme whose
maroon tail echoes their lipstick. "Makeup for me is part of relation-
ality, a way of being in and sharing, contributing to but also partaking
of—in a communist sense—the aesthetic sociality of makeup and styl-
ization," Gossett writes. "It is also a way of queering the body and moving as close as I can to being bioluminescent, the shock and vibrancy
and bursting of color, its explosive force, its confrontational beauty."[91]
Bioluminescence among marine animals—including, maybe, human-
nonhuman hybrids like merfemmes?—stands out to land-dwelling
eyes but serves as camouflage by counterillumination in the ocean,
where fish "light up their underside to match the intensity and wave-
length of the surrounding light perfectly" so they can swim away from
predators unseen.[92] And Gossett's purple lip and pastel nails pop as
queer counterillumination, standing out to straight eyes but partaking of queer "aesthetic sociality" that allows them to pod up, as Alexis
Pauline Gumbs writes of marine mammals, learning to "collectively
change direction abruptly to keep humans"—or homophobes—"from
following them" as they move through their element.[93]

"A trans femme writer, an archivist at the Barnard Center for Research on Women," and, at the time, "a PhD candidate in trans/gender
studies at Rutgers," according to their bio on We Are Fluide, Gossett
is an academic and organizer whose work crafts highly theorized,
electrically eclectic reflections "on how blackness destabilizes trans/
gender, the human, and the category of the animal."[94] In their essay
included in *Trap Door: Trans Cultural Production and the Politics of
Visibility*, an anthology coedited by their sibling Tourmaline, Gossett
explores the interrelation of animal and human freedom via the figure of the maroon. The English noun *maroon* comes from the Spanish
cimarrón, meaning wild, untamed creature (e.g., the bighorn sheep,
borrego cimarrón); or runaway slave. "The figure of the maroon," Gossett writes, "troubles both the human and the undomesticated animal

as property. The maroon is escaped property, property on the run."[95] Afro-zoological resistance, Gossett reminds us, can include interspecies lessons in escape: physical escape, counterilluminating to change directions; and ideological escape, evading colonial divides between human/nonhuman, straight/queer, Black/white. These are lessons shared by the marine mammals who, Gumbs tell us, "have most effectively escaped observation . . . the deep diving beaked whales, many of which have never been positively identified by western scientists, the Atlantic gray whales who disappeared during the slave trade and have just recently reappeared." The resistance of those who "refuse to be seen, to be known, to participate when politics as we know them have prioritized recognition by and access to the dominant paradigm. What becomes possible when we are immersed in the queerness of forms of life that dominant systems cannot chart, reward, or even understand?"[96] Cannot chart or understand, when merfemmes and trans femmes are counterilluminated by bright vegan lipstick.

In February 2020, Juliana Huxtable announced the launch of a new party, Off, at Trauma Bar und Kino in Berlin. The press release for the first event included a poem in Huxtable's signature all-caps: "BREAK US OFF / BRING TO A SUDDEN HALT / CAN WE PLEASE MAKE ROOM FOR SOMETHING NEW," the last stanza implored.[97] Of course, that *sudden halt* and *something new* found Huxtable weeks later when Germany entered COVID-19 lockdown. "The weekend before lockdown was implemented I was DJing in Amsterdam, and since then it's been a really chaotic kind of psychological pendulum," she told Philip Maughan of *Highsnobiety*. "There was a month where all I did was read and write. I started a new novel, then I did absolutely nothing for a month. Then I worked on music really voraciously, but then I stopped doing that." Maughan reflects on Huxtable's year: "One unexpected positive of 2020 has been its invitation to form new relationships with the non-human." "I love that there's been so many forest raves this year," Huxtable tells him, "though I'm using 'rave' for lack of a better term. I love that it's also hiking. It's a weird nature trail."[98] A weird nature trail, of course: because isn't that what Huxtable's been blazing all along? And wasn't *more weirdness*—more conjuring of science fictions, communing with forests, hiking toward pleasure—what environmental justice needed in 2020? In an article on the "strangest ways to fight climate change," Sara González points out, "It's time to consider the viability of actions that have not yet been explored, despite how surprising or strange they may seem. From genetically modified humans that create less environmental damage to recycling our own urine . . ."⁹⁹ To HuCow vegan feminism and intersex succubus-positive ecologies, maybe? Don't sleep on blue-lip, Black witch-cunt technologies for change, sisters. They may be the weird nature trail we'll need to wind our way through the 2020s.

CONCLUSION

Where Is the *Black* in Black Femme Freedom?

Running on fire, running, running, running: flames at her feet, flames at her fingertips, lace-front flames streaming behind her, Sha'Carri Richardson crossed the finish line at the 2021 Olympic Track and Field Trials, and in the blink of a mink-lashed eye, a Black femme was the fastest woman in America. "I'm a fucking Olympian!" Richardson shouted into the wind as she blew past the finish line in 10.86 seconds.[1] As she did, it felt like she was winning for us *all*: all us Black femmes, Black queers, Black women, Black troublemakers, unapologetic Blacks who spent the last four years pushing, flexing, sweating, visualizing, strategizing, running against winds, keeping our eyes on the finish line. And now we'd *made it to the other side*. Like (almost) every femme I know, Richardson honored Black women as the fire-stoking forces who guided her through her (Olympic) trials. When she tore past the finish straight into the stands and her grandmother's arms, "that probably felt better than winning the races, just being able to hold her after becoming an Olympian," Richardson confessed. "My grandmother is my heart. My grandmother is my superwoman."[2] When reporters marveled at her distinctive styling—long nails, mink lashes, piercings, tattoos, and tangerine lace front long and thick enough to brush aside Trump's orange shadow—Richardson credited her girlfriend for her winning trial-day look. "My girlfriend actually picked my color. She said it like spoke to her, the fact that it was just so loud and vibrant, and that's who I am," she claimed. "She felt like orange was loud and encouraging, and honestly, dangerous."[3] Seeing ourselves reflected and magnified in her glow, Black women greeted Richardson's win with fierceness and joy. "Sha'Carri Richardson, a dark skin black girl with long weave and nails, is ranked in the top ten fastest women and is cocky as hell," Makayela Bouldes revered. "I'm in love."[4]

But the collective euphoria of Richardson's victory was short-lived. On July 1, the sprinter tested positive for THC (a psychoactive component of cannabis), and the US Anti-Doping Agency (USADA) disqualified her win at the trials and barred her from Olympic competition. Richardson smoked marijuana in the legal-cannabis state of Oregon after learning of her biological mother's death from a reporter: "It sent me into a state of emotional panic. I didn't know how to control my emotions or deal with my emotions during that time. I greatly apologize if I let you guys down."[5] News outlets and social media erupted in outrage as athletes and politicians, celebrities and Black Twitter denounced the racism of Richardson's expulsion for a legal act of self-care. Pointing to a double standard that kept a Black femme from Tokyo while white Olympic soccer player Megan Rapinoe promoted CBD products, journalist Florence Ashley lanced, "White supremacy is banning Sha'Carri Richardson for smoking weed while Megan Rapinoe gets praised for her use of CBD. Highly reminiscent of how crack cocaine is infinitely more heavily criminalized than powder cocaine to ensure the disproportionate incarceration of Black people."[6] US representatives Alexandria Ocasio-Cortez and Jamie Raskin coauthored a petition demanding the USADA revoke Richardson's "punishment, which is not supported by any scientific evidence . . . after she inspired the country with her performance in the Olympic Trials last month." It stressed, "The continued prohibition of marijuana while your organizations allow recreational use of alcohol and other drugs reflects anti-drug laws and policies that have historically targeted Black and Brown communities while largely condoning drug use in white communities."[7] On her way to represent Joe Biden's America in 2021, Richardson was halted by a war on drugs declared by Richard Nixon in 1971. "Drug testing is yet another tool of the drug war, and it's a failure," declared Kassandra Frederique, executive director of the Drug Policy Alliance. "Sha'Carri's suspension serves as a cautionary tale and a reminder of how insidious the drug war is in our everyday lives, far beyond the carceral state."[8]

"Black femme freedom. Defend and protect Black girls always. Period. Period. Period," Jessica Marie Johnson captioned a July 2, 2021, Instagram post of Richardson raising a power fist.[9] In the lead-up to the 2021 Olympics, Black femmes watched the fastest woman in America cut down in ways we *knew* were patently racist; and *knew*, too, are leveled disproportionately at dark-skinned women. Even before the drug test, "the synthesis of her excellence (turbocharged gait, unrepentant demeanor) and aspect (mocha skin, faux lashes, rangy acrylics)"—a combination that "pierced the heart of a segment of viewers aware of how the United States so often regards these features"[10]—rankled a countercurrent who, like troll "Patrick_bateman," challenged, "Who wants ghetto looking trash like this representing America on the world stage??"[11] *Ghetto*—like *intimidating, loud, militant, masculine*—is consistently cathected onto dark-skinned Black women, sociologist JeffriAnne Wilder finds,[12] and novelist Sheridan Davis asks Richardson's haters, "How come we don't see y'all saying that [about] light-skinned female athletes?"[13] Such stereotypes about dark-skinned girls, Lance Hannon, Robert DeFina, and Sarah Bruch document in their research on African Americans' suspension rates, "can subconsciously influence a teacher's assessment of appropriate disciplinary action" and contribute to "odds of suspension . . . 3 times greater for young African American women with the darkest skin tone compared to those with the lightest skin."[14] So was any Black femme surprised when, as Education Post's Tanesha Peeples put it, "Sha'Carri Richardson was tossed out of the Olympics the same way Black kids are tossed out of public schools?"[15] The same way misogynoir and colorism intersect to leave girls and women who are "blackity black black on the track"—as Richardson captions her own Instagram post[16]—vulnerable to being "profiled, punished, and scrutinized . . . everywhere . . . education, health care, employment, cultural appropriation, and the legal system," musician Aja Graydon underscored after Richardson's suspension.[17]

Like *womanism*, *colorism* is a term coined by Alice Walker in *In Search of Our Mothers' Gardens*, glossed there as "prejudicial or preferential treatment of same-race people based solely on the color of their skin."[18] But the volume's opening definition of *womanism*—literally and figuratively placed before *colorism*—describes an antidote before naming the poison: the second entry declares a womanist "traditionally a universalist, as in: 'Mama, why are we brown, pink, and yellow, and our cousins are white, beige and black?' Ans. 'Well, you know the colored race is just like a flower garden, with every color flower represented.'"[19] Because I was finishing *The Color Pynk* while watching my lifetime's fastest Black femme lose a race to misogynoir, I dove back into *Our Mothers' Gardens* and was left asking, How does Black femme-inism imagine a brown, pynk, and lace-front-orange color palette for this century? What does it mean to queer and femme-inize our responses to colorism as deliberately as Richardson queers answers about her hair? Since *Our Mothers' Gardens*, some scholarship has explored colorism and (cis-het) gender; almost none considers colorism and Black queer gender and sexuality. One notable exception, Jamal Hailey, Joyell Arscott, and Kalima Young's "In Between the Shade: Colorism and Its Impact on Black LGBTQ Communities," is rich with suggestions on what scholars haven't yet researched but should. Noting that "media depictions of darker-skinned lesbian and bisexual women often situate them as hyper-masculine" and align Black masculinity with criminality, the researchers pose a barrage of questions that reverberate for Richardson's case: "What are the consequences of darker skin bias on Black lesbian and bisexual women's engagements with the carceral system? How does the double marker of same-sex orientation and darker skin affect their strategies of survival within these systems? Does it extend to their sentencing? . . . [How does] colorism affect their job opportunities and stability?"[20] Similarly, they remark, while "in recent years the experiences of transgender and gender diverse communities have taken center stage as TGNC individuals have become more visible in their fight for equality and better representation in media," attention "is centered on the experiences of White or lighter-skinned individuals," thus "overlooking the experiences of Black and darker-skinned transwomen."[21]

I wrote *The Color Pynk* as a love song to radical Black femmes of every depth of melanin, shade of hair, octave of voice, length of penis, or sign of the zodiac. I love us so, *so* hard and so, *so* much. But ironically, my book on Black femme-ininity was made easier to pitch, write, and publish because I do so with light-skin privilege. I connected to the University of Texas Press while working as a professor at UT Austin, a job whose baseline requirement is a PhD; and whatever femmephobia I fought to get that PhD, my light skin and loosely curled hair rendered my intelligence more plausible to my teachers from predominantly Black elementary schools through very white graduate programs. My PhD makes me credible as a writer; but my *light skin itself* makes me credible as a femme. Darker-skinned femmes, TJ Bryan owns, are persistently "masculine[ized]—automatically viewed, treated, and cruised as butches."[22] But while people may question my Blackness when I speak about Black femme-ininity—because Black folk *stay* questioning everyone's Blackness regardless of skin color—they never question my femmeness. In his own love song of a book, *¡Venceremos?*, Jafari Allen tells the story of a Black queer Cuban who lives two gendered personas with two different skin-color identifications. Walking through the world as Octavio, Allen's interviewee identifies as *negro*; walking as Lili, she applies light foundation, narrow lip liner, and loosely curled wigs to become *mulata*. "The woman he imagined for or as himself, even as negro, with negro parents, is mulata. To be 'successful,' if not completely believable, Lili must practice, perform, and wear culturally uncontested signs and symbols of attractiveness and desirability . . . which in Cuba is La Mulata. Though he and his mother share a rich brown skin color, Octavio cannot even imagine being a tobacco-colored woman," Allen reflects.[23] When Richardson dons the longest wig, nails, lashes, and swag of any Olympic athlete, this femme wears a hyper-femme-ininity so unapologetically *extra* it defies the unimaginability of tobacco-colored womanhood. And when her girlfriend chooses her vibrant hair color, she supports Sha'Carri's femme-ininity with the deep love all Black femmes deserve.

Rendering my own deep love, I end *The Color Pynk* with verses of appreciation for Black femmes whose creative work intentionally pushes back against colorism. I wish I could say that to do so, I pored through show after show, song after song, memoir after memoir that call out colorism and center dark-skinned femmes' stories. But while Black femmes unfailingly create from shorelines where so much—racism, classism, misogyny, erotophobia, transphobia, fatphobia, ableism—converges, the colorism bleeding through all these often remains "the light-skin elephant in the room; seldom talked about but no less visible when we walk down the street, turn on the television, roll over next to your partner in bed, scroll IG, go to the racial justice workshop," as Black trans podcasters Ericka Hart and Ebony Donnley put it.[24] So I focus on texts from two of my favorite sources—reality television and popular music—by Black femme water signs who (with typical water sign unfilteredness) go against the tendency to treat colorism as an undercurrent and bring it to the surface; and I purposefully overread their texts, drawing out every drop of insight I can. I start with the comeuppance of "light-skinned Miami bitches" in *Joseline's Cabaret: Miami*, executive produced and headlined by reality television star and musician Joseline Hernandez. This proud Scorpio, who rose to fame on the *Love & Hip Hop* franchise and left after being denied opportunities to produce there, curates story lines on her own series that draw in viewers with promos of sexy, light-skinned stars—then demote and drag those "stars" for their colorism. From this "ratchet reality" takedown I sweeten toward a "sexy-soulful-amplified take on colorism" in singer Shea Diamond's "Keisha Complexion," a dreamy Pisces ode to glowing melanin.[25] Diamond, whose career took off when megapop songwriter Justin Tranter heard her sing a cappella at a Trans Lives Matter rally, released "Keisha Complexion" as the lead track from her first EP to "share my journey of learning to love the dark skin I was blessed with in spite of the mental programming of colorblind people that refuse to see the beauty in dark skin and have tried to ensure we keep pouring milk in our coffee as black is too strong!"[26]

Both the Scorpio and the Pisces, the television star and the singer, come dressed to dismantle colorism in undress: Joseline wears a black bra and panties, Diamond a pink negligee, as they vocalize their defenses of melanin. That these femmes wear lingerie while laying colorism bare seems apt. In *An Intimate Affair: Women, Lingerie, and Sexuality*, Jill Fields observes, "Private and sexualized, yet essential to the shaping of the publicly viewed silhouette, intimate apparel—a term in use by 1921—is critical to making bodies feminine."[27] For Black women and femmes, light-skin privilege serves a similar function to the one Fields ascribes to lingerie: proximity to whiteness has been critical to making our bodies legible as feminine.

Of course, not every Black AFAB person wants to embody femininity any more than every Black person wants to wear lingerie; but (to return to Joan Nestle's metaphor) femme-ininity should be a garment we should be able to don regardless of skin color. Noting that early twentieth-century euphemisms for underwear and its production included *white goods* and *women's trade*, Fields remarks, "The use of both terms—*white goods* and *women's trade*—to refer to the production of apparel clearly linked with female bodily difference parallels the close association of American femininity with whiteness."[28] But of course, bras, panties, slips, corsets, and other "foundational garments" are no longer fabricated primarily in white; foundations of femininity—and femme-ininity—line clothing racks "like a flower garden, with every color flower represented." If you're phobic of all that color, Richardson, Hernandez, and Diamond are here to tell us, Black femme-inism is coming to enrich your palette.

"I'M NOT LIGHT SKINNED, I'M CARAMEL": DRAGGING COLORISM ALL THE WAY DOWN

"Welcome to Joseline's Cabaret Miami, Bitch"—the series premiere that aired January 19, 2020—opens in the fluorescent-lit, orchid-purple locker room of Miami strip club G5ive, where former dancer Joseline Hernandez earned her title the "Puerto Rican Princess" a decade earlier. In the establishing shot, a cracked, wall-mounted mirror reflects a dressing table cluttered with handbags and plastic bags, half-empty plastic cups, and clear platform stilettos, where two naked dancers stand with their backs to the camera as they disinterestedly untangle and step into fishnets. The camera cuts to a close-up of another dancer's breast as she presses a pasty over her nipple before the first title screen appears. "The ladies know me on camera and off camera so they know I'm really real," Hernandez explains the difference between her show and *Love & Hip Hop*. "It's not fake, it's not flawed, it's not phony, it's not faux, it's for real."[29] Like the overflowing dressing table, *Joseline's Cabaret* is unapologetic about displaying the baggage Black femmes bring to their interactions and altercations, tensions and alliances; like the dancer's exposed breast, it matter-of-factly shows femme-for-femme vulnerability and eroticism other reality shows cover over. A self-declared feminist, Joseline designed her show as an empowerment vehicle for a cadre of Miami strippers, streetwalkers, and hustlers she counts as friends. "I really thought it was just a good idea . . . putting the music together with the cabaret and the ladies in my life and just building a nice story line around that, I just thought it was fucking genius. And it is, it is!" she owns. "I just figure why not bring my real lifestyle, which is coming from the strip club, right?"[30] Housed in a separate room of G5ive from the strip club, the cabaret, Joseline notes, "is some classy shit" where patrons pay for entry to enjoy dancers' artistry, not their full nudity.[31] "At the end of the day," she says, "having the cabaret is empowerment, it's powerful, and it's modern. Let's make something happen!"[32]

But suddenly the opening montage of dressing room realness cuts to black. "What the fuck you hos doing back here?" Joseline's voice-over demands in the dark. The scene fades back to the dressing room, a medium close-up of Joseline in a sequined, cupless bra and jeweled pasties accusing, "You all bitches always stay out of order. Like your hairdos tonight, is out of order. Why the fuck is y'all bitches so upset?" The camera pans to her adversaries, light-skinned, straight-haired dancers Daisy and Chazzity—"Y'all think you're hotter than everybody, but you're not," Joseline reads—and the conflict escalates until Joseline grabs Chazzity's hair and pulls her to the locker-room floor. The screen freezes in a medium close-up of Joseline mid-pull as the sound of a record scratch introduces an imperious new voice-over: "All I wanted to do is help these bitches and they're questioning *me*? The thanks I get is disrespect? Let me take you back to the beginning, and tell you why I had to walk these two-dollar-ass hos like a motherfucking dog."[33] Reneging on its title, *Joseline's Cabaret: Miami* doesn't end with the cabaret's debut on the G5ive stage. Instead, the story arc of *Miami*'s only season builds around the backstage conflicts that lead Joseline to "walk these two-dollar-ass hos" Daisy and Chazzity like dogs, kicking them out of the troupe and disbanding the cabaret days before it opens. "If colorism were a person," journalist Shamika Sanders imagines, "it would be *Joseline's Cabaret Miami* dancers Daisy and Chazzity"[34]; and in a cabaret that's *real* "classy shit," Joseline decides, colorism needs to be dragged *all the way down* before it pushes center stage.

Not merely a set of (bad) attitudes, colorism is a set of practices—"diverse sets of ritualistic exclusionary practices that [hierarchize] complexion by color," notes historian Laila Haidarali.[35] In "Welcome to Joseline's Cabaret Miami, Bitch," the locker room becomes the first setting where the cast rehearses rituals of colorism that punctuate the series. The premiere follows Joseline as she recruits dancers, starting with (then) close friend Daisy, whom she appoints "bottom bitch" and deputizes to bring in Chazzity. She heads to G5ive and meets darker-skinned dancers Lucky, Jaa, and Sapphire, persuading them to join the cabaret despite preexisting tensions with Daisy and Chazzity: "Y'all should be sucking each other pussy, not fighting," she advises. The Puerto Rican Princess convenes her newly enlisted dancers in the locker room to "let them know what's going on." Sapphire is the most vocal about her desire to leave strip club work. "Since I've been down here in Florida the game is so different from what I'm used to," she explains. "You do have men who try to be more disrespectful with certain colors than others." Cutting her off, Daisy initiates one of colorism's most noxious rituals: discounting dark-skinned femmes' lived experience. She points to Lucky and speaks for her: "Me and Lucky are completely different. She's dark skinned—well she's not dark, she's brown skinned and I'm light skinned, but we've worked at the same clubs. . . . Her doing extra because she's a brown-skinned girl, I don't see that." (Lucky never agrees.) Calling Sapphire's stories "ghetto shit," Daisy shares her own ideas on why patrons show her and Jaa less respect. Sapphire comes off too "tomboy and manly," she opines, and Jaa needs a makeover: "You looking like somebody's auntie that smokes Black & Milds at a barbecue," she laughs. "Bitch *you* need a makeover, with your pale ass," Jaa rebuts.[36] The "bottom bitch" discounts workplace colorism even as she perpetuates it, associating Sapphire's melanin with masculinity and Jaa's with dowdy auntiness. "Misogynoir is predicated on the idea that Black women are too masculine and too dark to be desirable," notes Moya Bailey, and Daisy echoes this idea as she throws colorist stereotypes around the club like dollar bills.[37]

In the premiere, Joseline stands determined not to let colorism undermine the cabaret's Black femme empowerment. "I hear you girls. It's dark skin and light skin, dancing and [street] walking and the club and I get it,

I get it," she empathizes. "This is why I'm trying to get to a point where we can put something together, where we can move past this conversation."[38] But when her bottom bitch laughs off repeated demands to stop bullying other dancers, Joseline devises another tactic to end "this conversation": she sanctions Daisy and Chazzity by inviting Sapphire, Jaa, and Lucky to dance in her music video while excluding the light-skinned duo. The next day Daisy and Chazzity arrive at rehearsal unrepentant and attitudinous, eager to perform another colorist ritual: invoking reverse colorism. "I feel like Joseline definitely chose a side," Chazzity sulks in her confessional, challenging, "You want to leave us out because you say we're being mean to these two but you're being mean, you're leaving *us* out!"[39] Ignoring the difference between excluding someone because of their color and because of their color*ism*, Chazzity's complaint about feeling rejected "sends the message that light-skinned suffering—an offshoot of white fragility—is in greater need of addressing than actual anti-Blackness," as Benji Hart writes of light-skinned tears about bad treatment from darker folk.[40] Daisy's comeback is more complex and problematic. "Ever since you befriended Dusty and Crusty . . . you messy," she reproaches Joseline, accusing Lucky, Jaa, and Sapphire, "Y'all are so dumb that y'all don't realize that Joseline's using y'all to look better. It's Beyoncé," she points to Joseline, "Kelly and Rowland," she gestures to Lucky and Jaa.[41] Botching the names of Destiny's Child, she charges that Joseline, too, operates from color consciousness that values lightness even as she discriminates against it: that the Puerto Rican Princess wants to be the lightest (Beyoncé) in her video so she can shine brightest, slinking her way to the top of the color hierarchy.

At this point Joseline calls out the duo's colorism point-blank. "Ya'll was out of line for treating them the way y'all treating them because y'all light skin," she accuses, and when Chazzity demands to know what her "skin got to do with anything," Joseline shoots back, "Because I know how y'all light-skinned Miami bitches act." "What do you know, because you *are* a light-skinned bitch like us!" Chazzity shouts. "Bitch, I don't act like y'all. I don't act like y'all!" Joseline gestures sweepingly as she repeats her claim for emphasis. The scene cuts to Joseline's confessional: "There's something about light-skinned bitches that you can't tell them *shit*. And I'm not light skinned, I'm caramel. I'm Puerto Rican [*scoffs*], I was born on the island. I got a tan."[42] In this twenty-second clip, Joseline offers a light-skinned Black femme primer on how to respond to colorism. First, recognize that while light-skinned femmes aren't responsible for our skin color, we *are* responsible for how we act on our privilege. Yes, Joseline's skin color has benefitted her: Hunter Shackelford acknowledges that while the Puerto Rican Princess's "platform was limited through the gaze of black femme ratchetry and hypersexualization" in *Love & Hip Hop*, "her light skin and beauty allows for her to have the limited platform she has now."[43] But from that platform, she flamboyantly undermines "the structures that imbue [her] with a greater humanity just for being light."[44] When Daisy complains that Joseline's solidarity with Lucky, Jaa, and Sapphire makes her messy, she's not wrong: Joseline is messing up "sets of ritualistic exclusionary practices that [hierarchize] complexion by color" and that Daisy depends on to outearn her colleagues.

Joseline's primer levels up as she differentiates herself from "light-skinned Miami bitches" by explaining, "I'm not light skinned, I'm caramel." Exemplifying Hilda Lloréns, Carlos García-Quijano, and Isar Godreau's claim that many Puerto Ricans' "self-description of skin color [is] at odds with how others would describe them,"[45] Joseline's emphatic rejection of light-skinned-ness declares a self-perception and "*feeling* of color" that defies paper-bag tests.[46] *Light-skinned* is a relative, oppositional term that relies on othering dark-skinned-ness for meaning; but *caramel* is a definition on Joseline's own terms, a shade of brown that's sweet, fluid, and changeable. Sometimes a color descriptor, *caramel* is more commonly a flavor. When Chazzity and Daisy first commiserate about other cabaret dancers, Daisy offers, "You know Joseline's really open-minded, she's—*flavorful.*" "She needs to be selective, not flavorful!" Chazzity protests.[47] Joseline's propensity for embracing flavor in herself and others is inclusive, not selective; she gathers *all* the chocolate, caramel, cinnamon, molasses, and sugar sweetness of brown for her Black femme empowerment cabaret. But Joseline doesn't stop at describing herself as caramel: she explains, "I'm Puerto Rican, I was born on the island. I got a tan." The last phrase is a loose translation of *quemaita*, a Puerto Rican term for a brown-skinned woman of African descent that literally means *a little sunburnt*. Joseline's evocation of her Puerto Rican–ness reminds viewers that, like race, colorism varies throughout the diaspora: she may be considered light skinned in Florida but not in Puerto Rico, purportedly the whitest of the Caribbean islands. "Ultimately, the classification of human complexion by color relies on imprecise and changing cultural values and standards; on sensory interpretations that differ according to time, place, and subject; on language that, despite its growing expansive range, remains finite in its ability to 'fix' color," Haidarali notes. Joseline's proud Puerto Rican–ness includes her dedication to a culturally specific color solidarity she doesn't abandon just because Miami's pigmentocracy offers other options.[48]

"Let's focus on the cabaret, not the bullshit," Joseline commands after her impromptu colorism lesson. The dancers reluctantly gather and Joseline sets simple choreography they botch spectacularly: "Rehearsal was a fucking mess," Chazzity admits, and Sapphire adds, "We look like a *hot ass mess.*" After minimal progress, Joseline breaks for the night. While she says good night to Lucky and Sapphire, Chazzity and Daisy gossip in the locker room until Joseline enters, demanding, "What the fuck you hos doing back here?" The story loop opened in the premiere closes as viewers rewatch the locker-room fight with the context amassed over the five episodes Joseline needed to "take you back to the beginning and tell you why I had to walk these two-dollar-ass hos like a motherfucking dog." "Do I feel bad?" she asks rhetorically in her confessional. "Do I feel bad that I chose the wrong hos? Yes."[49] *Taking a fight behind* Lucky, Jaa, and Sapphire is Joseline's recognition that, as light-skinned activist Benji Hart reflects, "it is dark-skinned Black people who are expected to absorb the aggressions of white supremacy—from employers and landlords, police and politicians, and from other Black people, usually Black people that look and act like me."[50] *Taking their fight* is Joseline's re-aiming of colorist aggression back in the direction it came from—grabbing it, turning it around the way you pull a leash to walk a dog when she won't listen to your commands. No, Joseline isn't sorry for walking Chazzity like a dog. But she dreads telling Lucky, Jaa, and Sapphire about the incident because "they not gonna like the fact that I had to get into a fight behind them. . . . They gonna want to confront those bitches."[51]

Joseline's meeting with Lucky and Sapphire (Jaa doesn't show) goes in a different direction, though. Lucky—on her fifth glass of champagne when her boss arrives—assumes Joseline fought the light-skinned duo for reasons other than their bullying and naively says so. "What the fuck you mean I got in a fight not because of you and Jaa, bitch? I've been rooting for you and Jaa the whole time," Joseline erupts. "I didn't get into a fight because of you and Jaa? Because they been dogging you out, calling you Raggedy Ann, calling you nothing, garbage hos, and I'm sitting out there *taking your fight*? Y'all bitches ran like two-dollar-ass, scary-ass bitches and I was there taking up for y'all, letting them know that I believe in y'all."[52] Outrage at Chazzity and Daisy, deep gratitude to the Puerto Rican Princess: this is Joseline's expected reaction to her decision to wrestle light-skinned privilege to the locker-room floor. But for light-skinned, caramel, *quemaita* femmes, fighting for the *Black* in *Black femme freedom* isn't something to do for accolades. In his op-ed "Why I'll Never Thank White 'Allies,'" Hari Ziyad declares, "I am not grateful for shows of support conditioned upon my gratefulness, or support pre-requiring my thanks—which is always Black labor, too."[53] Lucky and Sapphire work for Joseline in the cabaret, yes; but in the fight against colorist "bullshit," the extra labor of gratitude isn't theirs to perform. By the next day, Joseline realizes her overreaction and apologizes to Lucky. "She doesn't really seem like the type to apologize back but the fact that she did, it really showed me a vulnerable side to Joseline where she's willing as a woman to accept responsibility for her actions," Lucky reflects graciously.[54] Their reconciliation isn't enough to salvage the cabaret, though. Ultimately the mess of *Joseline's Cabaret: Miami*—sloppy dancing, snatched weaves, drunk misunderstandings—dissolves the show before it begins. Instead of ending with the cabaret's debut at G5ive, the finale fades out with Joseline's voice-over: "My vision for the future of the cabaret is some new girls . . . since these other bitches are acting not the way they need to be acting."[55]

Like the cracked locker-room mirror that reflects dancers at G5ive, sometimes Black femme spaces are so distorted by colorism that surface efforts at repair—duct tape, lectures, commands to do better—aren't worth continuing. Sometimes, you have to dismantle your cabaret and return for a second season where "light-skinned Miami bitches" aren't invited and your right-hand femmes are chocolate skinned and flavorful. (I'm describing *Joseline's Cabaret: Atlanta*, where Lucky and Sapphire return as cabaret captains.) Lovely as it would be if can't-tell-them-nothing "light-skinned bitches" peacefully set aside colorist rituals, sometimes you have to fight too—fight colorism as an offshoot of white supremacy. When you do, you open space to replace old rituals with new choreography and build a coalition of femmes who dance in sync. "The performance was great. Me, I was shocked that they actually did that good!" Joseline told hosts of the podcast *We Talk Back* after her Atlanta cabaret debut. Reflecting on Joseline's mentoring, one host remarks, "You identify so much with the underdog. Last season, to Daisy and Chazzity, [Lucky, Jaa, and Sapphire] weren't as put together as the light-skinned bitches in Miami and you celebrated them more." "I don't like fake people," Joseline responds simply. "I like sweet ladies. You not sweet, I'm not fucking with you." Why be flavorless *light skinned* when you can be sweet caramel, and why mess with femmes who don't choose the sweetness of Black too?

"LOVE MY KEISHA COMPLEXION": RITUALS FOR CURING MELANIN DEFICIENCY

Silky in a low-cut, blush-pink negligee offset by pearls, a plush robe, and tumbling curls, Shea Diamond croons into her lover's ear: "You know you really love that Keisha complexion."[56] This is the hook to "Keisha Complexion," a "joyous ode to Diamond's own dark complexion" that "grinds, . . . flirts, and . . . celebrates," *Refinery29*'s Rebecca Farley appreciated of the video's premiere on April 27, 2018.[57] For her first narrative video, Diamond told Farley, she wanted a concept that was *real*. A spectrum away from Joseline's high-drama reality of locker-room brawls, femme-on-femme drama, and general messiness, Diamond's vision of "real" is the quiet sweetness of an "every day homebody with no glam, no stage, and a sexy man that loves me."[58] Set entirely in the protagonist's house, the video stages a self-loving mise en abyme of Diamonds: titular Keisha arranges roses in the kitchen while her man flips through music videos on the living room TV, the star of each played by Diamond. "For me, it was important to express the fact that my love interest has such a strong sense of admiration for my beauty as he literally sees it . . . in the same light as any beauty on TV," Diamond offers. "He's able to see her outside of the visual restrictions [of] TV and media giving men limited access to depictions of beautiful Black skin."[59] "Got me admiring my own reflection," Diamond sings as the star of her video in a video. If *Joseline's Cabaret* plays out the colorist saga of a broken mirror, "Keisha Complexion" creates reflections where dark-skinned femmes meet their images with admiration and affirmation that, as Diamond puts it, "they aren't inadvertent beauties."[60]

Written after a breakup with a color-struck partner, "'Keisha Complexion' is very complicated. I was in a relationship where a guy thought I was beautiful, but he thought I should have been lighter. He did a number on me and my psyche, telling me that he preferred lighter women," Diamond explains. "I decided after that that I wouldn't allow anybody to rob me of knowing that I'm beautiful."[61] But the rejection Diamond sings back to is more than her ex's intimate colorism. Her love song to dark skin is a response to the "melanin deficiency of not only the music industry but all forms of media and major platforms that promote beauty . . . using their privilege and influence to ensure there are no dark spots 'visible.'"[62] Mainstream queer shows like *Pose* and *L Word: Generation Q* feature dark-skinned Black femmes as supporting characters, but none write, produce, direct, or otherwise have creative control of the projects. "How many dark-skinned artists do you see with my complexion?" Diamond asks. "That wasn't a rhetorical question. There aren't many. If you too dark, you asked to lighten your skin. If you weigh too much, you asked to lose some weight. If you're trans and you're my color, trying to do anything— absolutely anything, honey—it's not going to be an easy fight."[63] Like Joseline's cabaret, Diamond's song counters media-standard colorism with undiluted, keep-you-woke flavor: "This song is honoring the mother of everything. This is the strong coffee you're gonna get without any cappuccino. This is pure coffee. . . . [The video] shows this guy being attracted to her, not in spite of her dark skin, but because she's dark-skinned. That message is powerful alone." Where Joseline fights tooth and nail to defend *flavorfulness*, though, Diamond works to catch more (queen) bees with honey. "Coming to you in a pretty way, wrapped up in a bow," Diamond owns, "Keisha Complexion" still "has this political agenda in mind. You're grooving and being an ally at the same time."[64] "You know you really love that Keisha complexion," the bridge repeats in three different intonations, casting its spell to convert all listeners to color lovers.

But what color *is* a Keisha complexion? An ode to "the beauty of Black skin in its natural state, as pure as water and smooth as fine wine," the phrase "'Keisha Complexion' is a revamp—it's like doing reconstruction on . . . 'ebony complexion' adding an ethnic name to it, Keisha," Diamond informs.[65] Most common descriptors of dark-skinned women, JeffriAnne Wilder finds, are "names such as burnt, charcoal, and watermelon child" that "point to a historical bias [against] being dark and so reinforce controlling images of dark-skinned black women."[66] Lyricizing dark skin with a modifier that announces its bearer not as an object but as a subject—a proper noun instead of a common one—Diamond rebaptizes her complexion with a name as decidedly feminine as it is unapologetically Black. "Keisha, and its various spellings, was a name synonymous with the black American hood. *Kisha. Keesha. Kyeshia. Takisha. Nakisha. Mokeesha. Lakisha. Akisha. Makisha,*" novelist Keisha Bush meditates on her name.[67] When she foregrounds *Keisha* as the *first* title word of her *first* release from her *first* EP, Diamond writes into a long hip-hop conversation that evokes Keisha-ness as the essence of Blackity-Black womanhood—and a screen for misogynoir projections. "Keisha has served as a long-running motif in hip hop more often than most black women's names," Lakeisha Goedluck notes,[68] decrying rhymes like Dave East's "Keisha . . . Black but had them Spanish features" or YG's "Young Keshia, so fly, so diva / . . . Everybody in the hood wanna taste her, she was teasin."[69] But Goedluck champions her given name by reminding readers that the root of "so-called black names that end in '-isha' . . . is 'Aisha,' derived from an Arabic adjective that means 'alive' or 'well'" and popularized in the 1960s by Black activists who "helped make unique given names more valuable, more desirable— more empowered as names unshackled by the experience and legacy of slavery which stripped and replaced original names."[70] And Bush fondly recalls meeting a Black American in Senegal who appreciated, "My closest homegirl back home is named Keisha. . . . Keishas have got your back no matter what. Everybody needs a Keisha in their life."[71]

Yes, every Black person needs a Keisha in their life—a femme whose name sounds like Black community, Black pride, and Black alive-and-well-ness—and "Keisha Complexion" showcases one reason why: the Keishas in Diamond's video are artists at recasting colorist rituals that (in the singer's words) stay "fucking up the world of Black beauty." One of these is the persistent centering of light-skinned romantic heroines, a trope "Keisha Complexion" forces out of frame by transforming Keisha into *every woman* on any screen and the *only woman* her lover sees. Explaining her choice to cast herself as every femme character in the video, Diamond admits, "At first, my vision was, I wanted to have the representation of all these [dark-skinned] women. But then I thought, 'Well, the whole thing is to let people know that we're desired as well, so why not have it all men in the video?' And center it around this one [girl]."[72] Diamond's centering and multiplication of *this one girl* (herself) visualizes the kind of Black femme-inine self-regard Kevin Quashie calls *oneness*: "a sense of being capable of and related to everything."[73] As her lover flips through videos, Diamond's Keisha is simultaneously a sexy housewife in the kitchen, a lounging beauty floating in a pool, a regal diva with backup musicians serenading her, and a lollipop-sucking ingenue fanning herself while '90s-style hip-hop dancers flank her: she is *capable of* and *related to* everything and everyone she wants to be. Rather than closing her off, Keisha's flowering into *oneness* is what opens her to Black love—to a Black lover she connects with more deeply because his love starts with her deep skin. "If you knew me you'd gasp / I've never been so unabashed," Keisha sings as her lover embraces her from behind while she holds a yellow rose to her face. "When you say you love my Keisha complexion / In a way I ain't ever respected."

Unabashedly open to a lover's touch so hot she's "breaking a sweat," Keisha is just as unabashedly receptive to stimulation for her other senses—including bright, saturated colors and lights that set off her skin in every shot. The Keisha ingenue is shot under pink light and the Keisha bathing beauty in full sunlight, the Keisha housewife dressed in pale pink and the Keisha diva in bright-yellow with magenta flowers. "In the video, I thought it best to click Black skin in different lights and settings . . . [to] see our images through our eyes in a wide variety of shades and colors!" Diamond offers. "Allowing the viewers to really see the beauty in Keisha's beautiful skin in contrast to bright, vibrant colors and the essence of sexiness as her complexion is kissed by the sun."[74] The video's color palette flouts generations of advice against dark-skinned women sitting in bright sun and wearing bright colors—another colorist ritual "Keisha Complexion" rebukes. In Nella Larsen's 1928 novel *Quicksand*, protagonist Helga Crane recalls the proscription that "dark-complected people shouldn't wear yellow, or green, or red" and silently responds, "Something intuitive, some unanalyzed driving spirit of loyalty to the inherent racial need for gorgeousness told her that bright colours *were* fitting and that dark-complexioned people *should* wear yellow, green, and red," shades to bring out "the luminous tones lurking in their . . . skins."[75] Chafing against the sheer ugliness of colorism, Helga's embrace of color is also a declaration of her right to wear Black femme desire expansively, accessing a full spectrum of wants, loves, and experiences: "She resents the prohibition of bright colors by those who want it understood that black women do not love red. She does. She further seeks the adventure that color usually symbolizes."[76] Never an apolitical aesthetic for Black women, bright color symbolizes "a path to freedom":[77] a rejection of the idea that, as Diamond puts it, vibrancy is "not something that was meant for me" because "I'm too dark, too trans, too fat, too old."[78]

Glowing in her bright lights and colors, poolside Keisha works a palm-leaf hand fan as, "unapologetically, she fans her face calling out colorism for . . . shattering the confidence of those with darker skin by making it more difficult for them to navigate and have equal access to the word beauty."[79] Alluring as she lounges in a lemon-yellow bodycon dress, diva Keisha slides matching yellow nails across her gold necklace as she sings, "Look at, look at me / Got me feeling like I'm on TV." Fans, yellow, gold: these are all symbols of Oshun, a divinity whose iconography burst into Black popular music when Beyoncé styled herself as the Yoruba orisha of sweet water, beauty, love, creativity, and abundance at the 2017 Grammys. While many Beyoncé stans and Yoruba practitioners (like me) rejoiced at this reflection of African divinity in mainstream media, Beyoncé-as-Oshun reinscribes diasporic imaginations of the orisha of beauty as a light-skinned femme fatale. Oshun "is renowned for her beauty and sensuality. She is also a river deity for the Oshun River in Osogbo, Nigeria. Now, what does she look like? Well, since she is an ancient divine deity birthed from people in Osogbo wouldn't we look to *their* ancient ideals of beauty to guide us as to what she may have looked like?" Najaa Young challenges. "A dark, even skin tone, big, beautiful, almond shaped eyes, high cheek bones, gap toothed . . . perhaps. However, in modern representations of Oshun (from Cuba to Compton) she is depicted as a mulatto or light skinned Black woman with long wavy hair . . . and on a good day we are lucky if she's depicted as *dark* as Beyoncé!"[80] Looking like a goddess, Keisha-as-Oshun emphatically *doesn't* look like Queen Bey. "Don't attempt to be a carbon-copy, watered-down version of Beyoncé—You can't out-Beyoncé Beyoncé; she has that covered! Be yourself, find your unique sound, perfect and create your own lane, and ride it like a Tesla," Diamond advises aspiring musicians.[81] And Diamond's *own lane* is embodying and singing a path of Oshun that honors the cosmic African mother of trans-femininity: since as "divine femme goddess of love, ultimate attraction, sensuality, joy, creative justice, and all of the sweetness life has to offer,"[82] nonbinary artist Kamil Oshundara writes, "Oshun is the protector of vulnerable women, children, and the mother of transwomen and non-binary femmes."[83]

From its opening shot of the *not*-yellow diva in yellow to the closing image of the housewife luxuriating in her bath, "Keisha Complexion" celebrates everyday rituals for Blackening Black femme freedom: rituals that rename complexions, recenter reflections, and recolor divine beauty from the quiet, "real," unassuming space of Keisha's home. And while Shea Diamond, whose name is its own ritual—an affirmation ("She [is] a diamond") repeated every time it's spoken[84]—is the only and every celebrant of these rituals here, she opens them for any femme who wants to cast herself as the next Keisha. A recording artist whose professional career began in her late thirties, Diamond consciously sings for a next generation of Black femmes: "impressionable youths that look up to us and . . . are already being told in music through the cis narrative they're not good enough. It's important to inspire and empower!"[85] "The mirror you avoided will one day bring you comfort," she promises youth "born with a beautiful Keisha complexion in a world where people worship lighter skin and think the darkest thoughts about those who don't have it."[86] Insisting on a group dance, Joseline *mentors* a next generation of performers where colorism has no place onstage; but insisting on shining solo, Diamond *models* a Blacker femme future where Keisha-complected stars don't need an ensemble—and *certainly* don't need light-skinned costars—to dazzle. "Look at me, look at look at me. . . . You know you really love that Keisha complexion," her song ends a cappella.

In her narrative videos released after "Keisha Complexion"—the incisive political critiques "American Pie" and "Don't Shoot"; the Black queer, joyful "Smile"—Diamond returns in full shine as the only femme character, a self-affirming signature of her visual landscape. Keeping that signature but adding a flourish, the future Diamond videos *I* dream up add cameos from other women—femmes and studs who lavish desiring gazes on the undisputed romantic lead. If "the whole thing is to let people know that we're desired . . . [m]aking trans seem desirable . . . [m]aking dark skin sexy and desirable," what would it look like to visualize Black women desiring Keisha too? To visualize that Black-on-Black, femme-on-femme, Oshun-on-Oshun sweetness we (can) never get enough of? *Look at me, look at look at me, you got me feeling like I'm on TV.* Ms. Diamond, if you're ever looking to cast a starry-eyed Black femme-inist professor pining at your feet, please know I'm available to you in any way you might require.

"I would say that the problem of the twenty-first century will still be the problem of the color line," Alice Walker predicted in 1983, "not only 'the relation of the darker to the lighter races of men in Asia and Africa, in America and the islands of the sea,' but the relations between the darker and the lighter people of the same races, and of the women who represent both dark and light within each race."[87] And the femmes who represent dark and light within the race too: because the self-aggrandizement of individual Daisies, the self-recovery of individual Keishas clearly, queerly echo a continent of conversations that speak to widening divides along skin-color lines. "There is a growing body of evidence that the racial and political attitudes of light and dark-skinned Black Americans have diverged sharply over the past three decades," sociologist Robert Reece finds in 2021.[88] In the Obama era, he notes, light-skinned and first-generation mixed-race people of African descent increasingly identified as *multiracial* instead of *Black*. Not just "personal" differences in how people identify, light-skin/dark-skin differences in self-understanding influence Black folks' politics. The year Trump was elected, a study documented "that light-skinned Black Americans are more conservative compared to darker skinned Black Americans. Light-skinned Black Americans are less likely to support economic redistribution policies and affirmative action policies, and they are more likely to embrace negative racial stereotypes about Black people."[89] Record numbers of Black men shifted to Trump in 2020, while Black women flanked Democrats, numerous polls show; and while no polls I know differentiate between light- and dark-skinned Black voters, I'd be unsurprised to learn that light-skinned folk similarly skew Republican more frequently than our darker-skinned counterparts. The same way I was unsurprised that though Stacey Abrams's organizing was crucial to Joe Biden's victory, lighter-skinned Kamala Harris—who (coincidentally) lived on the same Berkeley street and studied at the same ballet studio as I did in the 1980s—became vice president.

Femmes, who represents both dark and light within each race, and when and why and how? I urge us to keep thinking on these questions. Because of course, colorism operates in Black queer communities as insidiously as in other spaces: as Ericka Hart lays out in her podcast addressing colorism, "we have to talk about queer light-skinned people" because "all we [Black queers] do is mimic the cis hetero world in a lot of ways. Not just in our gender relationships, but in the ways of who is desired in queer communities: it's totally light-skinned people."[90] But, more importantly, because in the race to freedom dream against melanin deficiency, Black femme creativity will always pull ahead—with our metaphorical lace fronts flying and acrylics blazing our path. You *know* this: if anyone understands that the surface of your body determines *nothing*—that the brown of your skin, the shape of your chest, the bulge of your Calvins isn't your gender, your desire, your worth, your *you*—it's Black femme-inists. Black femme-inists, who, just in the space of this small book, sang how our brains' pynk matter fires pussy power; invented wild nonbinary vaginas from cloth, thread, limbs, and imagination; conjured escape from prison cells that refuse to free Black trans bodies; envisioned udders in place of genitals and play in place of gender. "Perhaps black women who are writers in the twenty-first century will present a fuller picture of the multiplicity of oppression—and of struggle. Racism, sexism, classism, and colorism will be very much part of their consciousness," Walker hopefully concluded her 1983 reflections on colorism. "They will have a record of the struggles of our own times. They will not think of other women with envy, hatred, or adulation because they are 'prizes.' They will not wish to be prizes themselves. . . . They will, in fact, spend a lot of time talking to each other, and smiling. Women of all colors will be able to turn their full energies on the restoration of the planet."[91] Black femmes, *this* is what we're here to do in the Biden era and beyond.

The endgame of the color pynk is *always* empowering the color Black. *Black* femme freedom, now.

EPILOGUE

For My Child

My dearest Nia,

Today is the twelfth anniversary of the happiest day of my life: the first full day I spent with you. Happy birthday, my Virgo Venus. I always felt you chose carefully when and where you entered this world. I conceived you the first month after I went to Louisiana to talk to our ancestors, the river, and the ocean about you; the first month after I chose a new donor; the first month after Barack Obama was elected the first Black president of the United States. I later joked with Black friends who gave birth and adopted in those late-aught/early-teen years, "Oh, we all had Obama babies": children welcomed in a moment of believing the American political landscape might have room for you to be seen as human, and how could we explain that level of naivete to you in 2016? But of course, this world isn't mine to explain to you; and you came here to change it, as definitively as you change your own name.

I wrote this book for you as I've written every book, every vision for a Black femme-inist future that loves you—but you inspired this one in a different way. Because it was you, Nia, who taught me the color pynk. When you were a baby, friends and family gifted me with pale-pink sleepers, changing pads, blankets, snowsuits, dresses—including a dress sewn to look like a strawberry, with a matching green-topped hat. That strawberry dress, I was convinced, was designed with a pink-and-white-cheeked baby in mind. I bought you everything *but* pink things: dressed you in baby blue and purple and red and yellow and green and orange, in

213

love with the browns of your hair and eyes and lashes and birthmarks and skin. But of course, as things always happen with mothers and children, as soon as you could talk you asked for everything you wore, every manicure, every toy you played with in "pink light." "It's a phase," I told myself—and in a way I was right, since for your upper-elementary years, now-babyish pink was banished from your room. But last year, the color pink returned to your walls, closet, and favor just as I was finishing *The Color Pynk*.

While flags were going up in our neighborhood declaring peoples' votes in the 2020 presidential election, I was buying other flags to hang in your room. The sunset lesbian flag swung at the head of your bed, three shades of orange, a bar of white, and three shades of pink coloring your aura at night. (The older, all-pink lesbian flag is never to be endorsed, you explained, since it was made by and for trans-exclusionary lesbians.) I bought a gray, white, and pink demigirl flag for the foot of your bed too. Your school backpack is subtly tie-dyed blue, white, and pink to call out to those who know trans colors (and ignore those who don't); among the many shirts jostling for space with skirts in your closet, one has a decal of an all-inclusive pride flag that nestles that same pink and blue next to brown and black. In the three presidencies that have marked your years so far, you've changed what and where and how and why the color pink means to you, a Black disabled queer child of your time; you've invented your own color pynk. I love you more today than I did yesterday, and tomorrow I'll love you even more than I do today, I tell you every night—and every night, it's true. I hope you continue to love yourself, your Blackness, and your pynk the same way.

All my love, your loving mother,
Me

AFTERWORD

Pynk Parlance, a Glossary

Candice Lyons

This text begins as it now ends, with deep gratitude for the work of Black femme-inist forebearers such as Alice Walker, whose writing has constituted, for generations of Black femmes, a particular kind of purple-tinted litany for survival. The necessity of these interventions is more evident than ever, as we continue, in a post-Trump social landscape still marked by anti-Blackness, transphobia, femmephobia, and queer antagonism, to mourn those for whom that survival did not manifest. From icons we've lost without ever truly knowing them at all to friends taken for daring to imagine alternate modes of existence, we are forever being reminded that "we were never meant to survive," at least "not as human beings."[1]

There *are* other possibilities, however; in fact, Walker conjures them herself in her 1982 novel *The Color Purple*, which offers an alternative (if fictive) queer past within which Black femmes might locate ourselves— one that maps Black queer femme-ininity as a site of pleasure rather than pain. In recent years, artists like Janelle Monáe have taken up that mantle and colored it pynk; in the video for her album *Dirty Computer*'s third single, Monáe crafts a bubblegum-hued utopia where Black femmes are free to love and be loved by one another, and where there are no sanctions for living as Monáe does—queer, Black, and "carefree as fuck."[2] Perhaps, then, the true legacy of Walker's work lies not in the existential terrain it created but rather the ones it enabled: glittering Technicolor dreamscapes where Black femme-ininity is marked by abundance rather than loss. Another litany for survival.

These final few pages are an attempt to trace these strategies, through which Black femmes are able to continue showing up in a world that both doubts and resents our existence. Taking its cues from Eve Tuck and C. Ree's generative "A Glossary of Haunting," my accounting of the terms that anchor this text "is a fractal . . . a story [rather than] an exhaustive encyclopedia."[3] The words defined below do not exist solely in the abstract; rather, they are clues to the ways Black femmes circumvent erasure and willful misinterpretation. Perhaps this afterword, in its intentional embrace of Black femme opacity, will be subjected to equal measures of both. That is, though "I am telling you a story . . . you may be reading a different one"[4]—a story of frivolity rather than fortitude, black and white rather than pynk and purple. Nevertheless, I urge you to "pay close attention, and then move very far away. I am only saying this once."[5]

Black E-Femme-Era (Ephemera)

n.—The means by which Black femmes are rendered legible. As fluid and as changing as Black femme gender itself. An empty tube of lipstick, a discarded skirt, a pile of braiding hair shedding wisps on its way to the waste bin. A challenge to the preeminence of permanence.

n.—Tenuous offerings, tiny moments of connection. Acts of naming gone so quickly it is easy to forget that they happened at all.

In 2017, to promote her new single "Love Galore," femme musician SZA appeared in a Genius Verified video in which she was asked to explain the song's lyrics. Toward the end of the recording, SZA recites a few rarely discussed lines from the track's penultimate verse: "Don't take it personal baby / I love on my ladies / Love to my ladies / I've dated a few."[6] Smiling coyly at the camera, the artist hesitates for just a moment before shruggingly admitting, "It's true."[7] The moment passes as quickly as it begins, seized on by other Black femmes and seemingly forgotten by everyone else. A pynk palimpsest. (See also *Femme Invisibility.*)

Black Femme Depression

n.—A uniquely Black shade of blue tinged with pynk. Loaded, much like anger, "with information and energy."[8] Simultaneously as isolating and as generative as the hair on a Black femme's head.

Released in October of 2017, Ethiopian American musician Kelela's album *Take Me Apart* offers a poignant glimpse into one Black femme's movement through the grief of a failed relationship—a theme the artist had explored earlier on her futuristic 2015 EP, *Hallucinogen*. *Take Me Apart*'s fourth single, "Blue Light," premiered in November 2017 with an accompanying video that finds Kelela standing alone in a barren, hyperpigmented blue room, her shoulder-length dreads framing her frowning face. As she begins to sing, the locs start to stretch and lengthen, twining their way around her arms and eventually onto the floor beneath her feet, weaving a "hair story" as much about growth as it is about entanglement. Black femme depression is blue, knotted, messy—yes—but it is also the space where new expanses of self are cultivated.

Femme Invisibility

n.—A child born of shortsightedness and compulsory heterosexuality. The means by which femmes are rendered illegible. A manifestation of the cis-heteropatriarchy's need to believe that femmes' sexual availability is a foregone conclusion.

In August of 2020, following the release of her and collaborator Cardi B's hit single "WAP," femme hip-hop artist Megan Thee Stallion took to Instagram Live to announce that she was in the market for a new girlfriend. Earlier that year, she had released her third EP, *Suga*, which included the popular single "Captain Hook," one of the artist's first public acknowledgments of her own queerness. Toward the beginning of the song's second verse, Megan raps, "I be texting with a bi chick / We both freaky, just trying shit (mwah)," before adding, "I got a man, I got a bitch / I'm a banana, they gotta split / One in your top, one in your tip / One for the club, one for the crib."[9]

The rapper was even more explicit in her late-summer IG Live, outlining exactly what she was looking for in a potential partner. "I like lil' petite tings with tattoos; that's my type," Megan confessed, later clarifying that she was specifically referring to "petite *Black* girls."[10] This brief but unambiguously queer admission was initially met with excitement online, with fans tweeting Megan their qualifications for the role of the Hot Girl's number one hot girl.[11] It wasn't long, however, before implications abounded that this declaration was merely a temporary swearing off of men prompted by Megan's public dispute with fellow musician and former friend Torey Lanez, who had recently been accused of shooting her. Shortly after, the story dropped from the radar almost entirely—femme invisibility in action.

> n.—A superpower, a tool. The means by which femmes build livable lives while avoiding queerphobic scrutiny. In this context, femme invisibility is "concealing parts of [one]self from [those who] are not always aware of how dangerous [they] can be," a process of "using [one's] arm to determine the length of the gaze."[12] That this invisibility exists simultaneously as a form of negation and possibility is one of the many paradoxes that shape Black queer life.

Pynking
> v.— A practice of rescripting. An addition of color.

The introduction to this text defines *pynking* as the weaponization of Black femme insight "to poke holes in a social fabric whose edges have always been too straight." Femme actress Zendaya Coleman offers a model for what this might look like in her 2021 interview with *Vanity Fair*. Tasked with answering a series of rapid-fire questions in a recorded exchange later made available on YouTube, the notoriously private Coleman—whose sexuality has been a source of speculation for years—paused when asked what quality she most likes in a man and deftly pivoted. "I most like in a *person*?"[13] she suggested instead, subtly pynking the original question's ostensible heteronormativity. Later, when asked what quality she most likes in a woman, Zendaya laughed and replied, "Same answer."[14] Pynking, in this way, can be seen as a response to and rejection of femme invisibility, a reminder that rumors of Black femmes' straightness have always been greatly exaggerated.

Womanist

n.—A Black feminist who knows that the work of getting free is a group
project. When Alice Walker coined the term in the late 1970s, her
words were as much a response to a waning sociocultural moment often plagued by stymied political imagination as they were a blueprint
for the future. In defining a *womanist* as one who loves other women
and resists separatism, Walker was leveling a concise critique against
women's and Black liberation movements that had failed to serve as
safe places for Black queer women.

In her video for "Pynk," Janelle Monáe extends this criticism to the state
mechanisms of surveillance and control that still make "being Black and
queer and living in the world . . . a dangerous proposition."[15] Offering a
stark and fantastical contrast to the rest of *Dirty Computer*—in which the
transgressive is monitored, contained, and ultimately destroyed—"Pynk"
and its unique brand of saporous Afrofuturism insist that cycles of oppression need not be replicated in our attempts to dismantle them. Instead,
Monáe pushes us to consider what becomes possible when we envision
freedom as a space rife with Black femmes who love themselves and each
other, regardless. In this way, Monáe situates herself within Walker's sub-
strative, titian intellectual palette and expands it, conjuring womanist
worlds that are heightened, brighter, but never—because such imagina-
tively quixotic femmes have always existed—new.

n.—A Black femme-inist. Loves music, loves dance, loves the moon and
the sun, loves struggle and rest, loves love, loves lust, and loves pynk.
In fact, pynk is their favorite part.

ACKNOWLEDGMENTS

Thank you to the teacher in all things. Thank you to the spirit
that moves in all things.

Shelby Autrey, BFree Yoga

FROM THE BLACK ATLANTIC

This book was conceived during an ancestor-blessed year spent at Harvard
University in Cambridge, Massachusetts, the city where my parents met
(and so conceived me). The 2018–2019 F. O. Matthiessen Visiting Professorship of Gender and Sexuality in Harvard's Studies of Women, Gender,
and Sexuality provided the inspiration and support to begin this project.
Thank you to Robin Bernstein, Michael Bronski, Robert Reid-Pharr, Amy
Newlin Parker, Francoise Lionnet, Caroline Light, Durba Mitra, Alice Jar-
dine, Marla Frederick, and Todne Thomas for your amazing collegiality,
brilliance, humor, and engagement during a year that changed my life and
career. Special, over-the-top thank yous to my undergraduate students in
Beyoncé Feminism, Rihanna Womanism and Femme Theory, who talked,
laughed, contested, colored, and Instagrammed our way through many
ideas explored in this book. And of course, gratitude to Deena and Joy
Poritzky for conjuring the feminist art of survival from your kitchen.

While at Harvard, I was inspired by amazing Black femme-inist speakers whose voices deeply colored my thoughts. Jen Nash's insights on seeking Black feminist abundance beyond academic limits were crucial to
the form of this book. Amber Musser's generosity in visiting my Femme
Theory class and thinking through Black femme bodyscapes opened
new, playful, precise possibilities for Blackening and queering academic
community. One of the most memorable moments of my year and *all* my
years came on my birthday, March 9, 2019, when I was given the gift of

meeting my Black femme idol, Janet Mock, when she was honored as Harvard University Artist of the Year. My sister Pisces's generosity, loving-kindness, and embodied Black femme abundance were never clearer to me than when my daughter, Nia, asked Janet to be her second mother and she agreed, asking Nia for one thing in return: that if history forgets her second mother, Nia will go in search of her the way Alice Walker did for Zora Neale Hurston. My heartfelt thanks to Ms. Mock for her continual work to create livable Black feminist futures where all mothers' gardens are tended.

While at Harvard I tried *not* to travel so as to stay close to my Nia and colleagues, but two invitations were too beautiful to refuse—and I benefitted manifold from accepting. How could I not rush to accept Rushan Kumar's invitation to the FemGeniuses Lecture Series at Colorado College? And do you think I hesitated a millisecond to accept Black femme freedom messenger Jessica Marie Johnson's call to Johns Hopkins University for the symposium "PYNK: A Queering Slavery Working Group Intensive"? These two days of interrogating "black womanhood, black femme, and black queer & trans* labors in the context of slavery, empire, and colonialism" pushed me to articulate foundational frameworks for *The Color Pynk*. Special thanks to copanelists Derrais Carter and Vanessa Holden, who I wish could be my copanelists on *everything*; and deep gratitude to Dr. Johnson and a growing witch baby, who together made this the pynkest event *ever. Maferefun Oshun.*

TO VIRTUAL FREEDOM DREAMING

Most of *The Color Pynk* was written in a state I never imagined I'd live in: the pandemic state of social distance, radical loneliness, Zoom, and virtual community. It was a difficult and tender place to write from, yet moments of Black femme connection over those eighteen months lit my way through this manuscript like the bioluminescent waves off California's central coast that spring. There's literally no way to overstate how radically filmmaker Tourmaline's spring 2020 visit to UC Santa Barbara's Feminist Futures Initiative recolored, expanded, and softened my quarantine self.

When the pandemic was declared that March, Feminist Futures contacted speakers and invited them to reschedule for the following fall, when life would be "normal." Tourmaline was the only one to refuse that invitation because she had a better idea: Why not employ the same technology disability justice activists had been using for years to turn this into an internationally accessible event? Because of her suggestion, participants tuned in across time zones and distance to witness the brilliant, generous, and beautiful Tourmaline overflow Black femme abundance for us all to bathe in like Cancers. I, too, planned to travel cross-country to give a talk that spring at the University of Miami, where I hoped to meet members of the art collective (F)empower. Though COVID prevented me from leaving California, its Zoomscape let me attend (F)empower's virtual healing circle "Heart Space: Meditation and Healing Circle for Black Folks," a "space for us to hold each other through the times," facilitated by the brilliant Emani Castillo. Thank you Emani, Helen Peña, and all (F)empower members who held me virtually while my former Minneapolis neighborhood burned.

By the second academic year of pandemic—the world still far from "normal" and my, Matt's, and Nia's classes crammed into our house—I revived my practice of limiting events. But again, those I couldn't refuse sustained me deeply. Brandeis's roundtable "P**** Valley: A Black Genders and Sexualities Studies Conversation," dynamically moderated by Shoniqua Roach and enlivened by copanelists Julian Glover, Mireille Miller-Young, and L. H. Stallings, broached conversations about gender and colorism that shape my introduction and conclusion. The following week—in time for Valentine's Day—UC Santa Barbara's Multicultural Center hosted a virtual event in its "Resilient Love" series: "Black Trans Lives Matter: A Conversation with CeCe McDonald and Elle Hearns," which I had the paradigm-shifting, soul-deepening chance to moderate. My beloved CeCe, my intellectual crush Elle, and I all coincidentally work pink, marking this as the pynkest of pynk conversations and an evening of radical Black femme love. Dr. Jillian Hernandez, whose monograph *Aesthetics of Excess* became the academic soundtrack powering my introduction, slipped into my inbox with an invitation to speak in the University of Florida's series "Radical Femininity: Women of Color Imaginaries, New

Political Iconographies." The dynamism of her next-generation femme-of-color scholarship and generosity of her engagement inspired me to glide to the end of this project with as much grace—and sartorial pleasure—as early 2021 allowed.

FINALLY, BACK TO THE BLACK PACIFIC

In February 2019, I gave my first lecture on material that would become this book: "The Color Pynk: Janelle Monáe, Janet Mock, and Black Femme Futures" was my job talk for the Department of Black Studies at the University of California, Santa Barbara. Thank you to Ingrid Banks, Vilna Bashi Treitler, and Christopher McAuley for your work as department chairs and support in bringing me to join the faculty. In my first year at UCSB I had the amazing opportunity to work with the newly formed Feminist Futures Initiative lovingly conceived by Leila Rupp, where I collaborated with Leila, Jenn Tyburczy, and Matt Richardson to bring amazing speakers, including Tourmaline. Thanks for imagining feminist futures together even as the world seemed to stand still. Nadège Clitandre and Claudine Michel were kind enough to welcome me to Haitian Studies in this historic site of its unfolding in the United States. Mireille Miller-Young and Stephanie Batiste, you not only shared your creative Black feminist scholarship with me: you put your Black feminism into practice by helping me navigate raising our beloved Black children in a year when their vulnerability was too present. Micaela Diaz-Sánchez and Terrance Wooten, my queer of color colleagues, collaborators, and water-sign kindred spirits, our conversations on campus, on text, over dinner, at Natural Café, as Micaela danced, as the hills burned, as our lives healed, were indispensable to *The Color Pynk*. As I finished my final revisions, Candice Lyons joined UCSB's Black Studies Department as a 2021–2022 Dissertation Fellow. Having the chance to work with Ms. Lyons again, to creatively, efficiently, and joyously femme the Black future together in the form of her afterword, was an absolute honor.

Moving to California in fall 2019 was a return to my home state and to family, who lovingly surrounded me as I colored everything pynk. My parents, Helen and Sheldon, drove from the Bay Area to become our first houseguests in 2019, drove back to surprise Nia for her 2020 quarantine birthday, and supported us from the North (Star) even when we couldn't see them. Dulce returned with me to California and follows me now as an angel, Zora keeping me safe in her absence. Layloni, Jocelyn, and Lupita, thank you for being new family in a new place, for Mango, Amara, sharing baby Salem, and renewing queer life in every way. My loving spouse, Matt, not only watched *Pose, Joseline's Cabaret, Love & Hip Hop, P-Valley*, and *L Word: Generation Q* over and over with me (for what he deemed entirely too many viewings), but remains my most insightful, fiercely femme-inist, unapologetically Black, tenderly Scorpio interlocutor, ever. You are my true helpmeet, kinder half, most honeyed Oshun, and I love you with all I have. Nia: you bring me to life over and over and over again, conjure me through Cambridge like Tituba and love me past Pacific shores too small to hold your name and your power. You are the one I have been waiting for, always, and always you are here for me as I am for you. Like the rest of the rainbow, *The Color Pynk* is for you.

NOTES

PROLOGUE. FOR ALICE WALKER

1. Alice Walker, *In Love & Trouble: Stories of Black Women* (New York: Open Road Media, 2001), 58, Kindle.

2. Walker, 51.

3. Alice Walker, *In Search of Our Mothers' Gardens: Womanist Prose* (Boston: Mariner Books, 2003), xi.

4. David Bradley, "Novelist Alice Walker Telling the Black Woman's Story," *New York Times*, January 8, 1964, https://www.nytimes.com/1984/01/08/magazine /novelist-alice-walker-telling-the-black-woman-s-story.html.

5. Zora Neale Hurston, *Their Eyes Were Watching God* (New York: Harper and Row, 1990), 111.

6. Alice Walker, *The Color Purple* (New York: Open Road Media, 2011), 49, Kindle.

7. Danielle Young, "We Should All Live by 'The Gospel According to Shug Avery,'" *The Root*, November 25, 2017, https://thegrapevine.theroot.com/we -should-all-live-by-the-gospel-according-to-shug-ave-1819921376.

8. Kaila Adia Story, "(Re)Presenting Shug Avery and Afrekete: The Search for a Black, Queer, and Feminist Pleasure Praxis," *The Black Scholar* 45, no. 4 (2015): 30.

9. Quoted in Ulrika Dahl, *Femmes of Power: Exploding Queer Femininities* (London: Serpent's Tail, 2008), 65.

10. Junauda Petrus quoted in "For Colored Girls Book Club + Junauda Petrus," For Colored Girls Book Club, accessed December 18, 2021, https://www .forcoloredgirlsbookclub.com/interviews/interview-with-junauda-petrus.

11. Barbara Christian, "The Race for Theory," *Feminist Studies* 14, no. 1 (Spring 1988): 78, 77–78.

12. Christian, 78.

INTRODUCTION. FEMME-INIST IS TO FEMINIST AS PYNK IS TO PINK

1. Walker, *Our Mothers' Gardens*, xi.

2. Walker, 290.

3. Alice Walker, "Turning Madness into Flowers #1," in *The World Will Follow Joy: Turning Madness into Flowers; New Poems* (New York: New Press, 2013), 19, Kindle.

4. Jessica Marie Johnson, *Wicked Flesh: Black Women, Intimacy, and Freedom in the Atlantic World* (Philadelphia: University of Pennsylvania Press, 2020), 173, Kindle.

5. Rhea Ashley Hoskin, "Can Femme Be Theory? Exploring the Epistemological and Methodological Possibilities of Femme," *Journal of Lesbian Studies* 25, no. 1 (2021): 6.

6. Reneice Charles, "Femme Fashion Is Queer Fashion," Autostraddle, November 8, 2018, https://www.autostraddle.com/femme-fashion-is-queer-fashion-438475/.

7. Quoted in Nicole Beilke, "Janelle Monáe Invents the Color 'PYNK' in Her New Video," 88Nine Radio Milwaukee, April 10, 2018, https://radiomilwaukee .org/discover-music/music-news/janelle-monae-new-video-pynk/.

8. Eve Barlow, "Best New Track: Janelle Monáe; 'PYNK' [ft. Grimes]," *Pitchfork*, April 11, 2018, https://pitchfork.com/reviews/tracks/janelle-monae-pynk-ft-grimes/.

9. Dyuti Gupta, "Today I Learnt: Womxn and Womyn Mean Two Different Things," SheThePeople, last updated March 8, 2021, https://www.shethepeople.tv /home-top-video/difference-womxn-womyn-diversity/.

10. Quoted in Kara Warner, "Janelle Monáe Says She's 'Working On' Mass Producing Those 'Vagina Pants,'" *People*, May 1, 2018, https://people.com/style /janelle-monae-says-shes-working-on-mass-producing-those-vagina-pants/.

11. Janelle Monáe, interview by Jazzy McBee, "Janelle Monae Is Pansexual, Protesting R. Kelly, and More," YouTube video, uploaded by JazzyMcBee, May 4, 2018, https://www.youtube.com/watch?v=UiT1g4DbqLc; all transcriptions are my own unless otherwise noted.

12. TJ Bryan, "It Takes Ballz: Reflections of a Black Attitudinal Femme Vixen in tha Makin'," in *Brazen Femme: Queering Femininity*, ed. Chloë Brushwood Rose and Anna Camilleri (Vancouver, BC: Arsenal Pulp Press, 2002), 148.

13. Moya Bailey, *Misogynoir Transformed: Black Women's Digital Resistance* (New York: New York University Press, 2021), 6, 1.

14. Bailey, 23–24.

15. Bailey, 19–20.

16. Bailey, 19.

17. Noah Brand, "Femmephobia," The Good Men Project, September 29, 2018, https://goodmenproject.com/featured-content/femmephobia/.

18. *Merriam-Webster*, s.v. "pink," accessed December 18, 2021, https://www .merriam-webster.com/dictionary/pink.

19. Peggy Orenstein, "The Ghettoisation of Pink: How It Has Cornered the Little-Girl Market," *Guardian*, June 18, 2011, https://www.theguardian.com /society/2011/jun/19/peggy-orenstein-pink-conspiracy-cinderella.

20. Petula Dvorak, "The Women's March Needs Passion and Purpose, Not

Pink Pussycat Hats," *Washington Post*, January 12, 2017, https://www.washington post.com/local/the-womens-march-needs-passion-and-purpose-not-pink-pussy cat-hats/2017/01/11/6d7e75be-d842-11e6-9a36-1d296534b31e_story.html.

21. Kaila Adia Story, "Fear of a Black Femme: The Existential Conundrum of Embodying a Black Femme Identity while Being a Professor of Black, Queer, and Feminist Studies," *Journal of Lesbian Studies* 21, no. 4 (2017): 417.

22. Laini Madhubuti, "Femme Invisibility," in *Naked: Black Women Bare All about Their Skin, Hair, Hips, Lips, and Other Parts*, ed. Ayana Byrd and Akiba Solomon (New York: Perigree, 2005), 141.

23. "Janelle Monáe Explains Dirty Computer Visuals, What Pansexuality Means to Her, and More!," YouTube video, uploaded by Power 106 Los Angeles, May 3, 2018, https://www.youtube.com/watch?v=TGhNbcIRKfI.

24. Christian, "Race for Theory," 68.

25. Christian, 68.

26. Kara Keeling, *The Witch's Flight: The Cinematic, the Black Femme, and the Image of Common Sense* (Durham, NC: Duke University Press, 2007), 145.

27. *Merriam-Webster* (@MerriamWebster), "We added shade to the dictionary," Twitter, February 7, 2017, https://twitter.com/MerriamWebster/status/8290562494 67637760?ref_src=twsrc%5Etfw%7Ctwcamp%5Etweetembed%7Ctwterm%5E829 056249467637760%7Ctwgr%5E%7Ctwcon%5Es1_c10&ref_url=https%3A%2F%2F www.huffpost.com%2Fentry%2Fmerriam-webster-shade_n_589a2e08e4b0c128 4f28f3df.

28. C. Namwali Serpell, "Notes on Shade," Post45, January 15, 2021, http:// post45.org/2021/01/serpell-notes-on-shade/?utm_source=rss&utm_medium=rss &utm_campaign=serpell-notes-on-shade.

29. Samuel R. Delany, introduction to *Shade: An Anthology of Fiction by Gay Men of African Descent*, ed. Bruce Morrow and Charles H. Rowell (New York: Harper Perennial, 1996), xvii.

30. Serpell, "Notes on Shade."

31. This conversation takes place in the video "Narrating Shade," accessed December 18, 2021, https://ensemble.syr.edu/hapi/v1/contents/permalinks/x8SX k97D/view. The video is included as link in Seth E. Davis, "Shade: Literacy Narratives at Black Gay Pride," *Literacy in Composition Studies* 7, no. 2 (December 2019): 56–89, https://doi.org/10.21623/1.7.2.4.

32. Jillian Hernandez, *Aesthetics of Excess: The Art and Politics of Black Latina Embodiment* (Durham, NC: Duke University Press, 2020), loc. 368, Kindle.

33. Joan Nestle and Barbara Cruikshank, "I'll Be the Girl: Generations of Fem," in *Femme: Feminists, Lesbians, and Bad Girls*, ed. Laura Harris and Elizabeth Crocker (New York: Routledge, 1997), 111–112.

34. Johnson, *Wicked Flesh*, 155.

35. Saidiya Hartman, *Wayward Lives, Beautiful Experiments: Intimate Histories of Riotous Black Girls, Troublesome Women, and Queer Radicals* (New York: W. W. Norton, 2019), 297, Kindle.

36. Tourmaline, "Filmmaker and Activist Tourmaline on How to Freedom Dream," *Vogue*, July 2, 2020, https://www.vogue.com/article/filmmaker-and-activist-tourmaline-on-how-to-freedom-dream.

37. Jill Casid (@jillhcasid), "It's a femmephobic denial of the pleasures in planning," comment on Instagram post by @omiseeke, July 21, 2021, https://www.instagram.com/p/CRmwjFDrYZM/.

38. Elsa Schiaparelli, *Shocking Life: The Autobiography of Elsa Schiaparelli* (London: Victoria and Albert Museum, 2007), 89–90.

39. Paulina Mormol, "The History of the Infamous N-Word in Terms of Political Correctness and Context-Dependence," in *Galicia Studies in Linguistics, Literature and Culture: The Students' Voices 3*, ed. Grzegorz A. Kleparski, Agnieszka Kallaus, Marta Pikor-Niedzialek, and Agnieszka Grasko (Rzeszów, Poland: University of Rzeszów, 2015), 63.

40. Elinor Rufus Hughes, "Mrs. Emily Gebhardt," *Kenyon Review* 15, no. 3 (Summer 1953): 415.

41. Carol Tulloch, *The Birth of Cool: Style Narratives of the African Diaspora* (London: Bloomsbury, 2016), 190, Kindle.

42. Keeling, *Witch's Flight*, 21.

43. Matt Richardson and Marlon Bailey, "'Will the Real Men Please Stand Up?': Regulating Gender and Policing Sexuality through Black Common Sense," in *Black Sexual Economies: Race and Sex in a Culture of Capital*, ed. Adrienne D. Davis and the BSE Collective (Urbana: University of Illinois Press, 2019), 116.

44. Safe Homes defines *nonbinary femme* as someone "holding a nonbinary gender identity and a femme gender expression, or claiming Femme as an identity outside of the gender binary." Safe Homes gender terms, accessed March 1, 2021, http://www.safehomesma.org/gender_alphabet.pdf.

45. Joshua Allen (@joshuaobawole), Instagram, January 28, 2021, https://www.instagram.com/p/CKmVmYfj4nC/.

46. Ericka Hart (@ihartericka), Instagram, December 3, 2020, https://www.instagram.com/p/CIW2p_nhacR/.

47. Hartman, *Wayward Lives, Beautiful Experiments*, 177.

48. Saidiya Hartman, "The Belly of the World: A Note on Black Women's Labors," *Souls* 18, no. 1 (2016): 169.

49. Hartman, *Wayward Lives, Beautiful Experiments*, 338.

50. Chloë Brushwood Rose and Anna Camilleri, introduction to *Brazen Femme*, 13.

51. Hoskin, "Can Femme Be Theory?," 10.

52. Anita González, "Interview with Sharon Bridgforth," in *Solo/Black/*

Woman: Scripts, Interviews, and Essays, ed. E. Patrick Johnson and Ramón H. Rivera-Servera (Evanston, IL: Northwestern University Press, 2014), 231.

53. Christina Radish, "Nicco Annan on the 'Unapologetically Authentic' Show 'P-Valley' & the Power of Uncle Clifford," *Collider*, September 6, 2020, https://collider.com/p-valley-nicco-annan-interview/.

54. Michael Cuby, "How Nicco Annan Crafted One of the Most Gender-Defying, Badass Roles on Television," *Them*, September 4, 2020, https://www.them.us/story/nicco-annan-p-valley-interview.

55. Nico Annan, interview by Tyler Doster, "Interview: Nicco Annan Is Breaking Non-binary Barriers on 'P-Valley' and Turning Heads and Looks as Uncle Clifford," *AwardsWatch*, January 8, 2021, https://awardswatch.com/interview-nicco-annan-is-breaking-non-binary-barriers-on-p-valley-and-turning-heads-and-looks-as-uncle-clifford/.

56. Brushwood Rose and Camilleri, introduction to *Brazen Femme*, 13.

57. "Without this club I don't have nothing," quote transcribed by Dale McGariggle, *TV Fanatic*, August 29, 2020, https://www.tvfanatic.com/quotes/without-this-club-i-dont-have-nothing-and-these-girls-these-girl/.

58. Adrienne maree brown, *Emergent Strategy: Shaping Change, Changing Worlds* (Chico, CA: AK Press, 2017), 13, Kindle.

59. Katori Hall, *P-Valley*, season 1, episode 1, "Perpetratin'."

60. Combahee River Collective, "The Combahee River Collective Statement," *BlackPast*, accessed March 21, 2021, https://www.blackpast.org/african-american-history/combahee-river-collective-statement-1977/.

61. Hoskin, "Can Femme Be Theory?," 11.

62. Veronica Jenkins quoted in Dahl, *Femmes of Power*, 62.

63. Hartman, *Wayward Lives, Beautiful Experiments*, 6.

64. Krista A. Thompson, *Shine: The Visual Economy of Light in African Diasporic Aesthetic Practice* (Durham, NC: Duke University Press, 2015), loc. 830, 841, Kindle.

65. Adolf Loos, "Ornament and Crime," in *Programs and Manifestoes on 20th-Century Architecture*, ed. Ulrich Conrads (Cambridge, MA: MIT Press, 1975), 24.

66. Lisa Marie Cacho, *Social Death: Racialized Rightlessness and the Criminalization of the Unprotected* (New York: New York University Press, 2012), 21.

67. Thompson, *Shine*, loc. 987.

68. Hartman, *Wayward Lives, Beautiful Experiments*, 33.

69. Janet Mock, *Surpassing Certainty: What My Twenties Taught Me* (New York: Atria Books, 2017), 11, Kindle.

70. Eve Lorane Brown, personal communication, December 7, 2020.

71. Treva Ellison, "The Labor of Werqing It: The Performance and Protest Strategies of Sir Lady Java," in *Trap Door: Trans Cultural Production and the*

Politics of Visibility, ed. Reina Gossett, Eric A. Stanley, and Johanna Burton (Cambridge, MA: MIT Press, 2017), 1, 17.

72. "Pay It No Mind - The Life and Times of Marsha P. Johnson," YouTube video, uploaded by Michael Kasino, https://www.youtube.com/watch?v=rjN9W2KstqE.

73. "Pay It No Mind."

74. Hartman, *Wayward Lives, Beautiful Experiments,* 117.

75. "Pay It No Mind."

76. "Pay It No Mind."

77. Hartman, *Wayward Lives, Beautiful Experiments,* 117.

78. "Pay It No Mind."

79. Hernandez, *Aesthetics of Excess,* loc. 3201.

80. Hernandez, loc. 2892.

81. Naomi Wolf, *Vagina: A New Biography* (New York: Ecco, 2012), 334, 279, Kindle.

82. L. H. Stallings, *Funk the Erotic: Transaesthetics and Black Sexual Cultures* (Urbana: University of Illinois Press, 2015), loc. 433, 3563, Kindle.

83. Audre Lorde, "The Uses of the Erotic: The Erotic as Power," posted by Vanessa Muradian, April 14, 2020, https://www.miamuse.com/blog/tag/Sexuality.

84. "Pay It No Mind."

85. Amber Jamilla Musser, *Sensual Excess: Queer Femininity and Brown Jouissance* (New York: New York University Press, 2018), 65.

86. Valerie Steele, "Pink: The History of a Punk, Pretty, Powerful Color," in *Pink: The History of a Punk, Pretty, Powerful Color,* ed. Valerie Steele (New York: Fashion Institute of Technology, 2018), 9–10, 12.

87. "Janelle Monae Is Pansexual."

88. "Janelle Monae Is Pansexual."

89. Pisces Isake Smith (@is_she_okay), Instagram profile, https://www.instagram.com/is_she_okay/.

90. "Janelle Monae Is Pansexual."

91. Jafari Allen, "Black/Queer/Diaspora at the Current Conjuncture," *GLQ* 18, nos. 2–3 (2012): 229.

92. Elle Moxley, interview by Charise Frazier, "SpeakHER50: Elle Hearns," *MadameNoire,* November 13, 2019, https://madamenoire.com/1109221/speakher 50-elle-hearns/.

PART ONE.
PUSSY POWER AND NONBINARY VAGINAS

1. Krista Suh and Jayna Zweiman, "The Sea of Pink," *Pussyhat Project,* October 6, 2020, https://www.pussyhatproject.com/blog.

2. Krista Suh and Jayna Zweiman, "Pussyhat FAQ," *Pussyhat Project*, accessed December 18, 2021, https://www.pussyhatproject.com/faq.

3. Banu Gökarıksel and Sara Smith, "Intersectional Feminism beyond U.S. Flag Hijab and Pussy Hats in Trump's America," *Gender, Place & Culture* 24, no. 5 (2017): 628–644.

4. Amiya Nagpal quoted in Gökarıksel and Smith.

5. Cáel Keegan quoted in Julie Compton, "Pink 'Pussyhat' Creator Addresses Criticism over Name," NBC News, February 7, 2017, https://www.nbcnews.com /feature/nbc-out/pink-pussyhat-creator-addresses-%20criticism-over-name -n717886.

6. Suh and Zweiman, "Pussyhat FAQ."

7. Elle Moxley quoted in Compton, "Pink 'Pussyhat' Creator."

8. Elle Moxley and Treva B. Lindsey, "Sister to Sister: Black Women in Solidarity," *Huffington Post*, February 12, 2016, https://www.huffpost.com/entry/sister-to -sister-black-women-solidarity_b_9213772.

9. Carmen Phillips, "Janelle Monáe's 'Pynk' Music Video Is Here to Wreak More Havoc on Your Queer Heart," *Autostraddle*, April 10, 2018, https://www.auto straddle.com/janelle-Monaes-pynk-music-video-is-here-to-wreak-more-havoc -on-your-queer-heart-417157/.

10. Janet Mock quoted in Catie L'Heureux, "Read Janet Mock's Empowering Speech on Trans Women of Color and Sex Workers," *The Cut*, January 21, 2017, https://www.thecut.com/2017/01/read-janet-mocks-speech-at-the-womens -march-on-washington-trans-women-of-color-sex-workers.html.

11. Indya Moore quoted in Josh Jackman, "Pose Star Indya Moore: Trans Women's Penises Are Biologically Female," *PinkNews*, February 19, 2019, https:// www.pinknews.co.uk/2019/02/19/pose-indya-moore-trans-penises-biologically -female/.

12. Indya Moore quoted in Bret Furdyk, "Transgender 'Pose' Star Indya Moore Sparks Penis Debate on Twitter," *ET Canada*, February 21, 2019, https:// etcanada.com/news/422370/transgender-pose-star-indya-moore-sparks-penis -debate-on-twitter/.

13. Within Our Lifetime, "Movement Mic Check Report: Rapid Response to Racial Disasters," 2018, 12, https://static1.squarespace.com/static/5a73ce6bbe 42d69316a2aa89/t/5f32b4dd6a06523b56ef3610/1597158633252/Movement+MIC+ Check+Report+2018.pdf.

14. Chana Kronfeld, *The Full Severity of Compassion: The Poetry of Yehuda Amichai* (Palo Alto, CA: Stanford University Press, 2015), 225.

15. Hunter Shackelford, "Queer Like Me: Breaking the Chains of Femme Invisibility," *Wear Your Voice*, November 22, 2016, https://wearyourvoicemag.com /queer-breaking-chains-femme/.

JANELLE MONÁE

1. "Janelle Monáe - Q.U.E.E.N. feat. Erykah Badu [Official Video]," YouTube video, uploaded by Janelle Monáe, May 1, 2013, https://www.youtube.com/watch ?v=tEddixS-UoU.

2. "Janelle Monáe at Women's March: 'I March Against the Abuse of Power,'" YouTube video, uploaded by Democracy Now!, January 23, 2017, https://www .youtube.com/watch?v=Z8Ev9aLqa8c.

3. "Janelle Monáe at Women's March."

4. Janelle Monáe quoted in "Janelle Monáe Celebrates Female Empowerment at #FemTheFuture Brunch," Rap-Up, September 23, 2016, https://www.rap-up .com/2016/09/23/janelle-monae-fem-the-future-brunch/.

5. Janelle Monáe quoted in Rebecca Milzoff, "Sister from Another Planet," New York, May 12, 2010, https://nymag.com/arts/popmusic/features/66012/.

6. Janelle Monáe, interview by Benjamino Marini, Vogue Italia, 2010, https:// www.vogue.it/en/vogue-black/spotlight-on/2010/06/janelle-monae?refresh_ce=.

7. Caroline Framke, "Janelle Monáe Doubles Down on Feminist Self-Love with Her New Video for 'Pynk,'" Vox, April 10, 2018, https://www.vox.com/culture /2018/4/10/17219874/janelle-monae-pynk-video-tessa-thompson-dirty-computer/.

8. Phillips, "Janelle Monáe's 'Pynk' Music Video Is Here."

9. Brittany Spanos, "Janelle Monáe Frees Herself," Rolling Stone, April 26, 2018, https://www.rollingstone.com/music/music-features/janelle-monae-frees -herself-629204/.

10. "Janelle Monáe - Dirty Computer [Emotion Picture]," YouTube video, uploaded by Janelle Monáe, April 27, 2018, https://www.youtube.com/watch?v=jdH 2Sy-BlNE.

11. Monáe quoted in Rebecca Bengal, "'You Don't Own or Control Me': Janelle Monáe on Her Music, Politics, and Undefinable Sexuality," Guardian, February 22, 2018, https://www.theguardian.com/music/2018/feb/22/you-dont-own-or -control-me-janelle-monae-on-her-music-politics-and-undefinable-sexuality.

12. Janelle Monáe quoted in Jenna Wortham, "How Janelle Monáe Found Her Voice," New York Times Magazine, April 19, 2018, https://www.nytimes.com /2018/04/19/magazine/how-janelle-monae-found-her-voice.html.

13. Janelle Monáe, "Americans," on Dirty Computer (Wondaland Records, 2018).

14. See Jacey Fortin, "Dress Like a Woman? What Does That Mean?," New York Times, February 3, 2017, https://www.nytimes.com/2017/02/03/style/trump -women-dress-code-white-house.html?auth=login-email&login=email,

15. Adam Geczy and Vicki Karaminas, Queer Style (London: Bloomsbury, 2013), 33, Kindle.

16. Elizabeth Lapovsky Kennedy and Madeline D. Davis, *Boots of Leather, Slippers of Gold: The History of a Lesbian Community* (New York: Routledge, 2014), 267.

17. Kennedy and Davis, 266.

18. Walker, *Color Purple*, 146.

19. Walker, 147.

20. Walker, 211.

21. Walker, 211.

22. Walker, 213.

23. Walker, 212.

24. Walker, 214.

25. Alison Turka, "Janelle Monáe's 'Black Panther' Premiere Look Is Too Fierce to Miss," *Elite Daily*, January 30, 2018, https://www.elitedaily.com/p/janelle -monaes-black-panther-premiere-look-is-too-fierce-to-miss-8060081.

26. Janelle Monáe, interview by Annie Mac, "Janelle Monáe Talks Prince, Politics and Black Panther with Annie Mac," BBC Radio 1, March 20, 2018, https://www .bbc.co.uk/programmes/articles/3tyr25Jt3HxB1bSTcKSZHZR/janelle-monae -talks-prince-politics-and-black-panther-with-annie-mac; emphasis mine.

27. Darnell-Jamal Lisby, "Gender Bending Icon Janelle Monáe Flips the Script Yet Again," *Cultured*, September 12, 2020, https://www.culturedmag.com/gender -bending-icon-janelle-monae-flips-the-script-yet-again/.

28. "Aneka & Ayo: My Dora Milaje Research Continues . . . ," *Sister from Another Planet*, July 11, [2017?], https://www.sisterfromanotherplanet.com/and -theres-aneka-ayo-dora-milaje-research-deepens/.

29. Sinclair Sexsmith, "Femme Invisibility & Beyond," *Sugarbutch Chronicles*, January 15, 2012, http://sugarbutch.net/2012/01/femme-invisibility-beyond/?utm _source=feedburner&utm_medium=feed&utm_campaign=Feed%3A+Sugar butch+%28Sugarbutch+Chronicles%29.

30. "Nakia," Marvel, accessed December 18, 2021, https://www.marvel.com /characters/nakia/on-screen.

31. Briana Shewan, "Can Femme Invisibility Be a Superpower?," *Mophead Femme*, October 24, 2018, https://www.mopheadfemme.com/blog/2018/10/24 /can-femme-invisibility-be-a-superpower.

32. Janelle Monáe (@janellemonae), "Liberation.Elevation Talk with @osope patrisse [Patrisse Cullors]," Instagram, September 18, 2020, https://www.instagram .com/tv/CFSx9QIlgQ7/?hl=en.

33. Monáe, "Liberation.Elevation Talk."

34. "Janelle Monáe Breaks Down 'Django Jane,' on Genius' Video Series 'Verified,'" Genius, April 23, 2018, http://so.genius.com/WUzpeqz.

35. *A Fantastic Woman*, directed by Sebastián Lelio (Chile: Fabula, 2017).

36. Mariah Barber, "The Invisible Femme," *Lesbionyx*, September 12, 2018, https://lesbionyx.com/the-struggle-is-queer/2018/9/11/the-invisible-femme.

37. Janelle Monáe quoted in Ivie Ani, "Janelle Monáe Is Redefining What It Means to Be a Genius [Interview]," *Okayplayer*, accessed December 18, 2021, https://www.okayplayer.com/originals/janelle-monae-redefining-genius-okay player-interview.html.

38. Monica Miller, "All Hail the Q.U.E.E.N.: Janelle Monáe and a Tale of the Tux," *Nka: Journal of Contemporary African Art*, no. 37 (November 2015): 64.

39. "Janelle Monáe Breaks Down 'Django Jane.'"

40. Barber, "Invisible Femme."

41. Barber.

42. Izzy Nastasia quoted in Samuel Hine, "Meet Brujas, the Bronx Skate Crew Making Streetwear for Post-Election America," *GQ*, November 17, 2016, https://www.gq.com/story/brujas-1971-streetwear-skate-crew.

43. Brujas online store, accessed July 8, 2019, https://shop.brujas.nyc/.

44. Brujas events page, accessed July 8, 2019, https://brujas.nyc/events.

45. Izzy Nastasia quoted in Ashley Haines, "The Brujas Skate Crew Is Radicalizing More Than Just Skateboarding," *Hypebae*, October 14, 2016, https://hypebae.com/2016/10/brujas-skateboarders-1971-hypebae-interview.

46. Bengal, "'You Don't Own or Control Me.'"

47. Strong Black Lead (@strongblacklead), ".@JanelleMonae and @Tessa Thompson_x just set me free," Twitter, April 10, 2018, https://twitter.com/i/events /983752852693770242?lang=en.

48. Keifer: Definitive Edition (@DannyVegito) quoted in Sam Manzella, "Lesbian Twitter™ Lost Its Mind over Janelle Monáe's 'Pynk' Video," *NewNowNext*, April 11, 2018, http://www.newnownext.com/janelle-monae-pynk-video-twitter -lesbians/04/2018/.

49. Dened rey moreno (@Hajabeg), "Ya'll Janelle Monáe and Tessa Thompson are at it again," Twitter, April 10, 2018, https://twitter.com/hajabeg/status /983753862631706624?lang=en.

50. Folu (@notfolu) quoted in Manzella, "Lesbian Twitter™ Lost Its Mind."

51. Warner, "Mass Producing Those 'Vagina Pants.'"

52. Shoniqua Roach, "Black Pussy Power: Performing Acts of Black Eroticism in Pam Grier's Blaxploitation Films," *Feminist Theory* 19, no. 1 (April 2018): 7–9, doi:10.1177/1464700117742866.

53. Leah Lakshmi Piepzna-Samarasinha, *Dirty River: A Queer Femme of Color Dreaming Her Way Home* (Vancouver, BC: Arsenal Pulp Press, 2015), 216, Kindle.

54. Spanos, "Janelle Monáe Frees Herself."

55. Bengal, "'You Don't Own or Control Me.'"

56. Bengal.

57. Aerosmith, "Pink," on *Nine Lives* (New York: Columbia Records, 1997).

58. Ulrika Dahl, "Femmebodiment: Notes on Queer Feminine Shapes of Vulnerability," *Feminist Theory* 18, no. 1 (April 2017): 35–54.

59. "Janelle Monáe - A Revolution of Love (Artist Spotlight Stories)," YouTube video, uploaded by Janelle Monáe, September 17, 2018, https://www.youtube.com/watch?v=QIz5MHKV1nk.

60. María Lugones, "Playfulness, 'World'-Travelling, and Loving Perception," *Hypatia* 2, no. 2 (1987): 3–19.

61. "Janelle Monáe - A Revolution of Love."

62. Shana L. Redmond, "This Safer Space: Janelle Monáe's 'Cold War,'" *Journal of Popular Music Studies* 23, no. 4 (December 2011): 393–411.

63. Roach, "Black Pussy Power," 10.

64. Audre Lorde, "The Uses of the Erotic: The Erotic as Power," in *Sister Outsider* (Freedom, CA: Crossing Press, 1984).

65. Amanda Duarte quoted in Alli Maloney, "#PussyGrabsBack Creators Amanda Duarte and Jessica Bennett Interview," *Teen Vogue*, October 21, 2016, https://www.teenvogue.com/story/pussygrabsback-creators-amanda-duarte -jessica-bennett-interview.

66. Inger-Lise Kalviknes Bore, Anne Graefer, and Allaina Kilby, "This Pussy Grabs Back: Humour, Digital Affects and Women's Protest," *Open Cultural Studies* 1 (2017): 538–539.

67. Monáe in Lisby, "Monáe Flips the Script Yet Again."

68. Keeling, *Witch's Flight*, 9.

69. Candace Bond-Theriault, "Janelle Monáe's 'Dirty Computer' Is the Black, Queer, Feminist Love Note We Need in 2020," *Self*, June 25, 2020, https://www.self.com/story/janelle-monae-dirty-computer.

70. Anya Nuttz (@queenanyanuttz), Instagram profile, accessed December 18, 2021, https://www.instagram.com/queenanyanuttz/.

71. Anya Nuttz (@queenanyanuttz), Facebook profile, accessed December 18, 2021, https://www.facebook.com/queenanyanuttz/.

72. Anya Nuttz (@queenanyanuttz), "Rapunzel, Rapunzel, let down your (pussy) hair," Instagram, May 18, 2017, https://www.instagram.com/p/BUQAU6jlH5a/.

73. Anya Nuttz (@queenanyanuttz), "Węt æñd Črëämÿ," Instagram, March 11, 2019, https://www.instagram.com/p/Bu35t9GhIxR/.

74. Rachel Devitt, "Girl on Girl," in *Queering the Popular Pitch*, ed. Sheila Whiteley and Jennifer Rycenga (New York: Routledge, 2006), 39.

75. See Gwen Aviles, "Lena Waithe Honors Black Drag Queens with Met Gala Outfit," NBC News, May 7, 2019, https://www.nbcnews.com/feature/nbc-out /lena-waithe-honors-black-drag-queens-met-gala-outfit-n1002851.

76. Janet Mock quoted in Angel Lenise, "Janet Mock Wants You to Know That Queer People Invented Camp," *Elle*, May 8, 2019, https://www.elle.com/fashion /celebrity-style/a27459266/janet-mock-2019-met-gala/.

77. Katie Dupere, "Janelle Monáe Wore Four Hats to the Met Gala," *Bustle*, May 6, 2019, https://www.bustle.com/p/janelle-monaes-2019-met-gala-outfit -included-four-hats-a-giant-face-17306442.

78. Quoted in Sam Manzella, "Are Janelle Monáe and Lupita Nyong'o an Item? An Investigation," *NewNowNext*, May 10, 2019, http://www.newnownext .com/janelle-monae-lupita-nyongo-dating-rumors/05/2019/.

79. Lupita Nyong'o quoted in Kat Sanders, "30 Days of Empowerment: Lupita Nyong'o," *Medium*, June 29, 2019, https://medium.com/dream-create-inspire-be -epic/30-days-of-empowerment-lupita-nyongo-4111ed14f43.

INDYA MOORE

1. Janet Mock, "Indya Moore," *Time*, April 16, 2019, https://time.com /collection-post/5567698/indya-moore/.

2. Indya Moore quoted in Danielli, "Indya Moore Is the First Trans Person to Grace an Elle Magazine Cover and Her Red Carpet Looks Prove Why," *Mitú*, May 16, 2019, https://wearemitu.com/entertainment/indya-moore-cover-elle -magazine/; Indya Moore quoted in Janelle Okwodu, "Last Week, Stars Found Their Power in Heroic Fashion," *Vogue*, April 29, 2019, https://www.vogue.com /vogueworld/slideshow/brie-larson-naomi-campbell-gigi-hadid-10-best-dressed.

3. Danielli, "First Trans Person to Grace Elle."

4. Danielli.

5. Meghan Giannotta, "What Is Ball Culture? Examining NYC's Vibrant Underground Scene in 'Pose,'" *AMNY*, June 21, 2018, https://www.amny.com /entertainment/what-is-ball-culture-1-19343425/.

6. Jon Bernstein, "'Nothing Like This Has Ever Happened: How TV Drama Pose Breaks New Ground," *Guardian*, June 1, 2018, https://www.theguardian.com /tv-and-radio/2018/jun/01/pose-ryan-murphy-transgender-actors-groundbreaking -new-show.

7. Janet Mock (@janetmock), Instagram, July 8, 2018, https://www.instagram .com/p/Bk-g9oGhS-y/.

8. Indya Moore quoted in Madi Skahill, "Indya Moore on Her Acting Career and How She Found Her Way to FX's 'Pose,'" *Los Angeles Times*, July 30, 2018, https:// www.latimes.com/fashion/la-ig-wwd-indya-moore-fx-pose-20180730-story.html.

9. Indya Moore quoted in Jada Yuan, "Indya Moore Just Wants to Be Free," *Elle*, May 9, 2019, https://www.elle.com/culture/movies-tv/a27378298/indya -moore-transgender-pose-interview/.

10. Yuan.

11. Nicki Minaj featuring Beyoncé, "Feeling Myself," on *The Pinkprint* (New York: Young Money Entertainment, 2014).

12. See, for example, Julie L. Mellby, "The Birth of Aphrodite, or Venus Rising from the Froth of the Sea," Graphic Arts, Princeton University Library, March 15, 2012, https://www.princeton.edu/~graphicarts/2012/03/the_birth_of_aphrodite .html.

13. Treva Carrie Ellison, "Black Femme Praxis and the Promise of Black Gender," *Black Scholar* 49, no. 1 (2019): 8.

14. Ellison, 13.

15. Ellison, 13.

16. Ellison, 12.

17. Indya Moore (@indyamoore), "And then, a nonbinary Wild Vagina bloomed," Instagram, April 24, 2019, https://www.instagram.com/p/Bwnmci6HP6K/.

18. See Stacy Lambe, "My Favorite Scene: 'OITNB' Writer Sian Heder on the Vagina Conversation That Led to an Education on Set," *ET*, July 28, 2016, https:// www.etonline.com/tv/194284_my_favorite_scene_oitnb_writer_sian_heder.

19. Janet Mock quoted in Malcolm Venable, "The Mind-Blowing 1990 Documentary You Must See Before Watching Pose," *TV Guide*, May 29, 2018, https:// www.tvguide.com/news/pose-fx-paris-is-burning/.

20. *Paris Is Burning*, directed by Jennie Livingston (New York: Off White Productions, 1990).

21. Janet Mock, interview by Anna Menta, "Janet Mock on Writing for Ryan Murphy's 'Pose,' Passing in the Trans Community, and Her Queen, Beyoncé," *Newsweek*, July 15, 2018, https://www.newsweek.com/janet-mock-pose-writer -interview-1019550.

22. Janet Mock quoted in Evan Real, "'Nothing Has Changed': Why 'Pose' Put Its Spotlight on Violence against Trans Women of Color," *Hollywood Reporter*, July 9, 2019, https://www.hollywoodreporter.com/tv/tv-news/pose-death -explained-ryan-murphy-janet-mock-violence-trans-women-color-1223057/.

23. *Pose*, season 1, episode 4, "The Fever," written by Janet Mock.

24. Jeffry J. Iovannone, "Justice for Venus Xtravaganza," *Think Queerly*, July 12, 2018, https://thinkqueerly.com/justice-for-venus-xtravaganza-1cbd45bc504a.

25. *Pose*, season 1, episode 2, "Access," written by Ryan Murphy, Brad Falchuk, and Steven Canals.

26. Mock, *Surpassing Certainty*.

27. Stallings, *Funk the Erotic*.

28. Saidiya Hartman, "Venus in Two Acts," *Small Axe* 12, no. 2 (2008): 1.

29. Janet Mock quoted in Benjamin Lindsay, "How Janet Mock Gave *Pose* Its *Sex and the City* Moment," *Vanity Fair*, July 9, 2018, https://www.vanityfair

.com/hollywood/2018/07/pose-season-1-episode-6-janet-mock-director-ryan
-murphy.

30. *Pose*, season 1, episode 6, "Love Is the Message," directed by Janet Mock.

31. Indya Moore quoted in Raquel Willis, "Indya Moore Becomes the First Trans Person to Keynote at Essence Festival," *Out*, July 8, 2019, https://www.out.com/events/2019/7/08/indya-moore-becomes-first-trans-person-speak-essence-fest.

32. Moore quoted in Jackman, "Pose Star Indya Moore."

33. Ana Valens, "Pose Star Indya Moore: Trans Women Are Biological Women," *Daily Dot*, February 19, 2019, https://www.dailydot.com/irl/pose-indya-moore-trans-women-biological-women/.

34. See Lauren Rearick, "Calvin Klein Selected Indya Moore as the Face of Its Pride Campaign," *Teen Vogue*, May 15, 2019, https://www.teenvogue.com/story/calvin-klein-indya-moore-pride-campaign.

35. Bailey Calfee, "The Best Genderless Underwear Brands You Should Support," *Nylon*, December 4, 2018, https://www.nylon.com/best-genderless-underwear-brands.

36. Thomas F. DeFrantz, "Bone-Breaking, Black Social Dance, and Queer Corporeal Orature," *Black Scholar* 46, no. 1 (2016): 66–67.

37. Yuan, "Indya Moore Just Wants to Be Free"; Moore quoted in Yuan.

38. Christina Tente, "'. . . And Just Set That Body on Fire!': Posthuman Perspectives on the Body, *Becomings*, and Sticky Encounters in Vogue Femme" (master's thesis, Lund University, 2020), 8.

39. Indya Moore, interview by Jess Cole, "Indya Moore: 'Representation of Marginalised People Shouldn't Only Begin and Centre around the Most Privileged Looking of Us,'" *i-D*, September 21, 2020, https://i-d.vice.com/en_uk/article/jgxzep/indya-moore-representation-of-marginalised-people-shouldnt-only-begin-and-centre-around-the-most-privileged-looking-of-us.

40. "Indya Moore Is a Convention Killer in #MYCALVINS | CALVIN KLEIN," Vimeo video, uploaded by AMBIT, September 12, 2019, https://vimeo.com/359579719.

41. Marlon M. Bailey, *Butch Queens Up in Pumps: Gender, Performance, and Ballroom Culture in Detroit* (Ann Arbor: University of Michigan Press, 2013), 175.

42. Tente, "'Set That Body on Fire!,'" 22.

43. Marlon M. Bailey, "Gender/Racial Realness: Theorizing the Gender System in Ballroom Culture," *Feminist Studies* 37, no. 2 (June 2011): 370.

44. Bailey, 369–370.

45. Tente, "'Set That Body on Fire!,'" 23.

46. Elijah Ezeji-Okoye, personal communication, March 2019.

47. Graham Gremore, "D.L. Hughley Has Meltdown, Calls Trans Actress Indya Moore a 'P*ssy' for Standing Up against Bigotry," *Queerty*, December 10,

2018, https://www.queerty.com/d-l-hughley-meltdown-calls-trans-actress-indya -moore-pssy-standing-bigotry-20181210.

48. Bailey, "Gender/Racial Realness," 382–383.

49. Gloria Wekker, *The Politics of Passion: Women's Sexual Culture in the Afro-Surinamese Diaspora* (New York: Columbia University Press, 2006), 192.

50. Indya Moore (@IndyaMoore), "& then Goddess @janetmock teleported from the universe of infinitely cunty magical stuff," Twitter, July 28, 2020, https:// twitter.com/indyamoore/status/1288162577776873472.

51. Indya Moore quoted in Kate Demolder, "Calvin Klein Casts Trans Model as Part of New Campaign," *Irish Tatler*, May 17, 2019, https://irishtatler.com /fashion/calvin-klein-trans-model.

52. Moore, interview by Cole.

53. Moore quoted in Taylor Henderson, "The Cast of *Pose* Gets Real about Colorism: 'It Needs to Be Seen,'" *Pride*, August 13, 2019, https://www.pride.com /tv/2019/8/13/cast-pose-gets-real-about-colorism-it-needs-be-seen.

54. Miss Major Griffin-Gracy in "Miss Major on Trans Day of Visibility 2019 - #SupportUsInTheLight #AlliesBeVisible," YouTube video, uploaded by Miss Major, March 27, 2019, https://www.youtube.com/watch?v=3zGZ5a9a0L0.

55. "Miss Major's Monthly Fundraising Circle," Friends of Miss Major Fundly page, accessed December 18, 2021, https://fundly.com/missmajor.

56. Spencer and Eleneke quoted in *Major!*, directed by Annalise Ophelian (Floating Ophelia Productions, 2015).

57. Miss Major Griffin-Gracy, CeCe McDonald, and Toshio Meronek, "Cautious Living: Black Trans Women and the Politics of Documentation," in Gossett, Stanley, and Burton, *Trap Door*, 32.

58. Miss Major Griffin-Gracy, interview by AJ Lewis, New York City Trans Oral History Project, December 16, 2017, https://s3.amazonaws.com/oral-history /transcripts/NYC+TOHP+Transcript+054+Miss+Major+Griffin-Gracy.pdf.

59. Miss Major, interview by Lewis.

60. *Pose*, season 1, episode 5, "Mother's Day," written by Steven Canals, Ryan Murphy, and Brad Falchuk.

61. Mey Rude, "How *Pose* Is Changing Media Representation of Gender Confirmation Surgery," *Them*, June 18, 2018, https://www.them.us/story/pose-gender -confirmation-surgery.

62. Dominique Jackson (with Mj Rodriguez and Indya Moore), interview by Out.com editors, "The Cast of *Pose* Takes Center Stage and Makes History," *Out*, July 17, 2018, https://www.out.com/out-exclusives/2018/7/17/cover-exclusive s-cast-pose-takes-center-stage-makes-history.

63. Quoted in Harling Ross, "Why the Naked Dress Trend Will Never Die," *Repeller*, July 20, 2017, https://repeller.com/naked-dress-trend/.

64. Moore quoted in "Modella trans conquista la copertina di Elle: 'Diamo voce alle minoranze,'" *Il Messaggero*, May 23, 2019, https://www.ilmessaggero.it/mind_the_gap/modella_trans_elle_indya_moore-4508703.html.

65. Quoted in Alex Frank, "This Breakout Star Dedicates Her Red Carpet Win to the Trans Community at the Golden Globes," *Vogue*, January 6, 2019, https://www.vogue.com/article/golden-globes-red-carpet-indya-moore-pose.

66. IAM (@indyamoore), Instagram post saved to Pinterest by Ted X, accessed December 18, 2021, https://www.pinterest.com/pin/360569513917957867/.

67. "The Future of Fashion: From Design to Merchandising, How Tech Is Reshaping the Industry," CB Insights, May 11, 2021, https://www.cbinsights.com/research/fashion-tech-future-trends/.

68. Teresa de Lauretis, *Technologies of Gender: Essays on Theory, Film, and Fiction* (Bloomington: University of Indiana Press, 1987), 2.

69. Rachel Lasebikan, "WEAR at Ars Electronica 2018," September 7, 2018, https://legacy.wearsustain.eu/2018/09/07/wear-sustain-arselectronica-2018/.

70. Indya Moore, interview by Hari Ziyad, "Interview: Trans Actress Indya Moore on Representation; Putting a Trans Face on an Anti-Trans Institution Isn't Enough," *Afropunk*, April 25, 2017, https://afropunk.com/2017/04/interview-trans-actress-indya-moore-on-representation-putting-a-trans-face-on-an-anti-trans-institution-is-not-enough/.

71. Eva Reign, "Trans Women and Femmes Speak Out about Being Fetishized," *Them*, July 21, 2018, https://www.them.us/story/trans-women-femmes-fetishization.

72. Moore, interview by Cole.

73. Indya Moore (@indyamoore), "a face that did not come to play with you hoes," Instagram, April 24, 2019, https://www.instagram.com/indyamoore/p/Bwn_stYnGT7/?hl=en.

74. Jeanne Vaccaro, "Feelings and Fractals: Woolly Ecologies of Transgender Matter," *GLQ* 21, nos. 2–3 (June 2015): 283–284.

75. Vaccaro, 281.

76. Indya Moore quoted in Monica Roberts, "Indya Moore Makes History Again," *TransGriot*, May 10, 2019, https://transgriot.blogspot.com/2019/05/indya-moore-makes-history-again.html.

77. Moore, interview by Ziyad.

78. Indya Moore, interview by Mike Hill, "POSE Star Indya Moore Says Colonialism Invented Gender Binaries," YouTube video, uploaded by Ebony Magazine, January 14, 2019, https://www.youtube.com/watch?v=IMRZIViQuec.

79. Jackson, interview by Out.com editors.

80. Janet Mock, "I'm a Trans Woman, but Please Stop Asking Me about My Genitalia," *Elle*, January 9, 2014, https://www.elle.com/culture/career-politics/a14059/transgender-women-body-image/.

81. Janet Mock, "Why I Asked Alicia Menendez about Her Vagina and Other Invasive Questions," *Neo-Griot*, May 1, 2014, http://kalamu.com/neogriot/2014/05/05/interview-video-janet-mock/.

82. Mock, *Surpassing Certainty*, 16–17.

83. Janet Mock, "Sex Workers Matter: Sharing My Own Complicated Experience," Janet Mock's website, accessed December 18, 2021, https://janetmock.com/2014/01/30/janet-mock-sex-work-experiences/.

84. Janet Mock, "On the Women's March 'Guiding Vision' and Its Inclusion of Sex Workers," *Janet Mock on Tumblr* (blog), January 17, 2017, https://janetmock.tumblr.com/post/156017232338/womens-march-sex-worker-inclusion.

85. Crunktastic (Brittney C. Cooper), "Pussy Don't Fail Me Now: The Place of Vaginas in Black Feminist Theory and Organizing," *Crunk Feminist Collective*, January 23, 2017, http://www.crunkfeministcollective.com/2017/01/23/pussy-dont-fail-me-now-the-place-of-vaginas-in-black-feminist-theory-organizing/.

86. Joan Morgan, "Why We Get Off: Moving Towards a Black Feminist Politics of Pleasure," *Black Scholar* 45, no. 4 (Winter 2015): 36.

87. Cardi B featuring Megan Thee Stallion, "WAP" (New York: Atlantic, 2020).

88. Rhea Cartwright, "'WAP' Highlights the Hypocrisy That Sex Is Taboo When Women Steer the Conversation," *Popsugar*, August 10, 2010, https://www.popsugar.com/love/why-cardi-b-megan-wap-video-is-feminist-47679645.

89. James Bradley quoted in August Brown, "James P. Bradley Slams Cardi B / Megan Thee Stallion's 'WAP,'" *Los Angeles Times*, August 7, 2020, https://www.latimes.com/entertainment-arts/music/story/2020-08-07/cardi-b-megan-thee-stallion-wap-congressional-candidate-james-bradley.

90. Raquel Willis (@raquel_willis), "Folks are really mad about Cardi and Meg owning their sexuality," Instagram, August 10, 2020, https://www.instagram.com/p/CDugU1EgVMG/.

91. Carmel Ohman, "Undisciplining the Black Pussy: Pleasure, Black Feminism, and Sexuality in Issa Rae's *Insecure*," *Black Scholar* 50, no. 2 (April 2020): 5.

92. Indya Moore (@indyamoore), "WAP FACTORY," Instagram, October 1, 2020, https://www.instagram.com/p/CFoYyCRnBZi/.

93. "Savage X Fenty Show Vol. 2," Savage X Fenty, October 1, 2020, https://www.amazon.com/gp/video/detail/B08JQNCY8R/ref=atv_dp_season_select_s201.

94. Tente, "'Set That Body on Fire!,'" 45.

95. Mike Belmont, "Astraea of Greek Mythology," Gods-and-Monsters, accessed December 18, 2021, https://www.gods-and-monsters.com/astraea.html.

96. Moore, interview by Cole.

97. Indya Moore (@indyamoore), "Do things my own way darling," Instagram, October 1, 2020, https://www.instagram.com/p/CFoTcvFHXDR/.

PART TWO. HYMNS FOR CRAZY BLACK FEMMES

1. Jen Christensen, "Doctors Want President Trump's Head Examined," CNN, updated January 16, 2018, https://www.cnn.com/2018/01/13/health/trump -mental-health-exam/index.html.

2. Donald Trump quoted in Daniella Diaz, "Trump: I'm a 'Very Stable Genius,'" CNN, updated January 6, 2018, https://www.cnn.com/2018/01/06/politics /donald-trump-white-house-fitness-very-stable-genius/index.html.

3. Quoted in Christensen, "Doctors Want Trump's Head Examined."

4. Karen Bass, "#DiagnoseTrump," Change.org petition, accessed December 18, 2021, https://www.change.org/p/diagnosetrump.

5. John Gartner Ph.D., "Mental Health Professionals Declare Trump Is Mentally Ill and Must Be Removed," Change.org petition, accessed January 16, 2019, https://www.change.org/p/trump-is-mentally-ill-and-must-be-removed.

6. *Unfit: The Psychology of Donald Trump*, directed by Dan Partland (2020).

7. s. e. smith, "Why We Shouldn't 'Diagnose Trump,'" *Bustle*, August 4, 2016, https://www.bustle.com/articles/176861-why-the-diagnose-trump-hashtag -hurts-people-with-mental-illness.

8. Dan Schindel, "Donald Trump Is a Bad President; Let's Leave Mental Illness Out of It," *Hyperallergic*, September 3, 2020, https://hyperallergic.com/584273 /unfit-documentary-psychology-donald-trump/.

9. Greg Procknow, "Trump, Proto-presidency, and the Rise of Sane Supremacy," *Disability and Society* 32, no. 6 (2017): 915.

10. Center for American Progress, "2017: The Year the Disability Community Reshaped American Politics," November 14, 2017, https://www.americanprogress .org/events/2017/11/07/442398/2017-year-disability-community-reshaped -progressive-politics/?fbclid=IwAR0sM8QB2jaTB84p6cwsM4kL5nLYibN3R0g Xlw4wwU4EALYc7cMe3XOs1x0.

11. Alice Sheppard, "Intersectional Disability Arts Manifesto," Alice Sheppard's website, accessed December 18, 2021, https://alicesheppard.com/intersec tional-disability-arts-manifesto/.

12. Tourmaline in "We Move Together: Disability Justice and Trans Liberation," conversation with Patty Berne, Reina Gossett [Tourmaline], Kiyaan Abadani, and Malcolm Shanks, May 11, 2017, http://bcrw.barnard.edu/event/we -move-together-disability-justice-and-trans-liberation/.

13. Alice Sheppard, "My Promise in Accepting the Juried Bessie Award," Alice Sheppard's website, July 11, 2019, https://alicesheppard.com/my-promise-in -accepting-the-juried-bessie-award/.

14. Sheppard, "Intersectional Disability Arts Manifesto."

15. Alice Sheppard, "DESCENT by Kinetic Light," Alice Sheppard's website,

accessed December 18, 2021, https://alicesheppard.com/disabilitydanceworks /kinetic-light/.

16. Tourmaline (@tourmaliiine), "ableism figures psychiatric disability as not 'real' disability," Twitter, September 2, 2020, https://twitter.com/tourmaliiine /status/1301350078335135750.

17. Tourmaline and Sasha Wortzel, "Tourmaline and Sasha Wortzel Talk about Their Film *Happy Birthday, Marsha!*," *Artforum*, March 20,2018, https:// www.artforum.com/interviews/tourmaline-and-sasha-wortzel-talk-about-their -film-happy-birthday-marsha-74735.

18. Bria Royal, *Black Girl Mania: The Graphic Novel* (Chicago: CreateSpace, 2017), i.

KELSEY LU

1. Ann Cvetkovich, personal communication, November 16, 2016.

2. Ann Cvetkovich, *Depression: A Public Feeling* (Durham, NC: Duke University Press, 2012), loc. 98, Kindle.

3. Cvetkovich, personal communication.

4. Leah Lakshmi Piepzna-Samarasinha, *Care Work: Dreaming Disability Justice* (Vancouver, Canada: Arsenal Pulp Press, 2018), 192, Kindle.

5. Vickie M. Mays, Susan Cochran, and Michele Roeder, "Depressive Distress and Prevalence of Common Problems among Homosexually Active African American Women in the United States," *Journal of Psychology and Human Sexuality* 15, nos. 2–3 (January 2003): 27.

6. Piepzna-Samarasinha, *Care Work*, 196.

7. Piepzna-Samarasinha, 197.

8. Cvetkovich, *Depression*, loc. 336.

9. Geoffrey Jacques, poem presented at University of California, Santa Barbara, November 2019.

10. Lu quoted in Hannah Ongley, "Kelsey Lu Turned Her Depression into a Breathtaking Music Video," *i-D*, April 27, 2018, https://i-d.vice.com/en_uk /article/8xkpjk/kelsey-lu-depression-video-shades-of-blue.

11. Lu quoted in Tara Joshi, "Kelsey Lu: 'The White, Cis, Male Heteropatriarchy, It's All Being Deconstructed," *Guardian*, September 5, 2020, https:// www.theguardian.com/music/2020/sep/05/kelsey-lu-the-white-cis-male -hetero-patriarchy-its-all-being-deconstructed.

12. Kelsey Lu, interview by Sally Beauvais, "West Texas Talk: Kelsey Lu on Live Performance, Mix-Making, and Her New Song Shades of Blue," Marfa Public Radio, April 18, 2018, https://marfapublicradio.org/blog/west-texas-talk /kelsey-lu-on-live-performance-mix-making-and-her-new-song-shades-of-blue/.

13. Kelsey Lu quoted in Jessica Andrews, "Kelsey Lu Talks Sexual Identity, Personal Style, and Performing at the III Points Music Festival," *Teen Vogue*, December 6, 2017, https://www.teenvogue.com/story/kelsey-lu-interview-style-iii-points-music-festival.

14. Lu quoted in Andrews.

15. Quoted in Ongley, "Lu Turned Her Depression into Video."

16. Babatunde Lawal, "Orilonse: The Hermeneutics of the Head and Hairstyles among the Yoruba," in *Hair in African Art and culture*, ed. Roy Sieber and Frank Herreman (New York: Museum for African Art, 2000), 95.

17. Ayana D. Byrd and Lori L. Tharps, *Hair Story: Untangling the Roots of Black Hair in America*, revised and updated (New York: St. Martin's, 2001), 20.

18. Evan Ross Katz, "Four of Kelsey Lu's Best Looks (So Far)," *Vice*, April 19, 2019, https://garage.vice.com/en_us/article/43jdd9/kelsey-lu-best-looks.

19. William H. Gass, *On Being Blue: A Philosophical Inquiry* (New York: New York Review Books, 2014), loc. 148, 154, Kindle.

20. Andi Schwarz, "Low Femme," *Feral Feminisms*, no. 7 (Spring 2018), https://feralfeminisms.com/low-femme/#:~:text=Low%20Femme%20explores%20the%20effects,by%20social%20and%20political%20phenomena.

21. Gloria T. Hull, ed., *Give Us Each Day: The Diary of Alice Dunbar-Nelson* (New York: W. W. Norton, 1984), 430.

22. Hull, 20.

23. Hull, 359–360.

24. Hull, 123.

25. Alice Dunbar-Nelson, "Brass Ankles Speaks," Literary Ladies Guide, uploaded July 22, 2019, https://www.literaryladiesguide.com/full-texts-of-classic-works/brass-ankles-speaks-alice-dunbar-nelson/.

26. Hull, *Give Us Each Day*, 25.

27. Hull, 30.

28. StyleLikeU (Elisa Goodkind and Lily Mandelbaum), Patreon page, accessed December 18, 2021, https://www.patreon.com/stylelikeu.

29. Kelsey Lu, interview by StyleLikeU, "Escaping Jehovah's Witnesses & Finding Savoir In Her Own Creativity: Kelsey Lu McJunkins," YouTube video, uploaded by StyleLikeU, accessed December 18, 2021, https://www.dailymotion.com/video/x50071k.

30. Lu quoted in Ongley, "Lu Turned Her Depression into Video."

31. Kathryn Lindsay, "Kelsey Lu's 'Shades of Blue' Music Video Might Be the Next 'Lemonade,'" *Refinery29*, April 27, 2018, https://www.refinery29.com/en-us/2018/04/197586/kelsey-lu-shades-of-blue-music-video.

32. *Daughters of the Dust*, directed by Julie Dash (Geechee Girls Production, 1991).

33. Cvetkovich, *Depression*, loc. 336.

34. Yolanda Renee, "That Is Not a Protective Style!," *Curly Nikki*, accessed December 18, 2021, https://www.curlynikki.com/2016/01/that-is-not-protective-style.html.

35. Kelsey Lu, interview by Evan Nicole Brown, "Look and Listen: Kelsey Lu," *Office*, April 29, 2018, http://officemagazine.net/look-and-listen-kelsey-lu?page=8.

36. Bryan, "It Takes Ballz," 156.

37. TJ Bryan quoted in "Biography," bio page for TJ Bryan, Queer Media Database Canada-Québec Project, accessed December 18, 2021, http://www.mediaqueer.ca/artist/tj-bryan.

38. Lu, interview by Brown.

39. Cvetkovich, *Depression*, loc. 477–478.

40. Cvetkovich, loc. 477, 488.

41. Lawal, "Orilonse," 98.

42. Landon Peoples, "Kelsey Lu Is a Classically Trained Musician, but She's Also a Rising Fashion Star," *Refinery29*, September 24, 2018, https://www.refinery29.com/en-us/2018/09/209833/kelsey-lu-musician-style-interview.

43. Lu quoted in Peoples.

44. Busayo Olupona quoted in Chioma Nnadi, "This Centuries-Old African Natural Hairstyle Is Staging a Stateside Comeback," *Vogue*, October 27, 2017, https://www.vogue.com/article/hair-threading-irun-kiko-busayo-olupona.

45. Paul W. Andrews and J. Anderson Thomson Jr., "Depression's Evolutionary Roots," *Scientific American*, August 25, 2009, https://www.scientificamerican.com/article/depressions-evolutionary/.

46. "My Orisha Journey: The Spiritual Meaning of Depression," YouTube video, uploaded by day aka oyabunmi (Day Dream Alston), April 15, 2019, https://www.youtube.com/watch?v=oteToFAFqVU.

47. Imade Nibokun quoted in So Sad Today, "'I Thought Depression Was a White People Disease': A Conversation with Depressed While Black," *Vice*, March 15, 2018, https://www.vice.com/en/article/ywxmgx/i-thought-depression-was-a-white-people-disease-a-conversation-with-depressed-while-black.

48. Lynette Nylander, "Avant-Pop Star Kelsey Lu on Reclaiming Her Freedom," *AnOther*, February 12, 2020, https://www.anothermag.com/fashion-beauty/12238/kelsey-lu-musician-interview-profile-2020-grounded-blood-transfusion?fbclid=IwAR3dxBYlF8kpU9ta5ACOW-K-tYl1ys_qB5quevh-UbuXf95XizVcl2COVI4.

49. Sherronda J. Brown, "Nothing about Being Black Is Easy, Including Our Hair Care," *Wear Your Voice*, March 5, 2019, https://wearyourvoicemag.com/natural-hair/.

50. Brown.

51. Brown.

52. Makeda Easter, "Solange. Blood Orange. Kelsey Lu. There's a New Wave of Genre-Defying Black Artists," *Los Angeles Times*, August 21, 2019, https://www.latimes.com/entertainment-arts/story/2019-08-20/kelsey-lu-la-black-art-scene.

53. Willobee Carlan, "Slingshot: Artists to Watch in 2019," WFDD, January 17, 2019, https://www.wfdd.org/story/slingshot-artists-watch-2019.

54. Quoted in Henry Bruce-Jones, "Kelsey Lu Questions the Romanticism of Home on New Track 'Due West,'" *Fact*, accessed December 18, 2021, https://www.factmag.com/2018/11/09/kelsey-lu-due-west/.

55. Marc Hogan, "Kelsey Lu: 'Due West,'" *Pitchfork*, November 9, 2018, https://pitchfork.com/reviews/tracks/due-west/.

56. "Women in Windows: Press Release," February 21, 2019, https://static1.squarespace.com/static/5ec35d5f52052b09275bd03f/t/5f7cc4959b662b5af63065ce/1602012315284/WomenInWindows_2019_PressKit.pdf.

57. Andy Beta, "10cc's 'I'm Not in Love' Was the Real Song of the Summer," *Deadspin*, September 22, 2014, https://theconcourse.deadspin.com/10ccs-im-not-in-love-was-the-real-song-of-the-summer-1637590430.

58. J. Simpson, "Best New Song: Kelsey Lu—I'm Not in Love," The Guard, January 16, 2019, https://www.weareteguard.com/music/best-new-song-kelsey-lu-i'm-not-love.

59. Lauren Valenti, "Kelsey Lu's Serpentine Braid Is the Breakout Star of Her 'I'm Not in Love' Music Video," *Vogue*, January 11, 2019, https://www.vogue.com/article/kelsey-lu-im-not-in-love-music-video-long-braid-hair-beauty.

60. Valenti.

61. Sarah Sunday, "Unwrapping the Visual of Kelsey Lu's 'I'm Not in Love,'" *Musée*, accessed December 18, 2021, https://museemagazine.com/features/2019/1/29/unwrapping-the-visual-of-kelsey-lus-im-not-in-love.

62. Quoted in Czar Van Gaal, "Kelsey Lu Declares 'I'm Not in Love' in a New Short Film," *V*, January 11, 2019, https://vmagazine.com/article/kelsey-lu-declares-im-not-in-love-in-a-new-short-film/.

63. Mays, Cochran, and Roeder, "Depressive Distress," 35–36.

64. Shelley Stamp quoted in Noah Berlatsky, "Carrie at 40: Why the Horror Genre Remains Important to Women," *Guardian*, November 3, 2016, https://www.theguardian.com/film/2016/nov/03/carrie-stephen-king-brian-de-palma-horror-films-feminism.

65. Gemma L. Witcomb, Walter Pierre Bouman, Laurence Claes, Nicola Brewin, John R. Crawford, and Jon Arcelus, "Levels of Depression in Transgender People and Its Predictors: Results of a Large Matched Control Study with Transgender People Accessing Clinical Services," *Journal of Affective Disorders* 235 (August 2018): 308–315.

66. Colette Balmain, "It's Alive: Disorderly and Dangerous Hair in Japanese Cinema," (conference paper, Perspectives on Evil and Human Wickedness, Salzburg, Austria, March 2008), 9.

67. Bryan, "It Takes Ballz," 163.

68. Ingrid Banks, *Hair Matters: Beauty, Power, and Black Women's Consciousness* (New York: New York University Press, 2000), 88, 89, Kindle.

69. Hunter Shackelford, "Black Girl Interrupted: My Body, the World, and Nonbinary Me," *Wear Your Voice*, November 18, 2016, https://wearyourvoicemag .com/black-girl-interrupted-nonbinary/.

70. Rachel Hahn, "Kelsey Lu Puts a Punchy Twist on a Classic Suit," *Vogue*, October 28, 2019, https://www.vogue.com/vogueworld/article/kelsey-lu-instagram -green-kwaidan-editions-suit-nts-radio-the-tate-modern-london.

71. Alex Frank, "Kelsey Lu's Dreams Are Better Than Yours," *Pitchfork*, August 12, 2016, https://pitchfork.com/features/rising/9934-kelsey-lus-dreams -are-better-than-yours/.

72. Latonya Pennington, "How Femmephobia and the Gender Binary Caused Me to Hate Myself," Black Youth Project, March 24, 2017, http://blackyouth project.com/how-femmephobia-and-the-gender-binary-caused-me-to-hate -myself/.

73. Piepzna-Samarasinha, *Care Work*, 202.

74. *Euphoria*, season 1, episode 7, "The Trials and Tribulations of Trying to Pee While Depressed," directed by Sam Levinson.

75. Kelsey Lu quoted in Stephen Daw, "How Kelsey Lu Processed a Painful Past into a Message of Hope on Her Debut Album 'Blood,'" *Billboard*, April 22, 2019, https://www.billboard.com/articles/news/pride/8508060/kelsey -lu-interview-blood.

76. Clarkisha Kent, "How *Euphoria* Is Trying to Shatter What It Means to Be a 'Real Girl,'" *Entertainment Weekly*, July 31, 2019, https://ew.com/tv/2019/07/31 /euphoria-jules-shattering-what-it-means-to-be-a-real-girl/.

77. Clarkisha Kent, "On Fatphobia, Hair Discrimination, and Daily Negotiations with a Racist Society," *Afropunk*, April 2, 2019, https://afropunk.com /2019/04/clarkisha-fatphobia/.

78. Kent.

79. Clarkisha Kent, "An Ode to the Would-Be Carefree Black Girl in All of Us," *Afropunk*, April 12, 2019, https://afropunk.com/2019/04/blue-ivy-care free/.

80. Mock, *Surpassing Certainty*, 43.

81. Kelsey Lu quoted in Sydney Gore, "Kelsey Lu Breaks Down the Lyrics on Her 'Church' EP," *Nylon*, July 8, 2016, https://www.nylon.com/articles/kelsey -lu-church-ep.

TOURMALINE

1. Valerie Mesa, "Cancer Season 2020 Will Be the Best for These 3 Zodiac Signs," *Elite Daily*, June 18, 2020, https://www.elitedaily.com/p/cancer-season -2020-will-be-the-best-for-these-3-zodiac-signs-22949685.

2. Ari Felix, "A Love Note for the Weekend," Saltwater Stars, July 3, 2020, https://www.saltwaterstars.com/blog?offset=1595437328215.

3. Tourmaline, "Filmmaker and Activist Tourmaline on How to Freedom Dream," *Vogue*, July 2, 2020, https://www.vogue.com/article/filmmaker-and -activist-tourmaline-on-how-to-freedom-dream.

4. Tourmaline.

5. Tourmaline (@tourmaliiine), "Much of what exists in the public realm about Marsha and Sylvia I put online," Instagram, July 8, 2020, https://www .instagram.com/p/CCYkMY8B__c/.

6. Tourmaline (with Miss Major Griffin-Gracy, Barbara Smith, Alicia Garza, and Charlene Carruthers), interview by Out.com editors, "The Mothers and Daughters of the Movement," https://www.out.com/out-exclusives/2019/2/12/our -march-cover-stars-mothers-and-daughters-movement.

7. Tourmaline (@tourmaliiine), "This moment is a culmination and continuation of the countless forms of resistance and refusal," Instagram, May 31, 2020, https://www.instagram.com/p/CA3Nn1vhX_2/.

8. Anole Halper, "Marsha P. Johnson and Sylvia Rivera Were the Mothers of the Movement, but How Do We Tell the Story of Their Struggles with Their Minds?," *Trans Survivors*, June 25, 2019, https://trans-survivors.com/2019/06/25 /marsha-p-and-sylvia-rivera/.

9. Tourmaline, personal communication, April 2020.

10. Marsha P. Johnson quoted in Bianca Rodriguez, "Unforgettable Quotes by Marsha P. Johnson," *Marie Claire*, June 3, 2020, https://www.marieclaire.com /politics/a32745825/marsha-p-johnson-quotes/.

11. Chelsea Johnson, "The History of Headwraps: Then, There, and Now," *Naturally Curly*, June 16, 2020, https://www.naturallycurly.com/curlreading /hairstyles/the-history-of-headwraps-then-there-and-now.

12. Khanya Mtshali, "The Radical History of the Headwrap," *Timeline*, May 10, 2018, https://timeline.com/headwraps-were-born-out-of-slavery-be fore-being-reclaimed-207e2c65703b.

13. Mtshali.

14. Piepzna-Samarasinha, *Care Work*, 196.

15. Tourmaline, interview by Out.com editors.

16. Colin King, "They Diagnosed Me a Schizophrenic When I Was Just a Gemini: The Other Side of Madness,'" in *Reconceiving Schizophrenia*, ed. Man

Cheung Chung, K. W. M. (Bill) Fulford, and George Graham (Oxford, UK: Oxford University Press, 2007), 12.

17. LunarLampLight, "The Cancer Archetype—Feminine Authority and a Mother's Wisdom," Reddit, April 21, 2020, https://www.reddit.com/r/astrology /comments/g5ropu/the_cancer_archetype_feminine_authority_and_a/.

18. Piepzna-Samarasinha, *Care Work*, 195.

19. LunarLampLight, "Cancer Archetype."

20. Sir Lady Java, interview by Pasqual Bettio, "Pasqual's Eye on Sir Lady Java & T. Porter," YouTube video, uploaded by Tom Porter, May 24, 2016, https://www .youtube.com/watch?v=IIXMxouJxgA.

21. Brochure reproduced in "Sir Lady Java," Transas City, accessed December 18, 2021, http://transascity.org/sir-lady-java/.

22. Quoted in Ellison, "Labor of Werqing It," 10.

23. "Lena Meets Sir Lady Java at Festive L.A. Birthday Bash," *Jet*, August 10, 1978.

24. Carolyn Morrow Long, *A New Orleans Voudou Priestess: The Legend and Reality of Marie Laveau* (Gainesville: University Press of Florida, 2006), 21.

25. Sir Lady Java, interview by Bettio.

26. "Sir Lady Java," Transas City.

27. Sir Lady Java, interview by Bettio.

28. Ellison, "Labor of Werqing It," 12.

29. Tourmaline and Wortzel, "Talk about Their Film."

30. Tourmaline, "How to Freedom Dream."

31. Jeannine Tang, "Contemporary Art and Critical Transgender Infrastructures," in Gossett, Stanley, and Burton, *Trap Door*, 382.

32. Marsha P. Johnson in "Pay It No Mind."

33. "Pay It No Mind."

34. Sewell Chan, "Marsha P. Johnson," *New York Times*, March 8, 2018, https:// www.nytimes.com/interactive/2018/obituaries/overlooked-marsha-p-johnson .html.

35. "Pay It No Mind."

36. Felix, "Love Note for the Weekend."

37. Rhoda Olkin, H'Sien Hayward, Melody Schaff Abbene, and Goldie Van-Heel, "The Experiences of Microaggressions against Women with Visible and Invisible Disabilities," *Journal of Social Issues* 75, no. 3 (2019): 771.

38. Piepzna-Samarasinha, *Care Work*, 182, 125.

39. See Mecca Woods, *Astrology for Happiness and Success* (New York: Simon and Schuster, 2018), 77–79.

40. See Kay Sargent, "Designing for Neurodiversity and Inclusion," *Work Design*, accessed December 18, 2021, https://www.workdesign.com/2019/12/designing -for-neurodiversity-and-inclusion/.

41. Piepzna-Samarasinha, *Care Work*, 77, 78.

42. Hougan Sydney, "Erzulie Freda," October 5, 2014, http://hougansydney .com/voodoo-spirits/erzulie-freda.

43. Maya Deren, *Divine Horsemen: The Living Gods of Haiti* (New Paltz, New York: McPherson, 1970), 143.

44. Mambo Vye Zo Komande LaMenfo, *Serving the Spirits: The Religion of Haitian Vodou* (Lexington, KY: Mambo Vye Zo, 2011), 154.

45. Mambo Vye Zo, 150.

46. Piepzna-Samarasinha, *Care Work*, 179.

47. Tourmaline and Wortzel, "Talk about Their Film."

48. Jessica Marie Johnson, "4DH + 1 Black Code / Black Femme Forms of Knowledge and Practice," *American Quarterly* 70, no. 3, (September 2018).

49. Leah Lakshmi Piepzna-Samarasinha, "Disability Justice/Stonewall's Legacy, or: Love Mad Trans Black Women When They Are Alive and Dead, Let Their Revolutions Teach Your Resistance All the Time," *QED: A Journal in GLBTQ Worldmaking* 6, no. 2 (2019): 54–55.

50. Niv (Navild) Acosta and Fanny Sosa, *Siestas Negras*, no. 1, https://www .yumpu.com/es/document/read/61681023/siestasnegras-periodico.

51. Navild Acosta and Fanny Sosa, "Black Power Naps: Performance Space New York - January 2019," Black Power Naps, accessed December 18, 2021, https:// blackpowernaps.black/BPN-New-York-1.

52. Janine Francois, "Reparations for Black People Should Include Rest," *Vice*, January 8, 2019, https://www.vice.com/en/article/d3bbay/sleep-gap-black -slavery-reparations-black-power-naps.

53. Clara Mejias quoted in Agnish Ray, "Siestas Negras: A Conversation with niv Acosta and Fannie Sosa," *Schön!*, June 28, 2018, https://schonmagazine.com /siestas-negras-a-conversation-with-niv-acosta-and-fannie-sosa/.

54. Acosta and Sosa, *Siestas Negras*, no. 1: 6.

55. Fannie Sosa and niv Acosta, "A Place to Nap While Black," *Vice*, January 9, 2019, https://www.vice.com/en/article/a3mbap/black-power-naps-photos -mission-fannie-sosa-niv-acosta.

56. Piepzna-Samarasinha, *Care Work*, 181–182.

57. Sosa and Acosta, "Place to Nap."

58. Maxine Wally, "Tourmaline Reflects on the Power and Possibility of Black Art," *W*, June 25, 2020, https://www.wmagazine.com/story/tourmaline -filmmaker-salacia-moma-permanent-collection-keanu-reeves.

59. Wally.

60. Terri L. Snyder, "Suicide, Slavery, and Memory in North America," *Journal of American History* 97, no. 1 (June 2010): 43.

61. Tourmaline and Thomas Jean Lax, "Anything We Want to Be:

Tourmaline's *Salacia*," MoMA, June 25, 2020, https://www.moma.org/magazine/articles/360.

62. Lisa Ze Winters, *The Mulatta Concubine: Terror, Intimacy, Freedom, and Desire in the Black Transatlantic* (Athens: University of Georgia Press, 2016), 82.

63. See Josiah Henson, *The Life of Josiah Henson, Formerly a Slave, Now an Inhabitant of Canada, as Narrated by Himself* (Bedford, MA: Applewood Books, 2002); William and Ellen Craft, *Running a Thousand Miles for Freedom: Or, The Escape of William and Ellen Craft from Slavery* (Minneola, NY: Dover, 2014), 31.

64. Tourmaline posted the digitized interview to her Vimeo: "Randy Wicker Interviews Sylvia Rivera on the Pier," Vimeo video, uploaded by Tourmaline, January 31, 2012, https://vimeo.com/35975275.

65. Michael T. Kaufman, "Still Here: Sylvia, Who Survived Stonewall, Time and the River," *New York Times*, May 25, 1995, https://www.nytimes.com/1995/05/24/nyregion/about-new-york-still-here-sylvia-who-survived-stonewall-time-and-the-river.html.

66. Asian American Writers' Workshop, "AAWW Fave: Disability Justice (ft. Leah Lakshmi Piepzna-Samarasinha & Cyrée Jarelle Johnson)," May 13, 2020, in AAWW Radio, https://aawwradio.libsyn.com/aaww-fave-disability-justice-ft-leah-lakshmi-piepzna-samarasinha-cyree-jarelle-johnson.

67. Invisible Disabilities Association, "What Is an Invisible Disability?," accessed December 18, 2021, https://invisibledisabilities.org/what-is-an-invisible-disability/.

68. Therí Alyce Pickens, *Black Madness :: Mad Blackness* (Durham, NC: Duke University Press, 2019), loc. 1397, Kindle.

69. Piepzna-Samarasinha, *Care Work*, 248–249.

70. Nicole R. Fleetwood, *Marking Time: Art in the Age of Mass Incarceration* (Cambridge, MA: Harvard University Press, 2020), 38.

71. Fleetwood, 39.

72. Pickens, *Black Madness*, loc. 1723.

73. Omise'eke Natasha Tinsley, *Ezili's Mirrors: Imagining Black Queer Genders* (Durham, NC: Duke University Press, 2018), 106.

74. M. Jacqui Alexander, *Pedagogies of Crossing: Meditations on Feminism, Sexual Politics, Memory, and the Sacred* (Durham, NC: Duke University Press, 2005), 309.

75. "Come Join the Hottest Ladies Parading Mardi Gras," Krewe of Salacia Facebook page, July 23, 2020, https://www.facebook.com/KreweofSalacia/.

76. Ari Felix, "Love Letter to the Sun in Cancer," accessed July 2, 2020, https://www.saltwaterstars.com/blog?offset=1593821962015.

77. Tourmaline quoted in Sessi Kuwabara Blanchard, "Marsha P. Johnson's LGBTQ Legacy Is about How She Lived Her Life, Too," *Vice*, August 20, 2018,

https://www.vice.com/en_us/article/594aq8/marsha-p-johnson-happy-birthday-marsha-transgender-rights.

78. Tourmaline and Lax, "Anything We Want to Be."

79. Piepzna-Samarasinha, *Care Work*, 252.

80. Tourmaline quoted in Wally, "Power and Possibility."

81. Cherno Biko (@chernobiko), "Happy Birthday to The Girl Who Lived," Instagram, May 26, 2015, https://www.instagram.com/p/3J-ZOAGSZO/.

82. Sharyn Jackson, "From Locked Up to Legend: New Movie Tells Story of Mpls. Transgender Advocate," *Star Tribune*, October 23, 2016, https://www.startribune.com/from-lockup-to-legend-new-movie-tells-story-of-mpls-transgender-advocate/397826771/.

83. *Free CeCe!*, directed by Jac Gares (Jac Gares Media, 2016).

84. CeCe McDonald, as told to Dee Lockett, "The Traumatic Reality of Getting Sent to Solitary Confinement for Being Trans That *Orange Is the New Black* Can't Show," *Vulture*, June 28, 2016, https://www.vulture.com/2016/06/cece-mcdonald-as-told-to-orange-is-the-new-black.html.

85. CeCe McDonald, "Black Trans Lives Matter: A Conversation with CeCe McDonald and Elle Hearns," University of Santa Barbara, Multicultural Center, February 11, 2021.

86. Ari Felix, "Love Letter to the Sun in Gemini," accessed July 23, 2020, https://www.saltwaterstars.com/blog?offset=1589570996532&reversePaginate=true.

87. CeCe McDonald, foreword to *Captive Genders: Trans Embodiment and the Prison Industrial Complex*, 2nd ed., ed. Eric A. Stanley and Nat Smith (Oakland, CA: AK Press, 2015), 4.

88. McDonald in *Free CeCe!*

89. McDonald in *Free CeCe!*

90. Quoted in Sabrina Rubin Erdely, "The Transgender Crucible," *Rolling Stone*, July 30, 2014, https://www.rollingstone.com/culture/culture-news/the-transgender-crucible-114095/.

91. See Aaron Rose Philip (@aaron___philip), Instagram posts, "HAPPY BIRTHDAY @oaklandbae," July 2, 2020, https://www.instagram.com/p/CCJwkYXFiUL/; "!!!!!! rp @sinmiedomateo via @goodegawd," July 3, 2020, https://www.instagram.com/p/CCNOVPJl_jK/; "PLEASE BOOST/SHARE/DONATE TO HELP @blackqueerbpd," July 5, 2020, https://www.instagram.com/p/CCQ-wKmFWUW/.

92. Jean Maline, "Birthday Benz for Tourmaline," GoFundMe campaign, created July 3, 2020, https://www.gofundme.com/f/bday-benz-for-tourmaline?utm_source=customer&utm_campaign=p_cp+share-sheet&utm_medium=copy_link-tip.

93. Tourmaline (@tourmaliiine), "7 days left!," Instagram, July 13, 2020, https://www.instagram.com/p/CCmQnxhBbVU/.

94. Tourmaline (@tourmaliiine), "We shouldn't only have to ask for the things we need to survive," Twitter, July 8, 2020, https://twitter.com/tourmaliiine/status/1280945237997821953.

95. Tourmaline (@tourmaliiine), "wow! Thank you @jamesfalciano for this illustration," Instagram, May 22, 2020, https://www.instagram.com/p/CAgOPYdnX4s/.

96. Tourmaline (@tourmaliiine), "Black trans people are constantly told to turn our light down," Instagram, July 16, 2020, https://www.instagram.com/p/CCtI5yCh3Yy/.

97. Tourmaline (@tourmaliiine), "THANK YOU DREAMY COMMUNITY FOR GETTING ME THIS DREAM CAR!," Instagram, August 9, 2020, https://www.instagram.com/p/CDrR7vABj3j/.

PART THREE. BLACK FEMME ENVIRONMENTALISM FOR THE FUTA

1. Brooke Holland, "Santa Barbara Teens Rally for Action on Climate Change," *Noozhawk*, September 20, 2019, https://www.noozhawk.com/article/santa_barbara_students_march_global_climate_strike.

2. Jude Casimir, "Whitewashing Activism: Environmentalist Edition," *Beacon Broadside*, November 5, 2019, https://www.beaconbroadside.com/broadside/2019/11/whitewashing-activism-environmentalist-edition.html.

3. Naomi Thompkins, "Black Environmentalism," *Confluence*, October 9, 2020, https://confluence.gallatin.nyu.edu/sections/research/black-environmentalism?utm_source=rss&utm_medium=rss&utm_campaign=black-environmentalism.

4. Matto Mildenberger, "The Tragedy of the *Tragedy of the Commons*," *Scientific American*, April 23, 2019, https://blogs.scientificamerican.com/voices/the-tragedy-of-the-tragedy-of-the-commons/.

5. Thompkins, "Black Environmentalism."

6. Patty Berne and Vanessa Raditz, "To Survive Climate Catastrophe, Look to Queer and Disabled Folks," *Yes!*, July 31, 2019, https://www.yesmagazine.org/opinion/2019/07/31/climate-change-queer-disabled-organizers/.

7. Casimir, "Whitewashing Activism."

8. Berne and Raditz, "To Survive Climate Catastrophe."

9. Alexis Pauline Gumbs, *Undrowned: Black Feminist Lessons from Marine Mammals* (Oakland, CA: AK Press, 2020), 11, Kindle.

(F)EMPOWER

1. "23," on Saweetie, *High Maintenance* (Warner Records, 2018).

2. Scott Wilson, "Fires, Floods and Free Parking: California's Unending Fight against Climate Change, *Washington Post*, December 5, 2019, https://www.washingtonpost.com/graphics/2019/national/climate-environment/climate-change-california/.

3. Berne and Raditz, "To Survive Climate Catastrophe."

4. "Who We Are," (F)empower, accessed December 18, 2021, https://fempower mia.bigcartel.com/who-we-are.

5. Berne and Raditz, "To Survive Climate Catastrophe."

6. Helen Peña (@orangemooon), "Reading an article about climate change," Instagram, August 17, 2017, https://www.instagram.com/p/BYB7pxlHErd/.

7. Helen Peña quoted in "(F)empower MIA Shot by Lex Morales," *Chromat*, August 6, 2018, https://chromat.co/blogs/news/fempower.

8. Nicole Martinez, "The Radical Art Collective Fighting to Stop Miami from Becoming Atlantis," *Dazed*, May 15, 2019, https://www.dazeddigital.com/art-photography/article/44350/1/fempower-art-collective-climate-change-miami-2040.

9. Jorge Courtade, "This Collective Is Providing a Space for Miami's Queer, Femme Community," *Remezcla*, October 5, 2017, https://remezcla.com/features/culture/fempower-miami-queer-femme-community/.

10. Courtade, "This Collective Is Providing a Space."

11. Martinez, "Radical Art Collective."

12. Courtade, "This Collective Is Providing a Space."

13. Fem Fairy Garden (@femfairygarden), Instagram profile, accessed April 20, 2020, https://www.instagram.com/femfairygarden/.

14. Helen Peña quoted in Maria Esquinca, "Fighting Climate Gentrification with a Radical Community Garden," *Scalawag*, February 25, 2019, https://scala wagmagazine.org/2019/02/fempower-garden/.

15. Esquinca.

16. Tina M. Campt, *Listening to Images* (Durham, NC: Duke University Press, 2017), Kindle.

17. Alexis Pauline Gumbs, "We Can Learn to Mother Ourselves: The Queer Survival of Black Feminism 1968–1996" (PhD dissertation, Duke University, 2010), 12.

18. Gumbs, 2.

19. Carl Fisher quoted in Julio Capó Jr., *Welcome to Fairyland: Queer Miami before 1940* (Chapel Hill: University of North Carolina Press, 2017), Kindle.

20. Capó.

21. Capó.

22. M. Athalie Range quoted in Marina Novaes, "Report of the City of Miami Preservation Office to the Historic and Environmental Preservation Board on the Designation of the Historic Virginia Key Beach Park as a Historic Site," Miami Believe, 13, accessed March 17, 2020, http://miamibelieve.com/pdfs/Historic VirginiaKeyBeachPark.pdf.

23. Roshan Nebhrajani, "'White Sand, Black Beach': The Black History of Virginia Key," *The New Tropic*, February 12, 2017, https://thenewtropic.com/virginia -key-beach/.

24. M. Athalie Range quoted in Novaes, "Report of the City of Miami," 13.

25. Martinez, "Radical Art Collective."

26. Gregory W. Bush, *White Sand, Black Beach: Civil Rights, Public Space, and Miami's Virginia Key* (Gainesville: University Press of Florida, 2016), 43.

27. (F)empower (@fempowermia), "Welcome to your new local playground," Instagram, May 7, 2017, https://www.instagram.com/p/BToS4eblCGE/.

28. Grace Fussell, "The Origins, History, and Design Power of Neon Colors," Shutterstock, September 25, 2019, https://www.shutterstock.com/blog/neon -colors-history-design#:~:text=Fluorescent%20or%20neon%20colors%20are ,emit%20light%2C%20making%20them%20luminescent.

29. Campt, *Listening to Images*, 130–131.

30. (F)empower (@fempowermia), "It is that time of year again!," Instagram, February 1, 2020, https://www.instagram.com/p/B8CUj2LArdr/.

31. (F)empower (@fempowermia), "Zora Neale Hurston (1891–1960) was a writer and anthropologist," Instagram, February 6, 2020, https://www.instagram .com/p/B8O8b5RH-Ox/.

32. Zora Neale Hurston, "How It Feels to Be Colored Me" (1928), https://www .wheelersburg.net/Downloads/Hurston.pdf.

33. M. Alene Murrell, *Zora Neale Hurston in and around Jacksonville, Florida in the 1920's, 1930's and 1940's* (Apple Books, 2003), 165, 175.

34. Murrell, 50.

35. Murrell, 171.

36. Zora Neale Hurston, *Dust Tracks on a Road* (New York: Harper Perennial, 1996), 264.

37. Zora Neale Hurston, *Their Eyes Were Watching God* (New York: Amistad, 2009).

38. Edwidge Danticat quoted in CBC Radio, "Dismissed in Her Lifetime, African-American Writer Zora Neale Hurston Is Considered a Legend in Ours," *The Sunday Magazine*, May 18, 2018, https://www.cbc.ca/radio/sunday/the-sunday -edition-may-20-2018-1.4663712/dismissed-in-her-lifetime-african-american -writer-zora-neale-hurston-is-considered-a-legend-in-ours-1.4668643.

39. Sarah Anne Pfitzer, "Unnatural Disasters: Environmental Trauma and Ecofeminist/Ecowomanist Resistance in Zora Neale Hurston's *Their Eyes Were Watching God* and Jesmyn Ward's *Salvage the Bones*" (honors thesis, Belmont University, 2020), 5, https://repository.belmont.edu/honors_theses/9.

40. Zoe Ruffner, "14 Art Basel Beauty Staples for a Sunnier State of Mind," *Vogue*, December 6, 2018, https://www.vogue.com/article/art-basel-miami-beauty -packing-guide.

41. Naomi Rea, "What Would It Cost for the Art World to Offset Its Enormous Carbon Footprint? We've Compiled a Helpful Menu of Prices," Artnet, December 9, 2019, https://news.artnet.com/art-world/carbon-offset-art-world-1720782.

42. William Skeaping quoted in Kate Brown, "'All Culture Is Going to Trash as Soon as the Food Runs Out': Why Extinction Rebellion's Climate Activists Are Targeting Art Basel Miami Beach," Artnet, December 3, 2019, https://news .artnet.com/market/extinction-rebellion-art-basel-miami-beach-1718208.

43. (F)empower (@fempowermia), "DEC 6 + 7: (F)EMPOWER PRESENTS 2040: A 2-day exhibition and immersive installation," Instagram, November 23, 2018, https://www.instagram.com/p/BqikvuGHFg9/.

44. Martinez, "Radical Art Collective."

45. Margo Hannah (@margohannah_), "Here's what you missed if you didn't attend @projectz.miami," Instagram, December 14, 2018, https://www.instagram .com/p/BrY79ishkXw/.

46. Margo Hannah (@margohannah_), "@niquejeffries look inspired by some of your favorite 90s r&b groups," Instagram, December 23, 2018, https:// www.instagram.com/p/BrwUPmjBowS/.

47. Lawrence La Fountain-Stokes, "Puerto Rican *Rasanblaj*: Freddie Mercado's Gender Disruption," in "Caribbean Rasanblaj," ed. Gina Athena Ulysse, special is-sue, *Emisférica* 12, nos. 1–2 (2015), https://hemisphericinstitute.org/en/emisferica -121-caribbean-rasanblaj/12-1-essays/e-121-essay-lafountain-puerto-rican-rasan blaj.html.

48. Monica Uszerowicz, "(F)empower Is the Collective Inspiring a Black and Brown Feminist Awakening in Miami," *i-D*, December 3, 2018, https://i-d.vice .com/en_us/article/zmdydy/fempower-is-the-collective-inspiring-a-black-and -brown-feminist-awakening-in-miami.

49. Janaya Khan, "Black Radicalism as Vulnerability," *RaceBaitr*, July 6, 2015, https://racebaitr.com/2015/07/06/black-radicalism-as-vulnerability/.

50. Loka (Yesenia Rojas) quoted in Martinez, "Radical Art Collective."

51. Thompson, *Shine*.

52. Brown, *Emergent Strategy*, loc. 70.

53. Brown, loc. 479.

54. Lyn Mikel Brown and Dana Edell, "'I Love Beyoncé, but I Struggle with

Beyoncé': Girl Activists Talk Music and Feminism," in *Voicing Girlhood in Popular Music: Performance, Authority, Authenticity*, ed. Jacqueline Warwick and Allison Adrian (New York: Routledge, 2016), 59.

55. "Ego," on Beyoncé, *I Am . . . Sasha Fierce* (Columbia Records, 2008).

56. Margo Hannah, "Cut It," *Broke and Black*, June 19, 2016, http://broke blackblog.blogspot.com/search?updated-max=2016-08-02T18:18:00-07:00&max -results=4&reverse-paginate=true.

57. Margo Hannah, "Get Off My Areola!," *Broke and Black*, June 8, 2015, http://brokeblackblog.blogspot.com/2015/.

58. Becky Rutledge, *Miss Becky's Charm School: Using Southern Belle Secrets to Land Your Man* (New York: Kensington, 2007), 91.

59. Tinsley, *Ezili's Mirrors*, 13.

60. Stacey Cook, "Dreaming of Sustainability in a Material World," *National Geographic*, September 6, 2019, https://www.nationalgeographic.com/environment /2019/09/partner-content-dreaming-sustainability-in-material-world/.

61. Lida Pashkevych, Karan Khurana, O. V. Kolosnichenko, T. F. Krotova, and A. M. Veklich, "Modern Directions of Eco-Design in the Fashion Industry," *Art and Design*, no. 4 (2019): 13.

62. Elizabeth Broeder, "TRASHGiRRRRLLLZZ: A Manifesto for Misfit ToYZ," in *Burn It Down! Feminist Manifestos for the Revolution*, ed. Breanne Fahs (London: Verso, 2020), Kindle, loc. 505.

63. Mumbi O'Brien quoted in Martinez, "Radical Art Collective."

64. Mumbi (@mumb_iii), "Femme Future Protectors," Instagram, April 26, 2019, https://www.instagram.com/p/BwumMwplfzf/.

65. BLK MKT Vintage (@blkmktvintage), "Black Spring Break 1999 in Daytona Beach," Instagram, post January 25, 2020, https://www.instagram.com/p /B7w2bsDn-jI/.

66. BLK MKT Vintage (@blkmktvintage), "Spotted at our shop earlier today," Instagram, February 17, 2020, https://www.instagram.com/p/B8r631XHnkC/.

67. Kiyanna Stewart quoted in Genel Ambrose, "The Amazing Vintage Shop That Celebrates Black History Every Day," *Vice*, March 28, 2018, https://www.vice.com/en /article/9kgyq5/the-amazing-vintage-shop-that-celebrates-black-history-every-day.

68. Kiyanna Stewart and Jannah Handy quoted in Jaimee Swift, "Want to Collect Black Antiques? Don't Worry, the Creators of 'BLK Market Vintage' Got You Covered," *Huffington Post*, November 6, 2017, https://www.huffpost.com /entry/want-to-collect-black-antiques-dont-worry-the-creators_b_59ffc18be4 b0d467d4c22664.

69. Eliza Dumais, "These Women Are Rebranding the Antique Industry—& Shifting How We Curate Our Homes," *Refinery29*, August 30, 2019, https://www .refinery29.com/en-us/home-decor-vintage-maximal-inspo.

70. Gina Athena Ulysse, introduction to "Caribbean Rasanblaj," special issue, *Emisférica* 12, nos. 1–2 (2015), https://hemisphericinstitute.org/en/emisferica -121-caribbean-rasanblaj/121-introduction.html.

71. Kiyanna Stewart (@aunt_viv), "Me at any beach: okay, how black can I get?," Instagram, July 1, 2018, https://www.instagram.com/p/BksvlPFHRR-/.

72. Ashley Diane Varela (@cyb3r_butt3rfly), "Closing in on a quarter of a century," Instagram, March 30, 2020, https://www.instagram.com/p/B9Rm9G5g1qF/.

73. Ashley Diane Varela (@cyb3r_butt3rfly), "25," Instagram, March 6, 2020, https://www.instagram.com/p/B9aD-bdgP9b/.

74. Diane Roberts, "In Florida, We Love Our Beaches; Thanks to Our Governor, We Can Now Die for Them," *Washington Post*, April 22, 2020, https://www .washingtonpost.com/outlook/florida-beach-coronavirus-desantis/2020/04/22 /9a45c782-8429-11ea-ae26-989cfce1c7c7_story.html.

75. Carlos A. Gimenez, "Affadavit for Local State of Emergency," Miami-Dade County, October 23, 2020, https://www.miamidade.gov/global/initiatives/corona virus/emergency-orders/declaration-affidavit-10-23-20.page.

76. Ron DeSantis quoted in Eliza Relman, "'The Party Is Over': Florida Gov. Ron DeSantis Ends Spring Break amid the Coronavirus Pandemic," *Business Insider*, March 19, 2020, https://www.businessinsider.com/coronavirus-florida-gov -ron-desantis-ends-spring-break-partying-2020-3.

77. Roberts, "We Love Our Beaches."

78. Patricia Mazzei and Frances Robles, "The Costly Toll of Not Shutting Down Spring Break Earlier," *New York Times*, April 11, 2020, https://www.ny times.com/2020/04/11/us/florida-spring-break-coronavirus.html.

79. (F)empower (@fempowermia), "Dear warriors, in this moment, a veil is being lifted," Instagram, March 15, 2020, https://www.instagram.com/p/B9 xFzY7A98c/.

80. Cheryl Holder, "Many Black Communities Lack Resources to Protect Themselves from COVID," *Miami Herald*, April 6, 2020, https://www.miami herald.com/opinion/op-ed/article241805631.html#storylink=cpy.

81. Derrick Z. Jackson, "Fighting for a Just COVID-19 Response," *The Equation*, April 2, 2020, https://blog.ucsusa.org/derrick-jackson/fighting-for-a -just-covid-19-response.

82. (F)empower (@fempowermia), "Covid quarantine got you questioning whether you got the skills it takes," Instagram, March 23, 2020, https://www .instagram.com/p/B-E4pspA-wB/.

83. Helen Peña (@orange.mooon), "Civil disobedience," Instagram, March 27, 2020, https://www.instagram.com/p/B-QEEW4AAPV/.

84. Ashley Diane Varela (@cyb3r_butt3rfly), "Oshun's daughter," Instagram, April 14, 2018, https://www.instagram.com/p/BhjxGn_Hf8n/.

85. Toi Scott, *Queering Herbalism Vol. III: Women*, Feminine Healing Energy and Resistance; NYC Feminist Zine Fest Special Edition* (2015), 13.

86. Ashley Varela and Helen Peña quoted in Esquinca, "Fighting Climate Gentrification."

87. Sharla M. Fett, *Working Cures: Healing, Health, and Power on Southern Slave Plantations* (Chapel Hill, NC: University of North Carolina Press, 2002), 77–79.

88. Ashley Diane Varela (@cyb3r_butt3rfly), "This post is dedicated to the beautiful treehouse I lived in," Instagram, November 6, 2020, https://www.instagram.com/p/CHQdJJMLCwh/.

89. Ashley Diane Varela (@cyb3r_butt3rfly), "Blessings from yemaya and this lil butterfly," Instagram, May 20, 2020, https://www.instagram.com/p/CAa5lVoA8so/.

90. Leah Schnelbach quoted in Diana Spechler, "I Desperately Miss Human Touch; Science May Explain Why," *Guardian*, May 21, 2020, https://www.theguardian.com/commentisfree/2020/may/21/touch-starvation-lockdown-why.

91. Adrienne maree brown, *Pleasure Activism: The Politics of Feeling Good* (Oakland, CA: AK Press, 2019), 16, Kindle.

92. Adrienne maree brown, "Additional Resources for Facing Coronavirus/Covid19," adrienne maree brown's website, March 10, 2020, http://adriennemareebrown.net/tag/pleasure-activism/.

93. Eduardo Mejia quoted in Randy P. Conner, with David Hatfield Sparks, *Queering Creole Spiritual Traditions: Lesbian, Gay, Bisexual, and Transgender Participation in African-Inspired Traditions in the Americas* (New York: Routledge, 2004), 73–74.

94. Video, "Woman Holding 'We Are Free' Sign Arrested on Miami Beach," Local10, May 11, 2020, https://www.local10.com/news/local/2020/05/11/woman-holding-we-are-free-sign-arrested-on-miami-beach/.

95. Xandra Coe quoted in Annie Sprinkle and Beth Stephens, "What People Are Saying about *Here Come the Ecosexuals*," *Here Come the Ecosexuals!*, accessed December 18, 2021, https://theecosexuals.ucsc.edu/press/quotes/.

96. Melanie L. Harris, *Ecowomanism: African American Women and Earth-Honoring Faiths* (Maryknoll, NY: Orbis Books, 2017), loc. 366, Kindle.

97. Harris, loc. 388.

98. Ashley Diane Varela (@cybr_butt3rfly), "Intentionally envisioning," Instagram, accessed October 12, 2021, https://www.instagram.com/p/BoEVHkDAH2X/.

99. Fem Fairy Garden (@femfairygarden), "In the midst of the Covid-19 crises," Instagram, March 23, 2020, https://www.instagram.com/p/B-E8qrFglTb/.

100. Harris, *Ecowomanism*, loc. 1823.

101. Ashley Diane Varela (@cyb3r_butt3rfly), "I love being gay," Instagram, May 4, 2020, https://www.instagram.com/p/B_ypttKgoWx/.

102. Alexis Pauline Gumbs (@alexispauline), "find her (or surf lullaby #1)," Instagram, July 1, 2020, https://www.instagram.com/p/CCGb4iOAO8S/.

103. Gumbs, *Undrowned*, 7, 9.

104. Gumbs.

105. Gumbs, 8.

106. Gumbs, 11.

107. Gumbs.

108. Luke Ginger, "Hello Climate Change, Goodbye LA Beaches," Heal the Bay, May 13, 2020, https://healthebay.org/climate-change-la-beaches/.

109. June Jordan, "From Sea to Shining Sea," *Feminist Studies* 8, no. 3 (Autumn 1982): 540–541.

JULIANA HUXTABLE

1. Text reproduced by Hannah Black (@hannah_black___), "From 'Penumbra' our animal trial . . . this was so special," Instagram, May 23, 2019, https://www.instagram.com/p/BxobhKBlqTe/.

2. Quinn Schoen, "Hannah Black and Juliana Huxtable," *Performa*, June 6, 2019, https://performa-arts.org/magazine/reports-hannah-black-juliana-huxtable.

3. Black, "From 'Penumbra.'"

4. Charlene K. Lau, "Hannah Black and Juliana Huxtable: *Penumbra*," *Brooklyn Rail*, July–August, 2019, https://brooklynrail.org/2019/07/artseen/Hannah-Black-and-Juliana-Huxtable-Penumbra-Performance-Space-New-York-May-15-and-16-2019.

5. Kathryn Yusoff, *A Billion Black Anthropocenes or None* (Minneapolis: University of Minnesota Press, 2018), loc. 106, Kindle.

6. Juliana Huxtable, *Mucus in My Pineal Gland* (Capricious & Wonder, 2017), 17.

7. Mark Guiducci, "Meet Juliana Huxtable: Star of the New Museum Triennial," *Vogue*, February 27, 2015, https://www.vogue.com/article/juliana-huxtable-new-museum-triennial.

8. Juliana Huxtable, interview by Bella Spratley, "Juliana Huxtable: Play with Truth," *Metal*, no. 43 (Spring/Summer 2020), https://metalmagazine.eu/en/post/interview/juliana-huxtable.

9. Aph Ko, *Racism as Zoological Witchcraft: A Guide to Getting Out* (New York: Lantern Books, 2019), 18.

10. Ko, 48.

11. Juliana Huxtable, interview by Caroline Busta and @LILINTERNET, "Juliana Huxtable on Zoosexuality, Furries, and the Fetishization of Outrage,"

Art Basel, accessed December 18, 2021, https://www.artbasel.com/news/juliana -huxtable-project-native-informant-art-basel-hong-kong.

12. Giovanna Di Chiro, "Polluted Politics? Confronting Toxic Discourse, Sex Panic, and Eco-Normativity, in *Queer Ecologies: Sex, Nature, Politics, Desire*, ed. Catriona Mortimer-Sandilands and Bruce Erickson (Bloomington: Indiana University Press, 2010), loc. 2765, 2744, Kindle.

13. Huxtable, interview by Spratley.

14. Juliana Huxtable, interview by Sotheby's, in Ori Hashmonay, "Juliana Huxtable Takes on the Art Market with Topical Cream," Sotheby's, February 28, 2020, https://www.sothebys.com/en/articles/juliana-huxtable-takes-on-the -art-market-with-topical-cream.

15. Huxtable, interview by Busta and @LILINTERNET.

16. Glenda R. Carpio, *Laughing Fit to Kill: Black Humor in the Fictions of Slavery* (Oxford, UK: Oxford University Press, 2008), loc. 95, 178, Kindle.

17. Atlantis Narcisse quoted in John Eligon, "Transgender African Americans' Open Wound: 'We're Considered a Joke,'" *New York Times*, August 6, 2017, https://www.nytimes.com/2017/08/06/us/black-transgender-lil-duval.html.

18. Carpio, *Laughing Fit to Kill*, loc. 262.

19. "JULIANA HUXTABLE," YouTube video, uploaded by UCLA Design Media Arts, streamed October 23, 2018, https://www.youtube.com/watch?v=i1vsnI4lWww.

20. Jessica Pallingston, *Lipstick: A Celebration of the World's Favorite Cosmetic* (New York: St. Martin's Press, 1999), 34.

21. Janet Mock, *Redefining Realness: My Path to Womanhood, Identity, Love and So Much More* (New York: Atria, 2014), 124.

22. Jacob Tobia, interview by Elizabeth Entenman, "*Sissy* Will Make You Kick the Construct of Gender to the Curb with Six-Inch Stilettos," *HelloGiggles*, updated March 5, 2019, https://hellogiggles.com/reviews-coverage/sissy-jacob -tobia-interview/.

23. Michael Bullock, "Juliana Huxtable: Gender Camouflage," *Girls Like Us*, no. 6 (2014): 15.

24. Josefin Dolsten, "What It's Like to Come Out as a Trans Woman When Your Wife Is the Rabbi," *Times of Israel*, July 4, 2020, https://www.timesofisrael.com /what-its-like-to-come-out-as-a-trans-woman-when-your-wife-is-the-rabbi/.

25. Huxtable, interview by Busta and @LILINTERNET.

26. Ko, *Racism as Zoological Witchcraft*, 46.

27. "Randy Wicker Interviews Sylvia Rivera."

28. Ko, *Racism as Zoological Witchcraft*, 57.

29. Dean Spade quoted in Raquel Willis, "How Sylvia Rivera Created the Blueprint for Transgender Organizing," *Out*, May 21, 2019, https://www.out.com /pride/2019/5/21/how-sylvia-rivera-created-blueprint-transgender-organizing.

30. Sylvia Rivera, interview by Leslie Feinberg, "Interview: Sylvia Rivera," *The Queer Bible*, accessed December 18, 2021, https://www.queerbible.com /queerbible/2017/10/8/interview-sylvia-rivera-by-leslie-feinberg.

31. Juliana Huxtable quoted in Emma van Meyeren, "Juliana Huxtable and the Desire to Be: In Conversation with the Artist, Performer, DJ, Writer and Nightlife Icon," *Glamcult*, accessed December 18, 2021, https://www.glamcult .com/articles/juliana-huxtable-and-the-desire-to-be/.

32. Huxtable, UCLA lecture.

33. Quoted in Virginia Billeaud Anderson, "'Defending Democracy' at the Station," https://glasstire.com/2008/06/27/defending-democracy-at-the-station/.

34. Huxtable, UCLA lecture.

35. Juliana Huxtable, "A Split During Laughter at the Rally," video, 2017.

36. Will Furtado, "Non-Binary Coding: Juliana Huxtable on Taking Apart Our Notions of Identity," *Sleek*, December 1, 2017, https://www.sleek-mag.com /article/juliana-huxtable-interview/.

37. Juliana Huxtable quoted in Brian Droitcour, "Juliana Huxtable," *ART-news*, August 23, 2017, https://www.artnews.com/art-in-america/aia-reviews /juliana-huxtable-62377/.

38. Droitcoeur.

39. Droitcoeur.

40. Juliana Huxtable quoted in Aisha Harris, "Juliana Huxtable's Next Chapter," *New York Times*, August 10, 2020, https://www.nytimes.com/2020/08/10/t -magazine/juliana-huxtable.html.

41. Emory Douglas, "Position Paper #1 on Revolutionary Art," 1968, http:// www.itsabouttimebpp.com/emory_art/pdf/Position_Paper_on_Revolutionary _Art_No1.pdf.

42. "Juliana Huxtable: *Herculine's Profecy*," Kadist, 2017, https://kadist.org /work/herculines-profecy/.

43. Antwaun Sargent, "Juliana Huxtable's Bold, Defiant Vision," *Vice*, March 24, 2015, https://www.vice.com/en/article/exmjkp/artist-juliana-huxtables-jour ney-from-scene-queen-to-trans-art-star-456.

44. Solomon Chase, "Juliana Huxtable's Conspiracy Logic," SSENSE, accessed December 18, 2021, https://www.ssense.com/en-us/editorial/culture/juliana-hux tables-conspiracy-logic.

45. Huxtable, UCLA lecture.

46. Hil Malatino, *Queer Embodiment: Monstrosity, Medical Violence, and Intersex Experience* (Lincoln: University of Nebraska Press, 2019), 3.

47. Makayla Bailey, "Juliana Huxtable | Let's Skip the Essentialism and Devour the Semantics," *Flaunt*, October 7, 2019, https://flaunt.com/content/juliana -huxtable.

48. Michel Foucault, *Herculine Barbin* (New York: Knopf Doubleday, 2010), 97, Kindle.

49. Malatino, *Queer Embodiment*, 206.

50. David Ebony, "Surrounded by the Future: The New Museum Triennial Tackles Tech, Politics, and Gender," *Observer*, March 4, 2015, https://observer .com/2015/03/surrounded-by-the-future-the-new-museum-triennial-tackles -tech-politics-and-gender/.

51. "FutaWorld! Sci Fi 'Futas Taken by Aliens 4,'" Amazon, Kindle e-book product page, accessed December 18, 2021, https://www.amazon.com/FutaWorld -Sci-Fi-Futas-Taken-Female-ebook/dp/B07DB6BYZ8.

52. "FutaWorld! SciFi 'Futas Taken by the Alien' COMPLETE BUNDLE: 4 Stories of Futa-on-Futa, Futa-on-Female, Futanari Sci-Fi Tentacle Erotica (FutaWorld! Sci-Fi)," Amazon, Kindle e-book product page, accessed December 18, 2021, https://www.amazon.com/FutaWorld-SciFi-COMPLETE-BUNDLE-Female -ebook/dp/B07PYTJTZF/ref=sr_1_3?dchild=1&keywords=futaworld+sci+fi &qid=1614554057&s=digital-text&sr=1-3.

53. "FutaWorld! Fantasy 'The Futa Harem: Volume 1' 5-STORY BUNDLE: A Futanari, Futa-on-Female, Futa-on-Futa, Erotic Menage Story," Amazon, Kindle e-book product page, accessed December 18, 2021, https://www.amazon.com/Futa World-Fantasy-Harem-Futa-Female-ebook/dp/B07PGQDNZD/ref=sr_1_3?d child=1&keywords=futaworld&qid=1614554003&s=digital-text&sr=1-3.

54. Di Chiro, "Polluted Politics?," loc. 2739.

55. Di Chiro, loc. 3034–3038.

56. Di Chiro, loc. 3041–3045.

57. Brown, *Pleasure Activism*, 122–123.

58. Stephanie Toone, "Transgender Activist Raquel Willis Finds Strength in Telling Stories of Forgotten Trans Women," *Atlanta Journal-Constitution*, February 19, 2020, https://www.ajc.com/lifestyles/transgender-activist-willis-wants -tell-stories-those-forgotten/l7LzfLbt2In7pUk9PPDsIN/.

59. Raquel Willis quoted in Rosemary Donahue, "Raquel Willis Meditates with Her Plants Every Morning," *Allure*, August 16, 2020, https://www.allure.com /story/raquel-willis-my-beauty-ritual.

60. Raquel Willis (@raquel_willis), "In February 2018, I traveled to Whitakers, NC, with the powerful Black Organizing for Leadership and Dignity," Instagram, June 19, 2020, https://www.instagram.com/p/CBoFFjGALV2/.

61. Mart A. Stewart, "Slavery and the Origins of African American Environmentalism," in *"To Love the Wind and the Rain": African Americans and Environmental History*, ed. Dianne D. Glave and Mark Stoll (Pittsburgh: University of Pittsburgh Press, 2006), 11.

62. Alicia Garza and Ai-Jen Poo, "No Representation without Responsibility

with Raquel Willis," September 29, 2020, in *Sunstorm*, season 2, episode 4, https://ndwa2020.domesticworkers.org/category/sunstorm/ep-4-represent-responsibly-with-raquel-willis/.

63. Garza and Poo.

64. Juliana Huxtable quoted in Whitney Claflin, "Juliana Huxtable's Interfertility Industrial Complex: Snatch the Calf Back and the Pursuit of Desire," *Topical Cream*, September 19, 2019, https://www.topicalcream.org/features/juliana-huxtables-interfertility-industrial-complex/.

65. Claflin.

66. Celina Huynh, "Interview: Juliana Huxtable, Trans Artistic Goddess," *That's*, March 22, 2016, https://www.thatsmags.com/shenzhen/post/12787/juliana-huxtable-interview.

67. "Episode 2: Emancipation Reimagined," September 2019, in *The 730 Podcast*, https://open.spotify.com/episode/1kRf5fWJU7orsUuiKy9JyF?go=1&utm_source=embed_v3&t=0&nd=1.

68. Claflin, "Juliana Huxtable's Interfertility."

69. Claflin.

70. "The Future: Juliana Huxtable," *Hunger*, June 1, 2020, https://www.hungertv.com/editorial/the-future-juliana-huxtable/.

71. Juliana Huxtable, "Interfertility Industrial Complex: Snatch the Calf Back," digital video, 2019, https://contemporaryartdaily.com/2019/10/juliana-huxtable-at-reena-spaulings-2/.

72. Carol J. Adams, *The Pornography of Meat* (Brooklyn: Lantern Books, 2015), 68.

73. Huxtable, "Interfertility Industrial Complex."

74. Mark Hay, "Inside HuCow, the Fetish That Imagines Women as Cows," *Vice*, April 24, 2018, https://www.vice.com/en/article/d3599y/inside-hucow-the-fetish-that-imagines-women-as-cows.

75. Alex Blanchette, *Porkopolis: American Animality, Standardized Life, and the Factory Farm* (Durham, NC: Duke University Press, 2020), 91–92, Kindle.

76. See Thad Sitton and James H. Conrad, *Freedom Colonies: Independent Black Texans in the Time of Jim Crow* (Austin: University of Texas Press, 2005).

77. Ko, *Racism as Zoological Witchcraft*, 129.

78. Nicole Seymour, "Alligator Earrings and the Fishhook in the Face: Tragicomedy, Transcorporeality, and Animal Drag," *TSQ: Transgender Studies Quarterly* 2, no. 2 (May 2015): 269.

79. Nikki Sullivan, "Somatechnics," *TSQ: Transgender Studies Quarterly* 1, nos. 1–2 (May 2014): 187–190.

80. Lilia Trenkova, "The Womyn's Club: Vegan Feminism and Transphobia," *Collectively Free*, January 9, 2016, http://www.collectivelyfree.org/the-womyns-club-and-transphobia/.

81. Juliana Huxtable, conversation with Hannah Black, "Grounding Practice: Juliana Huxtable in Conversation with Hannah Black," Somerset House, June 10, 2020, https://www.somersethouse.org.uk/blog/grounding-practice-juliana -huxtable-conversation-hannah-black.

82. Juliana Huxtable (@julianahuxtable), "MY ANCESTORS ARE AN UNTRACE-ABLE MIX I WAS CUT OFF FROM," Instagram, February 17, 2020, https://www .instagram.com/p/B8rQpyyhG8f/.

83. Huxtable, conversation with Black.

84. Discwoman, "DiscUs 001 Frankie & Juliana Huxtable," Patreon, January 7, 2020, https://www.patreon.com/posts/discus-001-32965036.

85. Rasmus Rahbek Simonsen, "A Queer Vegan Manifesto," *Journal for Critical Animal Studies* 10, no. 3 (2012): 69.

86. Simonsen, 75.

87. Huxtable, conversation with Black.

88. Leo Solo, *Hucow Madame: Third Edition* (2020), 2, Kindle.

89. Solo, 30–31.

90. "About Us," We Are Fluide, accessed December 18, 2021, https://www .fluide.us/pages/about-us.

91. Che Gossett, "Queering the Body: Makeup Musings with Che Gossett," We Are Fluide, April 16, 2018, https://www.fluide.us/blogs/futurefluide/che-gossett -on-queering-the-body.

92. Ocean Portal Team, "Bioluminescence," Smithsonian Ocean Portal, accessed December 18, 2021, https://ocean.si.edu/ocean-life/fish/bioluminesc ence.

93. Gumbs, *Undrowned*, 42.

94. Che Gossett, "Blackness, Animality, and the Unsovereign," Verso, September 8, 2015, https://www.versobooks.com/blogs/2228-che-gossett-blackness -animality-and-the-unsovereign.

95. Che Gossett, "Blackness and the Trouble of Trans Visibility," in Gossett, Stanley, and Burton, *Trap Door*, 187.

96. Gumbs, *Undrowned*, 81.

97. Seb Wheeler, "Ziúr and Juliana Huxtable Have Started a New Berlin Party Called Off," *Mixmag*, February 5, 2020, https://mixmag.net/read/ziur-juliana -huxtable-berlin-party-trauma-bar-kino-news.

98. Philip Maughan, "Juliana Huxtable F*cks with Her Demons," *Highsnobiety*, November 13, 2020, https://www.highsnobiety.com/p/juliana-huxtable -interview/.

99. Sara González, "The Strangest Ways to Fight Climate Change," Open Mind, November 7, 2019, https://www.bbvaopenmind.com/en/scienceenviron ment/strangest-ways-to-fight-climate-change/.

CONCLUSION. WHERE IS THE *BLACK* IN BLACK FEMME FREEDOM?

1. "Sha'Carri Richardson, Now America's Fastest Woman, Scorches Her Olympic Trials Final | NBC Sports," YouTube video, uploaded by NBC Sports, June 19, 2021, https://www.youtube.com/watch?v=W5jWmeCZzp4.

2. Sha'Carri Richardson quoted in Tom Schad, "Sha'Carri Richardson Dominates 100 Meters in Style to Clinch Trip to Tokyo Olympics," *USA Today*, June 19, 2021, https://www.usatoday.com/story/sports/olympics/2021/06/19/shacarri -richardson-dominates-us-olympic-track-and-field-trials-100/7757848002/.

3. Richardson quoted in Schad.

4. Ms.independent (@_abrea), "Sha'Carri Richardson, a dark skin black girl," Twitter, June 20, 2021, https://twitter.com/_abrea/status/1406660717785255936 ?ref_src=twsrc%5Etfw%7Ctwcamp%5Etweetembed%7Ctwterm%5E140666071 7785255936%7Ctwgr%5E%7Ctwcon%5Es1_c10&ref_url=https%3A%2F%2Fwww .harpersbazaar.com%2Fcelebrity%2Flatest%2Fa36789007%2Fshacarri-richard son-is.

5. Sha'Carri Richardson quoted in Kevin Draper and Juliet Macur, "Sha'Carri Richardson, a Track Sensation, Tests Positive for Marijuana," *New York Times*, July 1, 2021, https://www.nytimes.com/2021/07/01/sports/olympics/shacarri -richardson-suspended-marijuana.html.

6. Florence Ashley quoted in Cedric "BIG CED" Thornton, "Social Media Rips Megan Rapinoe for Promoting CBD after Sha'Carri Richardson Was Banned for Marijuana Use," Black Enterprise, July 26, 2021, https://www.blackenterprise .com/social-media-rips-olympian-megan-rapinoe-for-promoting-cbd-after -shacarri-richardson-was-banned-for-marijuana-use/.

7. Jamie Raskin and Alexandria Ocasio-Cortez, letter to Travis T. Tygart and Witold Banka, July 2, 2021, https://oversight.house.gov/sites/democrats.oversight .house.gov/files/2021-07-02.UpdatedJR%20AOC%20to%20Tygart-USADA%20 and%20Banka-WADA%20re%20Marijuana%20Suspension.pdf.

8. "Drug Policy Alliance Statement on Sha'Carri Unjust Suspension from U.S. Olympics Team after Testing Positive for THC Consumed in Legal State," Drug Policy Alliance, July 2, 2021, https://drugpolicy.org/press-release/2021/07/drug -policy-alliance-statement-shacarri-unjust-suspension-us-olympics-team.

9. Jessica Marie Johnson (@jmjafrx), Instagram, July 2, 2021, https://www .instagram.com/p/CQ1-gFJlTrbjPHoSCUIol4ezcL7kMRa7f2reKoo/.

10. Lex Pryor, "Sha'Carri Richardson Can Outrun Everything Except a Broken System," *The Ringer*, July 9, 2021, https://www.theringer.com/2021/7/9/22569132 /shacarri-richardson-olympic-wada-drug-policy-ruling.

11. Comment on Sarah Kearns, "Over Half a Million People Sign Petitions to

Let Sha'Carri Richardson Run in the Olympics," *Hypebeast*, July 8, 2021, https://hypebeast.com/2021/7/petition-let-shacarri-richardson-run-olympics.

12. JeffriAnne Wilder, "Everyday Colorism in the Lives of Young Black Women: Revisiting the Continuing Significance of an Old Phenomenon in a New Generation" (PhD dissertation, University of Florida, 2008), 95.

13. "Y'all HATE Dark-Skinned Black Women | Sha'Carri Richardson," You-Tube video, uploaded by Sheridan S. Davis, June 24, 2021, https://www.youtube.com/watch?v=KvhKgo7lTOs.

14. Lance Hannon, Robert DeFina, and Sarah Bruch, "The Relationship between Skin Tone and School Suspension for African Americans," *Race and Social Problems* 5, no. 4 (December 2013): 281.

15. Tanesha Peeples, "Sha'Carri Richardson Was Tossed Out of the Olympics the Same Way Black Kids Are Tossed Out of Public Schools," Education Post, July 7, 2021, https://educationpost.org/shacarri-richardson-was-tossed-out-of-the-olympics-the-same-way-black-kids-are-tossed-out-of-public-schools/.

16. Sha'Carri Richardson (@carririchardson_), "Blackity black black on the track," Instagram, July 6, 2020, https://www.instagram.com/p/CCToRnMHrKa/.

17. Aja Graydon, "Cheer for Black Girls with Orange Hair, Long Nails, Tats, and Lashes," *Philadelphia Inquirer*, June 24, 2021, https://www.inquirer.com/opinion/commentary/cheer-black-girls-with-orange-hair-long-nails-tats-lashes-opinion-20210624.html.

18. Walker, *Our Mothers' Gardens*, 290.

19. Walker, xi.

20. Jamal H. N. Hailey, Joyell Arscott, and Kalima Young, "In Between the Shade: Colorism and Its Impact on Black LGBTQ Communities," in *Colorism: Investigating a Global Phenomenon*, ed. Kamilah Marie Woodson (Santa Barbara, CA: Fielding University Press, 2020), loc. 8630-8637, Kindle.

21. Hailey, Arscott, and Young, loc. 8669.

22. TJ Bryan, "It Takes Ballz," 147.

23. Jafari S. Allen, *¡Venceremos? The Erotics of Black Self-Making in Cuba* (Durham, NC: Duke University Press, 2011), 78.

24. "The Light Skin Elephant in the Room," July 12, 2019, in *Hoodrat to Headwrap: A Decolonized Podcast*, https://soundcloud.com/user-501838661/the-light-skin-elephant-in-the-room-colorism.

25. Camille May Baker, "Shea Diamond Speaks Her Truth," *Indypendent*, July 5, 2018, https://indypendent.org/2018/07/shea-diamond-speaks-her-truth/.

26. Shea Diamond, interview by Mathew Rodriguez, "Shea Diamond Drops 'Keisha Complexion' Video, Talks Colorism, Trans Beauty, and Tina Turner," *Into*, April 27, 2018, https://www.intomore.com/culture/shea-diamond-drops-keisha-complexion-video-talks-colorism-trans-beauty-and-tina-turner/.

27. Jill Fields, *An Intimate Affair: Women, Lingerie, and Sexuality* (Berkeley: University of California Press, 2007), 2–3.

28. Fields, 113.

29. Joseline Hernandez quoted in London Alexaundria, "'It's Not Phony': Joseline Hernandez Reveals What Separates Her Show from 'Love and Hip Hop Atlanta' and Why She Has No Regrets Doing Reality TV," *Atlanta Black Star*, May 7, 2021, https://atlantablackstar.com/2021/05/07/its-not-phony-joseline -hernandez-reveals-what-separates-her-show-from-love-and-hip-hop-atlanta -and-why-she-has-no-regrets-doing-reality-tv/.

30. Joseline Hernandez, interview by Breakfast Club, "Joseline Talks New Show about Strip Club Culture, Engagement + More," YouTube video, uploaded by Breakfast Club Power 105.1 FM, January 10, 2020, https://www.youtube.com /watch?v=ZuKb_EnEJoI.

31. Hernandez, interview by Breakfast Club.

32. *Joseline's Cabaret: Miami*, season 1, episode 1, "Welcome to Joseline's Cabaret Miami, Bitch," Zeus Network, 2020.

33. *Joseline's Cabaret*, season 1, episode 1.

34. Shamika Sanders, "Joseline Hernandez Can Teach a Lesson on Colorism," MAJIC 102.3/92.7, accessed September 28, 2021, https://mymajicdc.com/3944033 /joseline-hernandez-can-teach-a-lesson-on-colorism/.

35. Laila Haidarali, *Brown Beauty: Color, Sex, and Race from the Harlem Renaissance to World War II* (New York: New York University Press, 2018), 4.

36. All preceding quotations in this paragraph are from *Joseline's Cabaret*, season 1, episode 1.

37. Bailey, *Misogynoir Transformed*, 107.

38. *Joseline's Cabaret*, season 1, episode 1.

39. *Joseline's Cabaret*, season 1, episode 5, "Why We Not in the Video?!"

40. Benji Hart, "Black People Have Every Right to Distrust You for Being Light Skinned," *Radical Faggot*, October 17, 2016, https://radfag.com/2016/10/17 /black-people-have-every-right-to-distrust-you-for-being-light-skinned/.

41. *Joseline's Cabaret*, season 1, episode 5.

42. *Joseline's Cabaret*, season 1, episode 5.

43. Hunter Shackelford, "Hood Femmes & Ratchet Feminism: On Amandla Stenberg, Representation & #BlackGirlMagic," Hunter Ashleigh Shackelford's website, accessed September 28, 2021, http://ashleighshackelford.com/writing /2016/9/22/hood-femmes-ratchet-feminism-on-amandla-stenberg-representation -blackgirlmagic.

44. Hart, "Black People Have Every Right."

45. Hilda Lloréns, Carlos G. García-Quijano, and Isar P. Godreau, "Racismo en Puerto Rico: Surveying Perceptions of Racism," *Centro Journal* 29, no. 3 (September 2017): 164.

46. Haidarali, *Brown Beauty*, 6.

47. *Joseline's Cabaret*, season 1, episode 2, "The Last Supper."

48. Haidarali, *Brown Beauty*, 6.

49. All previous quotations in this paragraph are from *Joseline's Cabaret*, season 1, episode 5.

50. Hart, "Black People Have Every Right."

51. *Joseline's Cabaret*, season 1, episode 6, "Locker Room Brawl."

52. *Joseline's Cabaret*, season 1, episode 6.

53. Hari Ziyad, "Why I'll Never Thank White 'Allies,'" Black Youth Project, April 3, 2017, http://blackyouthproject.com/ill-never-thank-white-allies/.

54. *Joseline's Cabaret: Miami*, season 1, episode 7, "We'll Always Have New Girls."

55. *Joseline's Cabaret*, season 1, episode 7.

56. "Keisha Complexion," on Shea Diamond, *Seen It All* (Asylum Records, 2018).

57. Rebecca Farley, "Shea Diamond Wants You to Groove & Be an Ally at the Same Time," *Refinery29*, April 27, 2018, https://www.refinery29.com/en-us/2018/04/197353/shea-diamond-keisha-complexion-music-video-debut.

58. Diamond, interview by Rodriguez.

59. Diamond, interview by Rodriguez.

60. Diamond, interview by Rodriguez.

61. Diamond, interview by Farley.

62. Diamond, interview by Rodriguez.

63. Shea Diamond quoted in James Patrick Herman, "Trans Singer Shea Diamond Strikes a 'Pose'—and, She Hopes, a Nerve," *Variety*, July 4, 2018, https://variety.com/2018/music/news/shea-diamond-trans-singer-justin-tranter-interview-1202865265/.

64. Diamond, interview by Farley.

65. Diamond, interview by Farley.

66. Wilder, "Everyday Colorism," 87.

67. Keisha Bush, "Keisha vs. Kate: On Discarding and Reclaiming a Name," *Literary Hub*, February 1, 2021, https://lithub.com/keisha-vs-kate-on-discarding-and-reclaiming-a-name/.

68. Lakeisha Goedluck, "My Name Is Keisha and Pop Culture Ruined My Life," *gal-dem*, March 27, 2020, https://gal-dem.com/my-name-is-keisha-and-pop-culture-ruined-my-name/.

69. "Keisha," on Dave East, *Kairi Chanel* (Mass Appeal Records, 2016); "Keshia Had a Baby," on YG, *4Real 4Real* (4Hunnid Records and Def Jam Recordings, 2019).

70. Goedluck, "My Name Is Keisha."

71. Bush, "Keisha vs. Kate."

72. Diamond, interview by Farley.

73. Kevin Quashie, *The Sovereignty of Quiet: Beyond Resistance in Black Culture* (New Brunswick, NJ: Rutgers University Press, 2012), 120.

74. Diamond, interview by Rodriguez.

75. Nella Larsen, *Quicksand* (New York: Alfred A. Knopf, 1928), 38.

76. Cheryl A. Wall, "Passing for What? Aspects of Identity in Nella Larsen's Novels," in *Black American Literature Forum* 20, nos. 1–2 (Spring–Summer 1986): 101–102.

77. Julia Nordquist, "'A Plea for Color': Color as a Path to Freedom in Nella Larsen's Novel *Quicksand*" (thesis, Växjö University, 2008), http://lnu.diva-portal.org/smash/get/diva2:206076/FULLTEXT01.

78. Shea Diamond quoted in Jeffrey Masters, "Shea Diamond: 'Nothing Has Changed Since the Days of Sylvia and Marsha,'" *Advocate*, July 21, 2020, https://www.advocate.com/transgender/2020/7/21/shea-diamond-nothing-has-changed-days-sylvia-marsha.

79. Diamond, interview by Rodriguez.

80. Najaa Young, "Black Gods in the 21st Century: A Cautionary Tale about Folks," *Medium*, April 2, 2019, https://medium.com/@americanafricans/black-gods-in-the-21st-century-a-cautionary-tale-about-folks-532e63c3b8fe.

81. Shea Diamond, with Gabrielle Barnes, "Shea Diamond, Singer-Songwriter and Trans Rights Activist," Changing Wxman Collective, April 30, 2020, https://changingwomxncollective.org/the-glow-1/shea-diamond-singer-songwriter-and-trans-rights-activist.

82. Kamil Oshundara (@k6mil), "Oshun, (Ochún and Oxúm in Latin America) is the divine femme goddess of love," Twitter, February 14, 2018, https://twitter.com/k6mil/status/963969092351803392?lang=en.

83. Kamil Oshundara, "Honey Never Spoils: Oshun, the Orisha of Love," *Too Taboo*, February 14, 2021, https://k6mil.substack.com/p/honey-never-spoils-oshun-the-orisha.

84. Sondra Rose Marie, "Shine Bright Like a Diamond," *Tagg*, May 20, 2019, https://taggmagazine.com/shea-diamond/.

85. Shea Diamond, interview by Nora Rothman, "Shea Diamond Sparkles," *Earhart*, October 19, 2018, https://thisisearhart.com/independent-artist-features/shea-diamond.

86. Shea Diamond, "Musician Shea Diamond's Powerful Words to Trans Women: 'Honey, You Will Survive,'" *NewNowNext*, October 9, 2017, http://www.newnownext.com/letter-myself-shea-diamond/10/2017/.

87. Walker, *Our Mothers' Gardens*, 310–311.

88. Robert L. Reece, "The Future of American Blackness: On Colorism and Racial Reorganization," *Review of Black Political Economy* 48, no. 4 (2021): 10.

89. Reece.

90. Ericka Hart, in "Light Skin Elephant in the Room."

91. Walker, *Our Mothers' Gardens*, 311–312.

AFTERWORD. PYNK PARLANCE, A GLOSSARY

1. Audre Lorde, "The Transformation of Silence into Language and Action," in Lorde, *Sister Outsider*, 42.

2. Danielle Young, "Janelle Monáe Says Dirty Computer Is a Soundtrack for Carefree Black Women Who Are 'Beautiful As Fuck,'" *The Root*, April 26, 2018, https://www.theroot.com/janelle-monae-says-dirty-computer-is-a-soundtrack-for-c-1825566235.

3. Eve Tuck and C. Ree, "A Glossary of Haunting," in *Handbook of Autoethnography*, ed. Stacy Holman Jones, Tony E. Adams, and Carolyn Ellis (London: Routledge, 2016), 640.

4. Tuck and Ree.

5. Tuck and Ree.

6. "Love Galore," on SZA, *Ctrl* (2017).

7. "SZA 'Love Galore' Official Lyrics & Meaning | Verified," YouTube video, uploaded by Genius, June 15, 2017, https://www.youtube.com/watch?v=Kr5V6muCJR8.

8. Audre Lorde, "The Uses of Anger: Women Responding to Racism," in Lorde, *Sister Outsider*, 127.

9. "Captain Hook," on Megan Thee Stallion, *Suga* (2020).

10. "MEGAN THEE STALLION IS Looking for a GIRLFRIEND," YouTube video, uploaded by Goddess Raven Show, August 8, 2020, https://www.youtube.com/watch?v=49lhIyhi_Qo.

11. Taylor Henderson, "Megan Thee Stallion Says She Wants a Girlfriend, Describes Her Type," *Pride*, August 11, 2020, https://www.pride.com/celebrities/2020/8/11/megan-thee-stallion-says-she-wants-girlfriend-describes-her-type.

12. Tuck and Ree, "Glossary of Haunting," 640.

13. "Zendaya Answers Personality Revealing Questions | Proust Questionnaire | Vanity Fair," YouTube video, uploaded by Vanity Fair, February 23, 2021, https://www.youtube.com/watch?v=sxw-ZvRKI8A.

14. "Zendaya Answers Personality Revealing Questions."

15. Matt Richardson, *The Queer Limit of Black Memory: Black Lesbian Literature and Irresolution* (Columbus: Ohio State University Press, 2013), 167.

INDEX